VICTORIAN ESSAYS

G. M. YOUNG

VICTORIAN ESSAYS

Chosen and introduced by

W. D. HANDCOCK

LONDON

OXFORD UNIVERSITY PRESS

1962

Oxford University Press, Amen House, London E.C.4
GLASGOW NEW YORK TORONTO MELBOURNE WELLINGTON
BOMBAY CALCUTTA MADRAS KARACHI LAHORE DACCA
CAPE TOWN SALISBURY NAIROBI IBADAN ACCRA
KUALA LUMPUR HONG KONG

824
Y08v

First issued in *OXFORD PAPERBACKS* 1962

54004

July '66

Printed in Great Britain

CONTENTS

The Oxford University Press wishes to thank Rupert Hart-Davis, publisher of *Daylight and Champaign* (1937), *Today and Yesterday* (1948), and *Last Essays* (1950) for permission to use the following essays: Macaulay, Puritans and Victorians, No Servile Tenure, Mr and Mrs Dickens, Schoolman in Downing Street, The Mercian Sybil, The Victorian Noon Time, Sophist and Swashbuckler, The Faith of the Grandfathers, Tempus Actum, B. A. Kohnfeldt, Katherine Stanley and John Russell, Maitland, Topsy, The New Cortegiano (from *Daylight and Champaign*); Victorian Centenary, Age of Tennyson, Thackeray, Mr Gladstone, The Greatest Victorian (from *Today and Yesterday*); Eyes and No Eyes, The Liberal Mind in Victorian England, the Happy Family, Newman again, Thomas Hardy (from *Last Essays*).

The editor wishes to thank colleagues in the University of Exeter, and in particular Mr I. R. D. Mathewson, for the translations in the footnotes to the essays.

INTRODUCTION

G. M. Young's *Victorian England: the Portrait of an Age* first appeared in 1936, and was published as an Oxford Paperback in 1960. The present volume contains the Victorian pieces from the three volumes of essays that Young published in his lifetime. The two together constitute the *corpus* of his Victorian work. The *Portrait* has established itself as the most penetrating and comprehensive account that we have of the Victorian age. Indeed, in its sympathetic, though far from uncritical effort to explore all aspects of the age and view them in historical focus, it has been regarded as opening a new era in Victorian studies. Nothing, fortunately, is final in historical writing, but it may well be some time before anyone so variously equipped, with such powers of historical insight and composition, ventures on the same path again. But the very effort to keep all elements and aspects in place in a moving picture, which is the distinction of the work, made a taut structure and close, often highly allusive writing a necessity. Many may therefore find it pleasanter and easier to approach the work of the 'master of Victorian studies', as a recent American reviewer called Young, through the *Essays*, where he is more unbuttoned and at ease; those who know the *Portrait*, on the other hand, will find in the *Essays* expansions and elaborations of its themes.

Young never held a teaching post in a university for more than a year or two; his career until he was in his forties was as a civil servant; he published nothing till he was fifty; and even in his later years much of his time was given to public work and to letters in general. The historian profited, but historical output suffered. Life and writings were, nevertheless, of a piece with Young. Born in 1882, he went to St Paul's School; thence, in 1900 to Balliol College, as a scholar, and took a first in Classical Moderations, a second in *Litterae Humaniores,* and, in 1905, the blue riband of Oxford scholarship, an All Souls fellowship. His Civil Service career began three years later, when he joined the Board of Education in what, under the reorganization then in train at the hands

of Sir Robert Morant, was to become the Universities Department.
When the Board's Standing Joint Advisory Committee for Universities—the predecessor of the present University Grants Committee—was formed in 1911, Young became its first Secretary.
Thus began—or at any rate was confirmed—the interest he was
to take through the whole of his life in the adaptation of the university tradition created in the Victorian age to the needs of the
twentieth century. For Morant, the stormy petrel of the Civil
Service in his time, and the man to whom, under Balfour, the
country owes its present secondary school system, Young, to the
end of his life, had an admiration touched with veneration. It is
improbable that his general political views remained unaffected
by Morant's determined Tory-Radicalism. The second important
phase of Young's administrative career belongs to the later years
of the first World War. In those years, to an extent that even now
is impressive to remember, the country became engrossed in
thoughts of 'reconstruction'. The government set up two successive 'Reconstruction Committees', and, in mid-1917, a Ministry
of Reconstruction of which Young became Joint Permanent Secretary. The ministry was short-lived, and in early 1919 was fused
with the Ministry of National Service under Sir Auckland Geddes.
The tide of enthusiasm that had called it into being ebbed also, as
post-war prospects began to be seen in terms of intractable problems, rather than in those of golden opportunities, though not
before substantial achievements could be credited to it. So far as
Young is concerned, there can be little doubt that a commitment
that must have been personal, as well as official, left deep marks
on his mind. He had looked on the prospect of taking part in the
re-shaping of the nation's life, and seen it evade him; he had lived
through a period of great idealism and great disillusionment, and
where his final sympathies lay is shown by the phrase he later
coined for the post-war years—'the dirty twenties'. He remained
an idealist and a reformer, but a wary one, looking to growth
rather than to systems, to people rather than to machinery. In the
early post-war years he served a good deal abroad—in Baltic
Russia, in Austria and Italy. In the mid-twenties he left the
service.

The latter part of Young's life was spent between London, Wiltshire and Oxford, as a scholar and writer. In the early thirties he made his home in Wiltshire, and Wiltshire was to play a large part in his life. Urban as he was in disposition and upbringing, he loved countryside and country buildings and gardens, and his historical sense quickened to the evidence of undisturbed continuity in rural scenes and pursuits. The 'Old Oxyard', at Oare, near Marlborough, became a meeting place for neighbours and friends from London and Oxford; the downs and valleys became his familiar walking places; he made himself something of an expert on Wiltshire archaeology and history and took part in civic and educational movements in Swindon. Oxford became a second home to him after his re-election as a Fellow of All Souls in 1947. Life there followed a familiar pattern—the morning's work in reach of great libraries, the afternoon stroll round Colleges and gardens, which gave him the element of tranquil beauty that he needed each day, the social occasion of dinner, and above all, of coffee-room talk afterwards. All Souls, with its mixture of established scholars, its annual quota of young elected Fellows (whose company and conversation Young always sought), its regular infusions of visitors from the world outside, former Fellows and guests—and its lack of undergraduates, too, to worry and talk about and distract its attention from more serious matters—gave Young that meeting of worlds, of critical youth and established experience, that most stimulated his ranging and meditative mind. He met there, too, distinguished old associates and friends whose ways had gone differently from his own—Lionel Curtis, John Simon, Leopold Amery, Lord Salter and Lord Brand, who were frequently in residence. Young was not altogether free, perhaps, from the frailty he glances at in the apothegm prefixed to the *Portrait*—'Servants talk about People: Gentle folk discuss things' —but when coffee-room talk had been general and good, he might be heard saying, as he settled in his chair in his room, 'That was a real All Souls conversation.' The College, with its breadth and friendly commerce of interests, was, for him, the microcosm, perhaps, of the world as in his warmer fancies he hoped it might become.

Young did not begin publishing till the thirties and then the books came fast, covering an astonishing range of subjects, though always in the manner of essays rather than of treatises. In 1932 he published his *'Gibbon'*, the discharge of a personal piety: in 1934 *Early Victorian England,* two large volumes of essays by different hands on social history, which he edited, and to which was attached, as a final summary, the first half of what later was issued as the *Portrait*; in 1935 *Charles I and Cromwell*; in 1936 the *Portrait of an Age*; in 1937 *Daylight and Champaign*, the first of his collections of essays and addresses, followed, after the war, by *Today and Yesterday* (1948) and *Last Essays* (1950). In these years a good deal of public work came his way, as a Trustee of the National Portrait Gallery and of the British Museum, a member of the Historical Manuscripts Commission, the Standing Committee on Museums and Galleries, and the Royal Commission on the Press of 1947-49. He took a lot of trouble over these various tasks and thoroughly enjoyed them. Meanwhile he had embarked on his life of Baldwin, and this much-controverted volume—about which Young was never fully happy himself—appeared in 1952. In 1956 he published, in collaboration with the author of this note, *English Historical Documents, 1833-74,* but though his inspiration and guidance shaped the early work on this, the long and disabling illness from which he died prevented his taking any active part in its final preparation, and it can hardly be reckoned in the canon of his work. He died in 1959.

By disposition and classical training, Young was a humanist, rooting himself deliberately in sixteenth-century traditions. The intellectual core of his humanism was his belief in reason; 'Pensée fait la grandeur de l'homme', he quoted from Pascal; the historical function of the nineteenth century, in his view, had been 'to disengage the disinterested intelligence, to release it from the entanglements of party and sect—one might almost say of sex— and set it operating over the whole range of human life and circumstance'. The quotation might serve as the manifesto of his life. In matters of religion he was an unflinching rationalist, as is illustrated by several caustic references to what he regarded as the casuistry of Victorian apologetics. But his historic sense—something not native or intrinsic to humanism—and his deep human and aesthetic sensibilities, made him also a reverencing man—attached to old institutions and habits, appreciative of what had moulded the feeling, as well as the mind of the past. He was sensible, in particular, of all that religion had done, in the Victorian era especially, for the energizing and disciplining of mind and imagination. His humanism was more, too, than the accomplished scholar's sense of the unity of knowledge, or the polymath's pleasure in his own virtuosity. It was reinforced by his profound conviction, a conclusion from his historical studies, that society, including both its learned and literary classes and those conducting its practical activities, needed to be whole to be healthy; that unless there is reciprocity of respect and esteem between the different levels at which its life is lived, its energies cancel out instead of supporting each other, and a loss of vitality, with a failure to keep abreast of common tasks, is the result. Impulses, in any event, travel from layer to layer; the audience helps to make the play, whether for better or worse depends on the character of the relationship. In short, Young accepted the view that societies tend naturally to a 'culture'—that is, to a working unity of the social life in which modes of living, from the humblest to the highest, support and reinforce each other, and that social energies throughout the society tend to be more vigorous and fruitful in such conditions of unity. But cultural unity, in his view, does not come unsought; nature must be perfected by art, and to reach and remain at the natural end requires conscious and strenuous effort. Young gives, in fact, a radical twist to a conception which, in the hands of T. S. Eliot, for example, has had conservative implications. There are two passages in which he defines a culture. In the one, it is a 'body of assumptions, judgments, tastes and habits' that 'together form a framework of reference in which, and by which, men of all avocations can communicate with each other'. The order of the elements referred to is 'the order of massiveness and depth, which is the inverse order of mutability'—habits change fairly easily, tastes, judgments and assumptions less easily. In the other passage, Young speaks of a culture as an 'area of inter-communication, living and alert in all directions at once'.

Such inter-communication becomes possible, in his view, only when the 'clerisy'—he appropriates Coleridge's term for the learned and literary classes—accepts a public responsibility for knowledge as a whole—a duty, on the one hand, to understand its movement and its bearing on general issues of the conduct and quality of life, and on the other, to make that understanding as widely apparent as possible. The distinctiveness of Young's use of the conception of a culture is that the context in which he thinks of it is that of a dynamic modern society. For him, therefore, the vigour of a culture is revealed not in adherence to traditional patterns of conduct and thought (which might even amount to that 'froward retention of Custom' which could be 'as turbulent a thing as an Innovation'), but in responses at once new and characteristic to the constant challenges of a changing world. Only in a general temper of the public mind at once responsible, considering, and critical could such responsiveness be expected.

Victorian England had won its way to a culture. The common assumptions, which provided the basis of common understanding, were those of our insular security: the sanctity of the family; the rights and public duties of the leisured classes; the superiority of the representative to all other forms of government; and the unique and exclusive value of European civilization. Classical education provided a body of ideas and standards, a common language of thought, for the educated classes; the Bible served in the same way for the nation as a whole, in its more serious common concerns. The 'clerisy', as is evidenced by the great quarterlies, or by the 'Athenaeum' in the years from 1850 to 1880, took seriously its duty of keeping on terms with the newer science, theology, history and economics; public opinion responded in the value it set on rational and responsible conduct. For a variety of reasons—which Young touches on briefly in his essay *The New Cortegiano* and at greater length in the *Portrait*—after the sixties there was a decline in absorptive power, a failure to integrate new developments in knowledge, and to meet new challenges effectively. A large part of the cause of this lay, in Young's view, in the 'great Victorian omission'—the failure, before 1902, to provide a national secondary school system. 'Fundamentally, what failed in the late

Victorian age and its flash Edwardian epilogue, was the Victorian public, once so alert, so masculine, and so responsible.'

Today, in the twentieth century, the assumptions of the nineteenth, when they hold good at all, do so only in part; classical education, which Young continued to think the best training in precision of idea and thought, now plays a minority role even among the humanities in our universities; familiarity with the Bible and the services of the Church no longer exercises its sobering and refining influence on large sections of the population; scales and tensions have all changed. Whether the golden bowl could ever be mended, in his darker moments Young doubted. The chaos of specialisms and the resulting empire of unreason—things becoming too difficult to understand, and people giving up the effort to understand anything at all—had made disastrous inroads. 'Mentally, in its capacity for formulating, apprehending and exchanging ideas, our Sovereign Plebs is living in the slum.' 'It is all too plain', he wrote in 1948, 'and the experience of Education Officers in the Forces seems to me the clinching demonstration—that our schools have for years been discharging into the world young people without the slightest capacity for, or the remotest interest in what, for brevity, one might call scientific thinking. And the proof is this, that whether they believe or disbelieve, the grounds of their faith or scepticism are purely emotional, traditional, or it might seem accidental. What the schools have failed to teach is that a man has no more right to an opinion for which he cannot account than to a pint of beer for which he cannot pay.' But at other times Young still had hopes, and much of his writing centred round them. A generation was growing up whose parents, as well as themselves, had had a secondary education. It might again be possible to think of education as 'that which enables parents to help their children with their homelessons'. The universities, new and old, were forging new ties between 'clerisy' and people; the university man was now ceasing to be a 'distinguished variety' and becoming an accepted member of characteristic families throughout the land. To Young, the 'educated family', with its members engaged some in practical and some in learned avocations, its womenfolk sharing and influencing the common cultivated and responsible outlook, had been the fortress of the Victorian culture. He hoped it might be possible to return 'on a historic spiral' to something like this—to make the family serve again as a focus of the interpenetration of life and learning. It was a wide view; in its social implications a radical view. To Young, if not full of hope, it was the best hope: he was convinced that nothing fundamental could be done for education except through the family. But again, if there was to be a response of this sort from the public, there must be an 'offer'[1] from the 'clerisy', and essentially the offer must be of knowledge as a coherent and related body. The progress of specialized knowledge could and should not be stayed, but it was no discharge of their responsibilities on the part of the initiates in the different branches of it that they should confine their talk about it to themselves. People cannot be made specialists in everything, but they can be told what learning is and is about, and where it can be found, and learning itself—and this was very much a part of Young's point—gains in vigour and sense of purpose in an atmosphere of discussion to which, as occasion offers, all branches of it contribute. To Young it was always worth while to know a little more about more and more; his Humanism had for him something of the status of a social gospel. And he certainly thought that the power to make specialist knowledge interesting and significant to the layman was one of the tokens of mastery of it.

The other point, of contemporary importance as he conceived it, which Young preached in season and out, was the necessity of re-establishing, for all writing, specialized and technical or not, canons of plain prose style. A passage illustrates the general tenor of his advice. 'If a young man asked me how he could best form his style and train his literary judgment', he wrote in his essay on *Classical Criticism*,[2] 'I should say, "Avoid literary groups; shun criticasteries. Talk as much as you can to educated women older than yourself; and listen, whenever you have a chance, to men

[1] In his address on *Rights and Duties in the Modern State* in *Today and Yesterday*, Young put forward the view that in the 'offer and acceptance of superiorities' 'resides the cohesive power of every society'.
[2] In *Last Essays*.

whose profession requires them to use common words exactly—
officers, civil servants and lawyers—talking about common
things." ' Young's own style was based on the homely word and
illustration. It could be rich with allusion, and rise into singular
beauty at times, but its essence was mind speaking as plainly as
possible to mind.

It is hardly necessary to say that Young's conception of history
was a generous one. Though he wrote little in that kind himself,
he could accept the contention that in the broad sweep, at any rate,
the main stuff of history is political. Defending Gibbon against a
charge of over-emphasis that way, he wrote: 'As a naturalist will,
generally, attach more significance to the osseous structure of an
extinct species, than to the colour or texture of its skin, so the
historian must generally direct his attention to wars and migra-
tions, and the political revolutions of states.' In the *Portrait* he set
out to amplify and correct a traditional account that paid almost
exclusive attention to politics, but it cannot be said, even so, that
he neglects the 'osseous structure' of his subject. The general
effect of his writing, however, was to emphasize the many com-
petences, or at least interests, that the historian needs, the many
fields into which justice to his theme must carry him. He himself
grappled with theological issues, as befitted, indeed, a writer on
Gibbon and on Victorian England. Though he had no scientific
training—but would never have admitted himself disqualified
from scientific thinking—he was deeply conscious of the importance of the scientific revolution, and in one of his *London
Addresses*[3] pleaded for the teaching of the history of science, both
for the sake of its intrinsic interest and importance, and as some
means of bridging the gap between what Sir Charles Snow has
taught us to speak of as the 'two cultures'. In his Leslie Stephen
lecture on *Continuity*,[4] he even quoted a theory of the trade cycle,
though with the admission that it might not be considered a comprehensive one. He was prepared to admit that literary criticism
was not his trade, but very far from prepared to surrender the
historian's interest in the great figures of literature—or in the

3 In *Today and Yesterday*.
4 In *Last Essays*.

minor ones, for that matter. They are the standing sign-posts to
the thought and imagination of the past; to read them and understand what they said, why and how they said it, and the nature of
their hold on their times, was an indispensable duty for the historian and an indispensable element in the training of the historical imagination. It was a private duty imposed on the historian
additional to the duty incumbent on all of us to claim our birthright in our literary and aesthetic heritage. He was no very firm
believer in the 'Lessons of History', 'because the first lesson of
history, and it may well be the last, is that you never know what
is coming next'. Nor had he confidence in historical systems—
'the patch called history is so tiny in relation to the unrecorded
stretch, and the illumination of that patch so imperfect' that the
attempt to raise large structures upon it is the idlest presumption.
It is perhaps in his lecture on *Continuity* that the general statement
of his historical faith might be expected. In this, however, the
element of the contingent and the volitional is strongly emphasized. Continuity is a 'twofold process'; links between past and
present sometimes break down, and are made good again—or are
not—by a sentiment deliberately seeking to root itself in the past.
Continuity is chosen as well as chooses; it can be a matter of job-
bing backwards, as well as of majestic forward impulsion. Whatever his respect for it, history was, for Young, something made in
the last resort by hands, which might be careless or discriminating,
conventional or creative, in what they laid hold of in the past.
Young wrote a scathing review of Croce's *History as the Story of
Liberty,*[5] for which he was reproached in his college. He might,
in some moods, have accepted Croce's dictum that 'all history is
contemporary'.

It was not, indeed, for didactic purposes that Young valued
history, but rather as a key opening new doors to the mind and
imagination. He accepted G. M. Trevelyan's view of it, 'not as
the rival of the classics, or of modern literature, or of the political
sciences, but rather as the house in which they all dwell', and in
that spirit he looked to it to provide the connective tissue for a
modern culture replacing that based on the classical tradition—

[5] In *Last Essays*.

historical apprehension providing a common approach to diverse
intellectual interests and vocations, and recognized by them as
part of their picture of themselves. In matters of the future of the
West and of European culture, Young was a convinced European
and advocate of the importance of teaching European history; in
this context 'the historic view was not an indulgence of the human
fancy, but a dominant and imperative necessity of thought'.
European discussions would otherwise be those of people not
understanding each other. But while Young was prepared to
recommend historical studies and reading to his fellow-members
of the 'clerisy', he would certainly not have wished to impose
them, least of all as comprising, even potentially, an authoritative
body of knowledge. It was here that, while recognizing that only
the university schools could provide the essential initial academic
discipline in the subject, he was apprehensive lest their emphasis
should come to be too much on the latest refinements of accuracy,
the passing on of professional lore; lest historians should be left
with 'no higher aim than to teach the teachers of history how to
teach their successors'. His *mot* about research—'light dies before
that uncreating word'—should be taken as referring to the somewhat naïve faith, still to be met, that any detached piece of detailed
work gives its producer the indisputable title to the proud name
of historian. Academic historians, on their part, sometime spoke
of Young as more of a literary man than a historian. He would
have denied the distinction; and in any case the *Portrait* meets
the most rigorous standards of accuracy and thoroughness.
Indeed it makes some academic work on its subject seem rather
amateurish in comparison. Young's own prescription for the
apprentice-historian would have been to pitch him into some large
field of study with the instruction to read everything in it—perhaps
to teach, under rather more senior guidance than is generally
given—and leave him to choose his subjects of research later,
when his own curiosity had found them for him. The foundation
of historical training was, for him, keeping company with the
great historians; his prescription for the study of a subject or a
period 'reading till you can hear people talking'; the practice of
history 'an unceasing conversation or debate'; and the historian

himself an explorer reporting his travels. The business of history was to open, not to close the mind; to stimulate that historic imagination which is not content till it sees things in terms of human reality—'men's common thoughts of common things'. It was from this point of view that Young believed so strongly in the value and importance of local history. The thought that 'all that happened here and might have happened to us' literally brought history home to us; it could kindle minds not otherwise accessible; and Young believed enough in the liberal and liberating value of the historical imagination to think it important that it should be set on to work whenever and wherever possible. In an illuminating and penetrating phrase Young spoke of the historian as 'one for whom the past keeps something of the familiar triviality of the present, and the present has already some of the shadowy magnificence of the past'. Olympian as his mind might seem at stretch, it played very happily with familiar triviality, ready, in moments of relaxation, to grub up what it could where it could, though with the ranging imagination that could give moment to trivialities. The essays in this book differ in mood and weight. Some are formal, some lightly written. In all of them, it may be said, however, the quality of historical imagination is present: they uncover rather than cover their subjects, and send us back to reading and meditation.

W. D. HANDCOCK,

University of Exeter.

VICTORIAN CENTENARY

From *The Times*, 11 May 1937

AT the beginning of 1837 we are midway between the passing of the Reform Act in 1832 and the defeat of its authors, the Whigs, at the General Election of 1841. They had much to be proud of. By enfranchising the middle classes they could claim to have saved the country from such a revolution as that which, in 1830, had swept away the restored monarchy of France and put Louis-Philippe on the throne. The new Poor Law, by arresting the flow of indiscriminate relief, had delivered rural England from impending bankruptcy; agricultural unemployment was dropping, wages were in many counties rising, and, to give the great experiment in social amelioration its fair opportunity of succeeding, Nature was providing a sequence of good harvests. The standing vexation of tithes had been equitably mitigated; and the newly created Ecclesiastical Commission was preparing to deal with the other mischief of plural livings and the gross inequalities of clergymen's stipends. Finally, the Municipal Corporations Act had cleared away the antiquated, and often corrupt, machinery of local government and given the towns a clean and modern framework within which to exercise their civic energies. The electorate, which we may think of as one man in six: the forty shilling freeholder, the fifty pound tenant at will, and the ten-pound householder rated to the relief of the poor, had much to be grateful for, not much to complain of, and not very much to be interested in. It is a time of apathy, the product in part of prosperity, in part of reaction from the excited hopes and apprehensions of 1831. The storm had passed, the earthquake had come and gone; and, to outward seeming, everything was much the same, if not, as petulant Radicals sometimes asserted, rather worse.

Even Ireland, under the amiable administration of Lord Mulgrave, might be described as tranquil, though with a dangerous tranquillity depending less on the contentment of the people, or the efficiency of government, than on the authority of

O'Connell and his General, or National, Association. Throughout Great Britain the determination to maintain the Union with Ireland was overwhelming in its strength; to repeal the Act of 1800 and to leave the two islands united only by what O'Connell called 'the golden link of the Crown' was not within the range of public thought. Yet nothing less, if his assurances to his followers were to be believed, would content him; and his sovereignty over Irish Catholic opinion seemed to be almost absolute. The alternatives, therefore, were either to go on making concessions to Irish demands, in the hope that the chief demand, by being indefinitely postponed, would in the end be forgotten: or else, stubbornly to resist every measure which, by making Irish opinion more effective, would intensify the agitation for Repeal. With what show of reason or justice, it was asked on the one side, can you refuse to Ireland either a Poor Law or a Municipal Corporation Act? Is there any deep-seated peculiarity in the Irish people which makes them unfit for either? And on the other: But what assurance can you give us that Corporations, harmless and even useful as they appear, will not be perverted into political organizations, animated by an unflinching hostility to the English Connexion and the Church? United by the watchword 'No Repeal!', Whigs and Tories went down to do battle under the opposing banners of Justice for Ireland and the Church of Danger; and, as matters stood, the Tories were bound to win.

'The tongue of the Right Honourable Member for Tamworth governs England.' Even party invective, if it is to command a hearing, must have a kernel of truth; no one ever called Mr Fox a kill-joy or Mr Pitt undignified, or charged Canning with excessive modesty or Palmerston with irresolution. The suspicions with which old Tories, and strong Tories, regarded Peel were justified. He was not really at home in the Tory Party, because he would never have been at home in any party. But he played on the House of Commons like an old fiddle. He was not a man of wide outlook, or deep and far-sighted reflection; so far his Whig and Radical assailants were right. But he could make an administration work with the power and precision of a fine engine. By his side of the front Opposition bench were Lord Stanley, the most dashing, and

Sir James Graham, after O'Connell perhaps the most powerful, debater in the House. Both had sat in the Whig Cabinet, and left it on Church policy. Stanley was to be thrice Prime Minister. Graham might have been Prime Minister had he set his course that way. On the Treasury bench Lord John Russell, with courage equal to any encounter, but judgement not always equal to his courage, had to fight the battle of the Whigs with such help as he could get from Howick at the Colonial Office and Morpeth, Chief Secretary for Ireland. Palmerston rarely spoke except on foreign affairs, and, though a man of fifty-three, he was very far still from that ascendancy he was some day to exercise over Parliament, and the imagination of his country and the world.

The scene of these contentions was no longer the Chapel of St Stephen, which had been destroyed in the fire of 1834, but the old House of Lords hastily roofed and furnished, and whitewashed into the semblance of a conventicle in a manufacturing town. The Speaker, Abercromby, was an unfortunate successor to Manners-Sutton, who had kept a firm hold on the House through the agitations of three Reform Bills; he allowed members to argue with him and to debate points on which he ought to have ruled. 'This,' said Stanley, after one such wrangle, 'is the very oddest way of keeping order I ever saw in my life.' Twice in 1837 the business of the nation was suspended while cooler heads were persuading incensed colleagues, one of them Admiral Codrington, the victor of Navarino, not to carry their differences and their pistols to Putney Common or the gravel-pits at Notting Hill. Those who think that the tone of public life is lower today than it might be should study some faithful report of a debate when O'Connell had lashed the Tories into a howling frenzy; when, if ever the tempest lulled, some mischief-maker would awaken it again by quoting what O'Connell had said elsewhere; when young members, flown with insolence and wine, came down, from Brooks's or the Carlton, to bait or cheer the Radicals who had dined more soberly off a cutlet at the Reform; and early passengers through Old Palace Yard halted to listen to the farmyard noises proceeding from the Commons.

The virulence of debate was in no way assuaged, perhaps it was even exacerbated, by the knowledge that when the last word had been spoken in the Commons there still remained the Lords. During the long years of unchallenged Tory government the public had almost forgotten the Upper House; and Radicals hopefully believed that in the great defeat of 1830 its power had been finally shattered. Never have political expectations been so conspicuously disappointed. Behind the Right Hon. Member for Tamworth was the Duke, and the whole phalanx of Tory lords, very recent lords many of them, the offspring of Pitt's conviction that any man of £10,000 a year was entitled to be a peer if he liked; lords 'clutched from the counting houses of Cornhill' to make mirth for the Radical newspapers and furnish a topic for the fluent wit of young Disraeli.

Outgeneralled in the Commons, in the Lords the Government was outmanned and outgunned. Brougham had returned, to lash the friends whom he had abandoned or by whom he had been abandoned; and, by a refinement of malevolence, he chose to deliver his terrifying sarcasms from a place next to the Prime Minister. Lyndhurst was against them, and Lyndhurst was as formidable as he bid fair to be immortal. Born in Boston, when Boston was a British port, he was still youthful enough to take Disraeli's mistress off his hands; twenty years later he was pelting his ungainly Scottish successor, Campbell, with malicious wit over the Obscene Publications Bill; and he lived till 1863. Melbourne deserves the amused affection with which posterity has agreed to regard him: he was a man of many gifts, attractive and rare. But in no conceivable combination of circumstances could he have been a great Prime Minister or a vigorous party leader. Nor, as he himself had already most convincingly demonstrated, could the Duke of Wellington. But so long as the Duke was there no dangerous conflict between the Houses was likely to arise. Every one knew that if things ever came to a crisis he would say again: 'My Lords, about turn, march'; and march they would. And most people trusted his sound good sense, his known horror of civil dissension, to say it when it needed to be said.

On one topic he spoke with an authority unequalled in Europe, and in the general want of things to occupy the public mind that topic was disproportionately prominent. By the Quadruple Treaty of 1834, and its Additional Articles, we had undertaken, in concert with France, to support the Constitutional Government of Queen Isabella, then a child of four, against the absolutist Pretender Don Carlos. In 1835 the Foreign Enlistment Act had been suspended by Order in Council to enable a British Legion, some 10,000 strong, to be recruited as auxiliaries to the Queen's Army. The commander, Colonel de Lacy Evans, a Peninsular veteran who lived to be a Crimean veteran, was something of a Radical hero, having in 1835 won Westminster from John Cam Hobhouse, Byron's friend and fellow-traveller, who had resigned on a point of conscience which to a robuster age is almost invisible. Evans had struggled bravely, and not quite unsuccessfully, to turn his riff-raff into an army, while all the common incidents of civil war in Spain, the shooting of prisoners, murder of priests, and destruction of convents, were enacted on their familiar stage. Further to aid the cause of constitutional government we had liberally furnished the Queen with military stores, and a squadron under Lord John Hay was operating on the Biscay coast; his marines were sometimes useful in covering the flight of Evans's legionaries.

Wellington did not like it; he knew too much of war in Spain and of the Spanish character; and a reference in the King's Speech on January 27th to the success of our co-operating forces was enough to make cautious men uneasy. By intervening at all, Peel pointed out, we had set an example which the despotic Powers, Russia and Austria, might find it to their advantage to follow elsewhere—in the Turkish Empire, for example, or in Italy; and, once embarked, where were we to stop? Must there be more ships, more guns, more marines, assistance gradually extending to occupation? And all for what? To establish a government which the Spaniards, if they really wanted it, were well able to set up for themselves; or to support the Stock Exchange and give the Rothschilds and Ricardos a chance of recovering their Spanish advances? 'How is it,' Mahon once asked, 'that whereas Don Carlos began with an army of 30,000 and has officially lost 310,000 killed he still has an army of 30,000?' 'I can only suppose,' Peel suggested, 'that as 310,000 is the number of muskets supplied by Her Majesty's Government to the Queen, the Spaniards think it a decent compliment to assume that each musket killed its man.' But that they would ever pay for them seemed unlikely.

On March 17th the Carlists inflicted a crushing defeat on Evans and his legion at Hernani; and a month later another Peninsular veteran, Sir Henry Hardinge, rose to move that the legion be recalled and naval assistance limited to purely naval purposes. Palmerston's defence is a fine example of his gay and gallant eloquence, tossing old mistakes to oblivion and taking inconsistencies with the easy power of a thoroughbred; ranging and swooping from large prospects of history to the precise interpretation of an article; and always circling round the doctrine which, in years to come, was to distress and incense Victoria and her Consort so deeply, when it was applied to the young Italian nation. 'What,' he asked, 'is the great and fundamental difference between the champions of Divine Right and the advocates of the popular principle? Nothing more decidedly than this: that the first party consider nations to be like a private estate, the beneficial property of their possessor, and that hereditary rights must in all cases be held sacred; while the other party are of opinion that governments are established for the good of the many, and that there must reside in every community the power to change not only the forms of government but the order of the succession. This was the principle on which our own government was founded in 1688,' and where the relations of subjects and Sovereign were concerned, his own Sovereign not excluded, a Whig of 1688 Lord Palmerston would ever be. To brand the Tory opposition, too, as Carlists, as belated devotees of Divine Right and the Inquisition, was a telling touch, only a little spoiled by the fact that the Constitutional Government had abrogated the self-government of the Basques which Carlos was defending, and that, in their entire indifference to the rights of humanity in wartime, there was not a *real* to choose between Carlists and Cristinos. The fortune of war brought the controversy to a close. In May Evans retrieved his defeat by a victory on the same ground and took Irun and Fuenterrabia. What was left of the legion returned home, its departure expedited by a quarrel between its acting commander, O'Connell, and the Spanish general O'Donnell. Spain disappeared from the debates and Ireland resumed her natural pre-eminence as the grand exasperator of English politics.

In a rash and bitter phrase, not yet forgotten, Lyndhurst had stigmatized the Irish as aliens in blood, in language and in religion, thereby furnishing the members of the General Association with as good an argument for Repeal as their hearts could desire. But the Orangemen were in the field as well, and at a great synod in Dublin on February 24th they passed fourteen resolutions, arraigning the Administration in whole and in detail. They were fighting for the relics of ascendancy, which had been fatally impaired when in 1829 the Catholics received the rights of citizenship; for government by the minority; for a Protestant magistracy, Protestant jurors and sheriffs, and a Protestant Church. If words meant anything, and in Ireland it must be owned they do not always mean very much, the Orangemen desired the impeachment of Lord Mulgrave and the dismissal of all Catholics from public employment. It is unfortunately inevitable that when a long course of exclusive appointment and promotion is to be corrected, the correction should appear to the dispossessed as a new course of unmitigated jobbery on the other side.

In 1835 there was one Catholic magistrate in Ireland; Mulgrave appointed six, a step by itself enough to set every Orangeman whooping from Bloody Foreland to Sheep's Head. Mulgrave honestly intended to hold the balance even; he undoubtedly enjoyed the confidence of the Catholics and the affection of the people at large; and a gentleman, who keeps forty horses in his stable, and wastes the family estate on private theatricals, has at least three of the qualifications necessary for popularity in Ireland. But some of his appointments were unquestionably provocative, and he had brought himself into particular notice by an amiable practice of dropping in on gaols and discharging the prisoners. Those who are familiar with our Parliamentary ways can divine the consequences. Hour after hour, the question on the paper being the Municipal Corporations Bill, the House seethed and bubbled with the sufferings of Mr Carter and the merits of Mr

Pigot, with charges of favouritism and counter-charges of oppression; whether Pat Magrath had shot at the revenue man out of malice or bravado, whether Mr Tighe could be fairly described as a person, whether Mr Cassidy, magistrate, was an eminent grazier or a clerk in a distillery, and whether Mr Corboy had, or had not, come out of prison fatter than he went in.

The argument which rises out of the hurly-burly was stated in a terse sarcasm, by one of the Irish members. There were, he said, 7,000,000 Catholics in Ireland and 700,000 Protestants. Therefore the Catholics must not be town councillors but they must pay tithes. Give me Municipal Corporations, O'Connell had told the Association, and I will soon get all the rest. Seen in this light the appointment of Mr Pigot to be legal adviser to the Viceroy assumed a truly portentous significance. His career fully justified the choice: Chief Baron Pigot, as he was to become, was one of the best lawyers in Ireland. But he was an active member of the Association: the programme of the Association was Disendowment of the Church and Repeal of the Union: the Government had capitulated to O'Connell and the Papists; the Protestant religion was in danger. Agitation, which had swept away the Catholic disabilities in 1829, would take the field with redoubled power. Then, when they had served his turn, O'Connell would throw the Whigs aside and unite with the Radicals. Already the banquet halls where the Association feasted and declaimed were decorated with Radical banners; vote by ballot, extension of the suffrage, reform of the House of Lords; and in all the eight nights of the Irish debate the one speech which, read at this distance of time, seems to rise above declamation into real eloquence was delivered by a Radical, Carlyle's pupil, the young and brilliant Charles Buller. 'You tell us,' he said, 'that the concession of Municipal Corporations means the destruction of the Establishment. Give us then some reason why the Establishment should be maintained.' But there was none: it was the misfortune of the Conservative Party that it was committed to the support of an institution which could not be defended by argument or abandoned without dishonour. Hereditary bondsmen of the priesthood is not an argument. Minions of Popery is not an argument. Yet for want of better they had to serve.

But Radicalism itself was waning. The year before, Buller had gaily observed to a colleague: 'I see what it is, Molesworth: very soon you and I will be left to tell Grote.' The country was tired of agitation, and five elections in six years; the £10 householder was not disposed to see his new privileges swamped in a fresh extension of the suffrage; and, though moderate opinion was moving towards the ballot, it was moving reluctantly and with misgivings. To the English Radicals, the ballot was what Corporations were to the Irish: the first instalment, bringing all the others in sequence, until the Constitution had been remodelled on the lines of philosophic democracy. But between the obvious benefits of secret voting and its contingent and incalculable consequences, even liberally disposed men found it not easy to make up their minds. In the days of rotten boroughs, there was little intimidation of voters, because intimidation was superfluous. With the enlargement of the electorate it had become, especially in the smaller towns—and there were still boroughs with only two or three hundred voters—a serious mischief; an elector who could be put into the street for voting against his landlord or his customer was neither independent nor free. True, was the answer; but do you really desire the electorate to be entirely independent of the educated and propertied class? Remember, too, that the voters are acting virtually on behalf of a much larger unenfranchised class, who surely have the right to know how they cast their vote. Granted that some men now vote against their convictions, is not the example of the honest tradesman or yeoman who defies the consequences and follows his conscience of still greater importance in maintaining the spirit of independence? Is not occasional tyranny, restrained as it is by public opinion, better than a constant watch on the voter's doings, his conversation, the meetings he attends, and the newspapers he reads? You say that open voting allows the landlords to be bullies. We reply that the ballot will teach the landlords to be spies and the voters to be sneaks.

The ballot was under the special patronage of George Grote, banker and scholar, whose annual discourse on the subject was logically irrefutable. A generation later, when it had been conceded at last, his wife asked him whether he was not proud. His answer deserves to be remembered, for the Queen had few wiser subjects than the old historian. 'I have come to perceive,' he said, 'that the choice between one man and another, among the English people, matters less than I used formerly to think it did. Take a section of society; cut it through from top to bottom, and examine the composition of the successive layers. They are much alike throughout the scale. Take whatever class you will, the English mind is much of one pattern, and a House of Commons cannot afford to be above its own constituencies, in intelligence, in knowledge, or in patriotism.' It was the weakness of the Radicals that they aspired to be, not only above the constituencies, but above Parliament itself in knowledge and intelligence; naturally above the Tories, whom everybody acknowledged to be the stupid party—'poor, poor Bashaw', Lord Dudley was once heard murmuring to his dog: 'thou hast not an immortal soul, and Sir Thomas Lethbridge has'—but also above the Whigs, who could never be got to see that the ballot must be granted if the Reform Act was to yield its full effect, and the whole body of enlightened opinion brought to bear on Parliament. But by Whig doctrine not less than Tory, Parliament was meant to represent, not public opinion as an indistinguishable mass, but rather the several chief interests of the country; land, commerce, industry, with an acknowledged leaning towards the land as the stablest element in the social structure. Between this view and the Radical conception of Parliament as the organ of the actual numerical majority in the country at any moment, no accommodation was possible. 'Therefore,' said Roebuck, 'speaking openly and calmly, well knowing the consequences, being neither hurried nor confused, I say the Whigs have deceived the people.'

In politics, at all events, and perhaps in life, it is not so important to be right as to be right at the proper time. In their conception of public efficiency: in their notions of Imperial self-government, national education, and local administration: the Radicals were too far ahead of their age to be listened to, and they were becoming embittered by disappointment. At no time, perhaps, in the whole of the past century do we hear so much resentment, so much impatience, over the proceedings of Parliament and the make-believe of the party game. The early writings of Dickens and Carlyle are charged with disaffection bred by the wearying spectacle of two aristocratic factions divided only by political animosity and united in their resistance to organic change. If the Lords threw out the main measure of the Session, the Irish Corporations Bill, would the Whigs show fight? Everyone knew they would not. The Lords did not throw it out. They only postponed it till they had the rest of the Government's Irish legislation—Poor Law and Tithes—before them. As they were not forthcoming, the Corporations Bill lapsed. Another Session and still nothing done; and on their second measure, an ingenious device for abolishing Church rates by forming a fund out of the rents of Bishops' lands, the Government majority had fallen to five.

But the most useful legislation is not always that which occupies most time in Parliament, and this seemingly ineffective Session has to its credit a measure which removed one of the ugliest blots on our national life. The shadow of the gallows is so dark on the pages of early Victorian literature that it is with surprise we read that in England and Wales in 1836 there were only seventeen executions. But there were nearly 500 death sentences. In practice, the extreme penalty was only exacted for murder, or, very rarely, for robbery or murderous assault with aggravating circumstances. One such case was still fresh in memory, and, translated into fiction, is not likely soon to be forgotten. By New Year's Day in 1837, his twenty-fifth birthday not yet reached, Dickens was a classic from Calcutta to the Mississippi: and in March, to a public which was debating the Poor Law in all its bearings, he opened the story of Oliver Twist, the workhouse boy. From the workhouse he carried his readers swiftly to that academy for young thieves which the police had shortly before discovered in London, and its professor and proprietor, who, after reference to the Privy Council, had been duly sent to execution. Under the criminal law as reformed in 1837, though Bill Sikes could still have been hanged, Fagin could only have been transported. Six measures introduced by Lord John Russell brought the law into conformity with practice and with public opinion, and delivered the Courts from the odious mummery of passing sentences which no one expected to be executed. The horror of public hangings remained for another thirty years.

The Irish Corporations Bill gave its last gasp in the Lords on June 8th. If the King lived a few months longer, it seemed more than likely that, from mere exhaustion or a Radical revolt, the Whigs would be defeated, Peel would get his dissolution, and the Tories would return to office. But, as the law then stood, on a demise of the Crown a new Parliament had to be summoned, and King William died before the liberal impetus of 1830 was quite spent in the constituencies. The feelings of the young Queen were believed to be with the Whigs: she was thought to have a will of her own: and the notion that the Crown should possess a directing and even initiating voice in the Government was still current, not only among the ignorant. When in 1834 William IV, taking advantage of Melbourne's nonchalance, had dismissed his Whig Ministers and sent Hudson posting across Europe to bring Peel back from Rome, the prerogative so intemperately exercised had almost broken in his hands: almost, not quite. That Ministers are given by Parliament to the Crown, not by the Crown to Parliament, was a doctrine established in the course of Victoria's reign, not fully accepted at its opening. There was no stouter Radical in Parliament than Joseph Hume, the economist. Yet he spoke openly in the House of the strength afforded to the Government by the favour of the Sovereign. Two years later, so sound a Whig as Macaulay could speak to a Scottish audience of an Administration strong in the support of the Crown; though so candid an observer certainly could not claim that it was strong in anything else. The last three years of the Whig Administration were to be years of ignominy and gloom. Like a once popular individual, the last thing a once popular party ever realizes is that it has begun to be a bore.

The transference of the Crown from an elderly, undignified, and slightly crazy sailor to a girl endowed with remarkable self-possession and much force of character, could hardly be without its picturesque circumstances; and the early morning visit of the Archbishop and the Lord Chamberlain to Kensington, to the palace in a garden, brought a waft of Arcadia into the close and dusty air which seems congenial to the House of Brunswick. But there were other circumstances less agreeable. There was the immediate question of the succession; the heir presumptive, Ernest, Duke of Cumberland, bore, whether justly or not, a character more odious than any other member of his family; and he opened his reign as King of Hanover by suspending the Constitution of his kingdom. He was known to be an Orangeman, he was popularly believed to be a murderer, and, if the Queen happened to die childless, it was doubtful whether England would accept him as King, and almost certain that Ireland would not.

There was the Duchess of Kent, too, and Sir John Conroy, to be disposed of; and disposed of they were. There was the Civil List also. The financial entanglements of George III and his family were notorious, and it was difficult to make a new start without ripping up the old scandal of the pension list. Following the example of 1831, the Royal income was relieved entirely from all charges, such as the salaries of judges and ambassadors, more properly falling on the public, and the hereditary revenues were made over to the State. But the Queen retained her revenues as Duchess of Lancaster, and as trustee for the Duke of Cornwall when one should be born; and they were believed, in spite of much mismanagement, to be large. To grant a Civil List for a life which might witness great changes in the cost of living seemed improvident: to grant it for a peroid of years seemed to betray a want of confidence in the Sovereign. And why the Queen's mother should receive £30,000 a year and two houses rent free it was not easy to see. The whole business was uneasy and unpleasant, and the words with which the Speaker presented the Civil List Bill for the Royal Assent might be taken as a rebuke to the Queen's ancestors or as a warning to herself. 'In making provision,' he said, 'for the support of the dignity and honour of the Crown, we have acted in a liberal and confiding spirit, trusting that that which has been freely granted, will be so administered as to conciliate the favour and command the respect of your Majesty's people.' They are not courtly words. But between Liberals who had no veneration for the office, and Conservatives who had no affection for the person, of the Sovereign, the atmosphere surrounding the Monarchy at the death of King William was dry, bleak, and critical: and, beyond the natural if superficial popularity that any girl of eighteen in a novel position will command, for the Queen herself there was little feeling of any kind. Only in Ireland was she for a short while the object of a vague and rapturous hope; at the election in August the ballad singers were almost as busy with the Queen as with O'Connell, and the resounding emphasis with which the Liberator took the Oath of Allegiance at the Table did not go unobserved at Court.

From our safe distance in time we can now see that, of the two main attributes which the Constitution assigns to the Crown, its impartial elevation and its unifying symbolism, one was determined by the prudence and careful conduct of Prince Albert, the other by the natural course of history. The Queen began her reign with the unfortunate idea in her stubborn little head that H.M. Opposition was the Opposition to her Majesty. 'I hope to God', she wrote, 'that the elections will be favourable': if they had gone wrong she would have taken her first steps under the tutelage of Peel, so shy and awkward; and of the Duke, whose deafness ensured that his observations, though always to the point, were not always to the point under discussion. But the elections went right: though England returned a Conservative majority, the Government were twenty or thirty ahead. The Radicals sustained some awkward losses: Roebuck was out for four years; Grote barely scraped in; Westminster, Middlesex, Liverpool, Hull, all went Tory; and Hume had to borrow a seat from O'Connell. At the opening of the Session, Lord John boldly defied them: there was to be no Ballot and no extension of the Suffrage. 'Is this a coalition?' someone asked. 'I know nothing of any coalition,' he answered; but the historic parties were essentially in accord, and, call it coalition or not, the demand for constitutional change was to be resisted to the utttermost, whether it was urged by Radicals in the House, or more dangerously by the working classes out of doors.

Already that dark cloud of misery which hangs so heavy over the early Victorian years was rising in the West. For a while the impending depression had been concealed by the bustle of the new railroads and their demand for equipment and labour. The glory of the road, which shines for us in some of the most winning pages of our literature, the ringing hoofs, the ample hostelries, the iris-tinted rounds of beef, and the wayside gardens that welcomed the returning exile, were fading; and the white pennon was already flying across the countryside. Those who chose to avert their eyes from the hand-loom weavers and the sight of the famous industry perishing, might say without much exaggeration in 1836 that there was work for all who sought it; and the New Poor Law, by abolishing outdoor relief for the able-bodied, had certainly made them more eager to find it, even if it was only work on a Dorset farm at eight shillings a week, or else in a factory, to which children might be carried sleeping in their father's arms through the sleet of a winter morning. But there were signs that the years of abundance were ending; there were doubts whether the banks would stand the strain of a long depression, or the Poor Law carry the burden of widespread unemployment and its own unpopularity.

The first overt token of impending trouble was the failure of the Agricultural Bank of Ireland in the autumn of 1836. Shortly afterwards the Bank of England had to come to the rescue of the Northern and Central of Manchester. Simultaneously, overtrading, land speculation, and a mismanaged currency were drawing the United States to the verge of financial collapse, while the competition for American business was bringing enormous quantities of unsecured American paper on to the London market. Again the Bank of England had to come forward, this time to save the accepting houses, and moderate the volume of American bills, and the repercussion on America was so violent that in April every bank in the Union suspended payment. The Bank of England had let its reserves run dangerously low; gold was expected from America, and no gold came. But the warning shiver passed, with no general stoppage or widespread bankruptcy. By the end of the summer the country seemed to have righted itself and economists could analyse the cause of the crisis and learn its lessons. They were obtrusively plain; at home, the over-issue of notes and credit

2

by the provincial banks—it was about this time that the habit of paying by cheque took hold of us; in foreign trade, the abuse of open credits and accommodation bills; in both, over-trading and speculation. In these discussions the lines of Peel's Bank Act of 1843 were drawn.[1] The separation of the Issuing and Banking Departments, and the limitation of the fiduciary issue, had come to be generally accepted as the proper defence against financial distress.

The commercial and industrial ebb and flow of the world was of greater range than could be brought within any formula, unless it were that England should be the workshop of the world, and the rest of the world her customer. But the customer must be kept in funds, and the funds could only be provided by sales in the English market; of produce generally, of food in particular. There-fore—and, from the point of view of the industrialist, the argu-ment is irresistible—whatever protection our laws gave to home-grown food must be abolished; or only so much left as would give the landowner a fair set-off against the Poor Rate and other charges to which landed property was subject and industrial property was not. Between protection, under the sliding scale of 1828, and free trade, there was this middle way, the fixed duty on corn. But whether, without protection, the land could be kept in cultivation; and to what state England would be reduced if to occasional unemployment in the towns there was added a vast and permanent unemployment of the rural population, these were questions which had to be faced even if they could not be answered.

But what of the people who spun, and wove; who hammered the steel, and mined the coal which turned the wheels of the work-shop; who were outside the electorate of 1832, and clamouring, some of them very loudly, to be let in; whose discontent sometimes relieved iself in strikes, sometimes in riots; whose savage industry was a wonder, and almost a terror, to strangers from the leisurely South; that Other Nation whose habits and customs, science, armed with the new instrument of statistics, was beginning to register and explore? The British Association, meeting at Liver-pool in August, found itself discussing the state of education in

[1] This refers to Bank Charter Act 7 and 8 Vict., C.32, of 1844 [Ed.].

Bolton, Manchester, Liverpool, and York; the housing and domestic condition of six cotton towns and Bristol; wages in Nottingham during the depression; the causes, progress, and cost of the Preston strike; the relation between literacy and crime; the extent of juvenile delinquency. That the assembled scientists were deeply moved, and that the newspapers did not care to publish all the figures, we can believe and understand. But the final impression, on us and perhaps on them, is rather one of utter helplessness. There was no lack of genuine good will, made the more active in many minds by an equally genuine alarm. The contrast of affluence and misery was more than heartbreaking, it was terrifying. But where were they to begin?

Sooner or later all reformers came round to the belief that the one fundamental and remediable mischief was the lack of any system for educating the children of the poor. From this followed, in the first place, a fearful volume of juvenile crime; at any moment there were in the prisons of England and Wales about 12,000 youthful prisoners, some 2,000 being children under twelve, committed or imprisoned for offences from larceny of a coconut upwards, and herded very often with old and hardened sinners. Unchecked and reformed, they grew up to form the underworld of London and the great towns; to join the army of vagrants always on the tramp; to add their brutality to whatever agitation might be in progress. Somewhat higher were those who went from their beds, often in a cellar, to the brickfields or the gasworks, thence to the ginshop, from the ginshop back to the cellar, and knew no other life. Above them were the workpeople in the staple industries, for whom the hope of self-dependence was not altogether a delusive one; rising towards the Respectable Working Classes, whose womenfolk, at least, went to church or more often to chapel, who were careful with their wages, drank not, smoked not, enrolled themselves in Mechanics' Institutes, and did not marry till they could afford it. Always that Malthusian shadow of over-population, surplus labour, low wages, misery, famine, and fever haunted the minds of reformers, and shaped their ideals; the little house, if bare, yet clean; the little garden; money in the savings bank; and the children at school. All over England there were villages and small industrial towns under the eye of a resident master, where to a hopeful eye the ideal seemed to be taking body. But when that eye turned to the immense and shapeless growths of the Black Country, or explored the hardly human horror of Glasgow or Seven Dials, even complacency was silent.

To plough unflinchingly through the world of labour, throwing the surplus population, or, as we should say, the unemployed, into the new workhouses, and keeping them there in a state of reasonable discomfort until there were jobs for them outside, or ships, perhaps, to take them to Canada, was the formula to which the Poor Law Commissioners were bent on giving effect. Some of them might quail before the loud and bitter resentment which their doings, in particular their insistence on the separation of aged couples, provoked, and of which John Walter, proprietor of *The Times,* made himself the spokesman. Their secretary, Edwin Chadwick, quailed at nothing; and all over southern England, where the mischief of the old Poor Law had sunk deepest, his drastic surgery was commended by its results. But north of Trent, where the bread and children scale had not made its way, and the working population had kept some sense of independence, there, and in Birmingham and in the Black Country, the oscillations of employment were determined not by the seasons or the abundance or shortage of harvests, but by the markets, distant and uncontrollable, of the Continent, of America, of the Far East. Early in 1837 the lace trade of Nottingham suddenly collapsed, mainly for want of American buyers. The Poor Law formula, brought to the test, failed completely when applied to an industrial population, and in the teeth of the economists, the authorities of Nottingham fell back on public works. But what would happen if the depression returned and deepened all over the North: if the political agitation for the ballot, short Parliaments, and an extended franchise was reinforced and embittered by the cry for food; if the Midlands, which had mustered 200,000 strong in defence of the Reform Bill, mustered again for a more radical reform—these, too, were questions to which no man could give an answer, but which no thoughtful man could for long keep out of his mind.

The opposition to the Poor Law was partly constitutional and partly humanitarian. There was no precedent for a Government Department, and one moreover not represented in Parliament, exercising such extensive powers of regulation and control. The orders of the Commissioners had in effect the force of law, and the elected guardians were little more than the agents of an irresponsible central board. That the new administration often caused great hardship, especially to the aged poor, was scarcely to be denied. But in defence of the principle of the Act were ranged all the economists, and names of the greatest weight in Parliament; and it was reasonable to ask that a law supported by Peel and Graham for the Conservatives, Roebuck and Hume for the Radicals, should be given its fair run. Nor were the humanitarians all on one side. Against the humanity of sentiment was arranged a sterner, more stoical, but certainly not less generous, philanthropy, willing to accept or overlook some passing harshness and suffering, if the end was to restore and maintain the self-respect and self-dependence of the poor. Many of the controversies of our own day first make themselves heard in the assault and defence of the New Poor Law: the relations between Whitehall and the local authorities, the possibilities of industrial migration, the argument for and against public works, the account to be taken of savings in apportioning relief; and Stanhope, proclaiming the right of the unemployed man to maintenance in full comfort, seems to have strayed into the wrong century and the wrong House.

Not very willingly the Government granted a Committee of Inquiry into the working of the Act. It is the age of inquiry and of experiments in the method of inquiry, and the cost of investigation was becoming a substantial item in the Budget and a standing complaint against the Government. Three agencies were available. The Poor Law Commissioners with their thirty-nine Assistant Commissioners, and an admirably organized office, were better equipped for the purpose than any other Government Department. The Act itself had been prepared after inquiry by a Royal Commission, and for topics of some magnitude this model was preferred. But the traditional mechanism was a Select Committee of the House of Commons, usually fifteen in number, and often most perfunctorily attended: in 1837 eighteen such committees were sitting on matters ranging from aborigines to salmon fishing. It was not an efficient mechanism, and an honourable member who moved for a Select Committee to discover why the trains were late on the Birmingham and Liverpool Railway came near to reducing it to absurdity.

But neither was Parliament itself so efficient as the country had a right to expect. The last Session of King William's Parliament lasted eighty-eight sitting days. On one the Commons went home for want of a quorum: on seven they were counted out. Government business took twenty-eight days. The new House, which met in November, with 158 novices on the benches, seemed likely to waste even more time, and achieve even fewer results. Lord John made an appeal for greater regularity of business, and carried an amendment of the standing orders, securing three nights for the Government and a restriction of private members' motions. The back benchers never welcome a curtailment of their rights or their speeches, and a little revolt, of no consequence in itself, is worth recording for one circumstance. Disraeli went into the lobby with Gladstone and a mixed gathering of unbending Radicals and stern Tories, against Russell and Peel. But, as long experience should by now have taught us, the efficiency of the House rests ultimately on good will and a good Speaker, and in 1837 tempers were as acrid as the Speaker was feeble. The election had left O'Connell and his tail in a commanding position in the House: and a group known as the Spottiswoode Gang, and headed by old Burdett, once the people's champion, and now as sound a Tory as ever sat, were collecting funds to contest as many Irish returns as possible and so wear the Irish majority down. An unlucky novice, little Mr Blewitt of Monmouth, rose on December 6th to call attention to their proceedings. 'What qualifications,' he modestly asked, 'have I, a young and inexperienced member, to put myself forward thus prominently in the face of my country?' Long before Mr Blewitt, by way of Coke, Blackstone, a quotation from Lucretius, and our Virgin Queen in the spring-tide and blossom of her maiden intellect, had reached his resolution, the answer was obvious and the House was in hysterics. The next day the Speaker offered his resignation as no longer enjoying the confidence of the Commons. The warning should have been enough. But the storm awoke again, and another novice, no better advised than Mr Blewitt, rashly ventured to encounter it. What followed is still remembered, and will be remembered as long as English history is read. In the words of Hansard 'the impatience of the House would not allow the honourable member to finish his speech, and during the greater part of the time the honourable member was on his legs he was so much interrupted that it was impossible to hear what he said'. In all Hansard there is no such entry after or before, and the speaker was Benjamin Disraeli, twice Prime Minister.

The theme was still the Irish elections, expanding in debate over the whole topic of contested returns and petitions. At the General Election in August there were 210 contests, and sixty-seven results were challenged. By the law as it then was, each case had to go to a separate Committee of the House, and it was notorious that these committees were party bodies, bent on getting their man returned. Two years later Macaulay met Goulburn, who was to be Peel's Chancellor of the Exchequer, in the Mediterranean. Goulburn was abusing Election Committees as most partial and unfair. 'You really think so, Mr Goulburn?' 'Most decidedly.' 'Then,' said Macaulay, 'I cannot help thinking that it was rather hard to pass a vote of censure on O'Connell for saying so.' It is easy now to see that the remedy for what everyone in secret acknowledged to be disgrace to public life was the transference of petitions from the House to the Judges. But such a surrender of ancient privileges was hardly to be thought of then, especially at a moment when the House had already involved itself in a contest with the Law Courts, which might have been devised to bring Parliament into contempt. The Inspectors of Prisons, investigating Newgate, reported that the inmates were found solacing their leisure with the perusal of an obscene book, with plates, issued by one Stockdale; the report was laid, and in the usual course ordered to be printed by Hansard. Stockdale, conceiving his character as a publisher and a man to be at stake, took proceedings against Hansard for libel. On the question of obscenity he lost his first case, but Denman, Lord Chief Justice, who seven years later was to protect O'Connell from the vindictive pursuit of the Irish Government, ruled in the plainest language that if a man libelled another in his business it was no defence to say that a third party had bidden him to do it, even though that party was the House of Commons. Stockdale bought another copy of the peccant report, and renewed his proceedings. This time he won and was awarded £100 damages. Having discovered this easy way of adding to his income, there seemed no reason why Stockdale should not pursue it so long as copies of the report were to be purchased; and for nearly four years the public was entertained by the spectacle of the Commons spasmodically vindicating their privileges by committing an obscure printer to Newgate, along with his clerk and his attorney, for conduct which Queen's Bench had declared to be lawful.

It was well that with a Government so weak, in Parliament and in the country, the foreign outlook was peaceful. Over the Continent the skies were clear, though the advance of Russia in the Caucasus needed careful watching. But across the Atlantic all was not so well, and the first Session of Victoria's first Parliament was adjourned to strains of such eloquence as had not been heard for sixty years, when the North American colonies were in revolt, and was not to be heard again till, more than sixty years later, the Cape Colony was in revolt. 'This Government,' said Leader, 'will be held up to execration as the men who plunged England into a disastrous war, to punish a colony which, by their own incompetence, injustice, and misgovernment they had forced into open rebellion.' 'If war ensues,' Molesworth followed, 'may speedy victory crown the efforts of the Canadians, and may the curses of the Empire light on the heads of those Ministers who involve us in civil discord, and expend our national resources in an unholy struggle against liberty.' In plainer language, the Legislative Assembly of Lower Canada had refused to vote the supplies, and the Home Government by Order in Council had suspended the Constitution of 1791 and authorized the Governor to collect the taxes without their consent; the French had risen, or were rising, under Louis Papineau. The analogy was striking: the precedent ominous. The American packet commonly took nineteen days to cross from New York, and when Parliament rose, two days before Christmas, 1837, to reassemble on January 10th, few members who knew their history could feel confident that they would not meet to decide whether Canada was to be reconquered or abandoned. A dark ending to the year; a dark opening of the Imperial reign.

MACAULAY

Κούφα γὰρ δαπάνα νομί—
ζειν ἰσχὺν τόδ᾽ ἔχειν
ὅ τι ποτ᾽ ἄρα τὸ δαιμόνιον
τό τ᾽ ἐν χρόνῳ μακρῷ νόμιμον
ἀεὶ φύσει τε πεφυκός.[1]

IN 1853 Henry Vizetelly, a publisher not of the best repute, issued Macaulay's speeches in two volumes: they appeared simultaneously in New York. As Hansard had given his licence and most of the speeches had already appeared in the newspapers, Macaulay had no redress at law. There was no malice in the book, though much ignorance: the text was often taken from bad reports, and the historical allusions were sadly mishandled: but Vizetelly cannot be taxed with any graver crime than the desire to sell for a guinea what had cost him nothing. Other men might have been amused, annoyed, or flattered. Macaulay felt the indignation of a Roman Senator at hearing that his most admired pieces were being circulated by a Greek freedman with an imperfect knowledge of Latin syntax. To protect his reputation as an historian and stylist, he prepared an edition of his own, and he took the occasion to castigate the unprincipled Vizetelly as grimly and eloquently as if he had been a Quaker who had written a bad poem, or a Scotsman who had opposed a Whig Bill.

The result is a book of unique interest both as a literary classic

---

[1] For it costs little to believe that the divine, whatever it is, has power, and that what has been accepted over a long time is eternal, and rooted in the nature of things.   Euripides: *Bacchae*.

and an historic document. No one now—though the designers of the Reading Room seems to have thought otherwise—would place Macaulay either as a writer or thinker above or even on a level with Burke. But, long and illustrious as the roll of English orators is, there is no third whose speeches are part of our literature, and of the two there seems little doubt that as a master of the spoken word Macaulay was the more effective. Almost from his first appearance, he was in the front rank of Parliamentary figures. Yet though he was a good party man, who could be trusted to do his duty in the division lobbies, and in any office which did not keep him too long from his books, he did not, after his first fervour was spent, enjoy the life: he hated bad air and late nights, and he never much liked hearing other men talk. Without charm or elocution he became a Parliamentary favourite: without birth or manners he made his way into the inner, though never the innermost, counsels of the Whigs: a bad candidate and a negligent member, he compelled the electors of Edinburgh to beg for the honour of having him as their representative, and, when Edinburgh rejected him, the freeholders of Oxfordshire could hardly be prevented from returning him against his will. There is no parallel to the ascendancy which he exercised in the House, and if it seems extravagant to say that he owed it to his style, we can only ask: to what else did he owe it?

Certainly not to his manner, which by all accounts was exceedingly bad. Questiond by his nephew, Mr Gladstone tactfully replied that no one noticed it: their one thought was not to miss a word he said. An American visitor described him as 'a little man of small voice, affected utterance, clipping his words and hissing like a serpent'. A reporter of experience and good judgement, G. H. Francis, confirms the account. 'His voice is one of the most monotonous and least agreeable of those which usually belong to our countrymen north of the Tweed: pitched in alto and rather shrill, pouring forth words in inconceivable velocity: never stopping for words, never stopping for thoughts, never halting for an instant even to take breath, hauling the subject after him with the strength of a giant, till the hearer is left prostrate and powerless by the whirlwind of ideas and emotions that has swept over him.' 'Yet,' the same critic adds, 'no impression whatever has been made by the orator on your feelings, nor has he created any confidence in himself apart from the arguments he has used.'

The arguments are always of the most obvious kind, and it is worth while examining some of the most successful speeches to see with how few *loci communes* Macaulay operates. In the speech on the Anatomy Bill, a masterpiece in little, there are two: the poor are most in danger of burking; the poor are the greatest sufferers by bad surgery. Each is restated six times, and the demonstration is rounded off with a picturesque anecdote. Between the beginning and end of a very short speech, Macaulay has touched on the habits of murderers, France, Germany, Italy, the peasants of Russia and their Tsar, mountebanks and barbers, old women and charms, the squaring of the circle and the transit of Venus, Richard of England, Leopold of Austria, and the bricklayer who falls from a ladder. The listener has been borne at exhilarating speed, but in perfect security, through a variegated landscape and deposited at his destination before he has had time to wonder where he is going.

The fine speech on the Ten Hours Bill, of which Macaulay was justly proud, is more mature in composition, but in structure equally simple. A government can interfere too much or too little: it is difficult to know where to draw the line: in this case I think that a modified interference can be justified from admitted principles: nevertheless, it is an experiment and I advise caution. That is the framework: the rest is illustration, ranging from Athens to the London cab-ranks, from the Exodus to the French Revolution, and sparkling with coloured vignettes of men with pails and whitewash brushes, housemaids toiling up- and downstairs, settlers in Ohio, negroes in Louisiana, and the Sunday calm in England, 'while the plough lies in the furrow, while the Exchange is silent, while no smoke ascends from the factory'. The decoration is not laid on: like the pinnacles and flying buttresses of a cathedral, it is an integral part of the fabric. The speaker is thinking in images drawn from an inexhaustible store of historic reminiscence, and flashed on the mind of the listener with the force and dexterity of a born story-teller.

Macaulay's fertility in restatement and illustration, of which the speeches on Copyright furnish the best example, amused his contemporaries. There seems no reason why he should ever stop, and too often he stops on a point which a more delicate taste would have rejected as merely smart. The critic whom I have already quoted writes: 'He will sometimes spoil the effect of an eloquent passage by a sudden antithetical allusion, involving some vulgar idea, which catches him because of the opportunity it affords for alliteration and contrast and which he thinks humorous.' It is very true, and it will be found that these vulgar ideas commonly occur in the last sentence of a paragraph. The Attic ending did not appeal to Macaulay, and he likes to close not in a dying fall, but an explosion. It is a symptom of a certain commonness of mind which was perhaps the most deep-seated and most insidious defect in his constitution. Mr Gladstone called him φορτικός,[2] and though he hastened with suave sophistry to explain that he used the word in a laudatory sense, the epithet was in its proper sense entirely just. A Greek audience listening to the little man be-rating Peel and Wellington in these terms,

We have lived to see a monster of faction made up of the worst parts of the Cavalier and the worst parts of the Roundhead. We have lived to see Tories who because they were not allowed to grind the people after the fashion of Strafford turn round and revile their sovereign in the style of Hugh Peters . . .

would have shaken their heads and murmured φορτικωτέρως δημηγορεῖ.[3] In fact, if one had to define exactly what Aristophanes and Plato meant by the word one could not answer better than by saying: Macaulay on Croker, or Macaulay on Bacon.

It is observable that this vein is less obtrusive in the Speeches, where it might have been expected to be more conspicuous, than in the Essays. It was intensified by solitude and withdrawal from the clash of opinion. Macaulay was never more urbane than in the presence of a large audience: the banter in his last Edinburgh

2 'vulgar'
3 'His style of oratory is rather vulgar'

speech about Spencer Walpole's militia-men and Lord Maidstone's hexameters displays an easy humour which is very rare in his writings. His Parliamentary style is tighter and more mordant. But his best speeches, whether in the House or on the platform, display the natural excellences of his prose better than any passages in the *Essays* or the *History*. The diction is of flawless lucidity, slightly touched with an amplitude which reminds us that the speaker was born in the eighteenth century, when 'every point of senatorial deliberation was duly observed'. The movement of thought is slightly ahead of the audience, but not too far ahead: each paragraph has its own keynote, its appropriate cadences, and the language rises and falls from narrative to declamation, and back to straight hard-hitting argument, without effort, or interruption, or display.

There are indications in the essay on Machiavelli that Macaulay was on his way towards a more varied manner and a fuller harmony than in fact he ever achieved. His development was arrested by his entry into public life and his four years' exile in India. The Edinburgh Reviewer went into Parliament: he conquered Parliament with speeches in the style of his first reviews. His manner became set, and with his speaking, as with his writing, if a paragraph were taken at random it would be almost impossible to guess whether the speaker was in his thirty-second or his fifty-second year. Thus, in his own lifetime, he became a classic and a tradition: Londoners pointed him out to one another in the streets: when he rose in his place for the last time the members who crowded in to hear him, listened to what was not only an intellectual but an historic entertainment, the last echo of the oratory of 1831, itself an echo of the oratory of the heroic age. In Macaulay the tradition which begun with Halifax on the Exclusion Bill, and was continued, first through Bolingbroke, Pultency, and Chatham, and then through the second dynasty of Burke and Fox and Pitt; the tradition which was still maintained in Macaulay's youth by Brougham, Plunket, and Canning, sent up its last coruscation and expired. There were great speakers still to come: Bright more than once reaches a height where only Burke or the ancients afford a valid comparison. But professed oratory, the deliberate evolution of a theme in language meant to tell on the nerves of the hearers at once, and to stand the test of literature a generation later, when would that be heard again?

Bagehot said, with some truth and some malice, that Macaulay regarded English history as a process leading up to the debates in which he had taken part. He went up to Cambridge a Clapham Tory: after the straitest sect of our religion he was bred a Pharisee. Two brilliant contemporaries, Charles Austin and Lord Carnarvon, won him over to the Whigs. Thirty years before, George Canning had sat in the Temple weighing his chances, and had decided that for a new man with nothing but parts to commend him there were no prospects on the Whig side. But now, after a generation of office, Toryism was growing old. We who have lived to see what the winding up of a great war involves, can appreciate better than contemporaries could the dexterity with which Castlereagh disengaged Great Britain from continental commitments, the firmness with which disorder was suppressed at home, and the ability with which the finances of the State were restored. Lord Liverpool's last administration was one of the most capable that has ever held office in England, but it was an administration that only Lord Liverpool could keep together. Wellington and Eldon, Canning at the Foreign Office, Peel at the Home Office, Huskisson at the Board of Trade, Palmerston at the War Office, made a team of rare capacity. The stroke which robbed the team of their captain destroyed the cohesion of the party and released the nervous rancour of years. Canning shot upwards, carrying Robinson, Huskisson, and Palmerston with him. Peel went into opposition with Wellington and Eldon. Canning died, and Peel came back to accomplish Canning's policy, the emancipation of the Catholics. The ins and outs of the next few months are a burden to the memory, without meaning or purpose. The hour of the Whigs had almost come when Lord Lansdowne offered the young reviewer, Jeffrey's greatest discovery, a seat in the House as a member for Calne. Ten months later, the forty years of Tory government ended in panic, confusion, and flight.

The Reform was one of those transactions, of which history

does not present many examples, when the right thing was done in exactly the right way at exactly the right time. In the life of a nation the rational and irrational elements need to be kept in adjustment. Tradition, habit, instinct, and inertia, which are the grounds of public stability, may at times become an exasperation and a burden to the public intelligence, developing with the emergence of new ideas under the pressure of new circumstances. In the Constitution of 1830 the irrational element was in excess: the rational element was working with dangerous potency. Government was neither oppressive nor inefficient, but it was becoming absurd. All the arguments on both sides of the question came to this: the Constitution works well and people are used to it; the Constitution is unreasonable and people are tired of it. To Macaulay the situation in November 1830 appeared as the particular case of a secular problem, to find a mode of government which shall command the rational adherence of the intelligent, on whom government depends for its efficacy, and the habitual respect of the masses, on whom it depends for its existence. In England the problem had been brought to an issue by the emergence of the mercantile and manufacturing classes as a self-conscious entity. But in the problem itself there was nothing new; and Lord Grey and Lord John Russell, in abolishing nomination and enfranchising Manchester, were acting as the heirs and representatives of all great reformers in all ages back to the very origins of western polity, the Licinian Rogations and the enfranchisement of the Latins.

Sic fortis Etruria crevit
Scilicet et facta est rerum pulcherrima Roma.[4]

The pictorial quality of Macaulay's mind, the strong pragmatic element in his composition, his confident ignorance of philosophy and art, tend to mask both the depth and clarity of his metaphysic. Some metaphysic every historian must have, and in essentials Macaulay's is the metaphysic of Herodotus. The modern naturally has the keener sense of change and the problems which change involves: the ancient has a broader sympathy, a larger conception

[4] 'In this way, we may be sure, hardy Etruria grew great, and Rome became the glory of the world.' Virgil: *Georgic* ii

of human needs and satisfactions. Ionian cosmology was a grander discipline for the mind than Baconian trial and error. But essentially they view the stream of time from the same standpoint, and see in history, one the assertion, the other the perpetual reassertion, of a timeless rationality. 'The dawn appeared and they mustered the men. Themistocles spoke to them, in language of extraordinary eloquence. The substance was this: having contrasted the better with the worse in the whole range of human nature and its circumstances, he exhorted them to prefer the better. When he had ended, he ordered them to go on board.' So the great Ionian conceived the morning of Salamis, and so Macaulay conceived the closing of the gates of Londonderry.

So also, let it be acknowledged, did he contemplate the future, in 1931, with Ben Lomond laid out in allotments, with cranes and sirens, lorries and steam engines,

> Breaking the silence of the seas,
> Among the farthest Hebrides,

with factory towns, each encircled with a zone of villas complete with piano and laburnum tree, blackening the skies above Killarney. His first biographer entered thoroughly into his spirit when he headed one of his electoral speeches *Loveliness and Intelligence of Leeds*. An intellect less vigorous might have doubted the loveliness and intelligence of early Victorian England: an intellect more subtle might have been perplexed to account for its more obtrusive stupidity and squalor. Modern psychology would ask whether a man who seems so sure of everything was really sure of anything; whether he was not in fact declaiming to keep his spirits up, clinging to his professions the more passionately because in his heart he felt that he and his professions were being swept away together, and that Pascal's abyss was awaiting him if once he stopped reading to think.

To reason thus would be to forget that Macaulay was by birthright an historian, and the historian is one for whom the past keeps something of the familiar triviality of the present, and the present already has some of the shadowy magnificence of the past. Movement and continuity are the conceptions with which he works, and what aesthetic writers claim a passionate apprehension of form to be to the painter, a passionate apprehension of process is to the historian. Macaulay's view of life was somewhat narrow: Whig constitutionalism, Augustan humanity, Baconian induction furnished him with all the canons he required to measure its advance. That the nineteenth century was richer, more intelligent, more comfortable and more humane than any that had preceded it was enough, and that England led the world in riches, intelligence, comfort, and humanity was a source of endless pride and satisfaction. Like Cromwell's plain russet-coated captain, he understood what he was fighting for and loved what he understood. His mind was the mind of a scholarly English rationalist of the early railway age and pronounced political views; a belated Augustan like Byron captivated, but like Byron unconverted, by Shelley and Scott. But the springs of his genius were deeper, in an alert and vigorous humanism, which transcended and illuminated his pragmatic philosophy. Nothing recorded of him is more characteristic than a trivial entry in his diary. Roaming in the lanes round Esher he fell in with a party of hop-pickers whom he treated to a pot of beer. 'I liked their looks and I thought their English remarkably good for their rank in life. It was in truth the Surrey English, the English of the suburbs of London, which is to the Somersetshire and Yorkshire what Castilian is to the Andalusian, or Tuscan to Neapolitan.' Macaulay had no Wordsworthian illusions about peasants, or the goodness of the lower orders as such. But the sound of a few well-uttered words was enough to set his mind ranging in search of some kindred excellence, from the Surrey ale-house to the stage trodden by the highbred nobles of Calderon, and 'the gardens where Lorenzo meditated a song for the Mayday dance of the Etrurian virgins'.

His Whig scorn for the irrationality of mobs blazes in his speech on the People's Charter. But not less fiery is the humanist's scorn for those who would withhold from the people their birthright of leisure and instruction. Untouched by the new cosmology which was unseating man from his ancient pre-eminence as eldest child and vicegerent of the Creator, Macaulay in his heart believed in that perfectibility at which Carlyle gibed. As sceptical as

Gibbon, he left Vital Religion behind him at Clapham where it belonged, and took in its place a buoyant, because demonstrable, faith in human progress. *Il a son orgueil d'homme*: and out of this pride flowers the unexpected tenderness, the loving particularity with which he dwells on every instance of human goodness or ingenuity, courage in war, self-discipline in peace, of science and invention, craftsmanship and discovery, that comes his way; or tracks the human associations of every place he mentions, remembering that the gardens of Sir Thomas Browne were the pride of Norwich, that Johnson's father had kept a weekly stall in Birmingham market, and that Scott had seen the sword-dance of the borderers 'at Keeldar by the sources of the Tyne'.

This humanism was drawn and nourished from the fountainhead, from Florence, from Rome, and from Athens, and of the three perhaps Italy yielded the largest draught. Brougham, before he learnt to be jealous, had advised him to nourish his eloquence on Demosthenes and Dante; and Dante, more than even Shakespeare or the Greeks, was in literature the great passion of his life. It is easier to picture him in Florence of the fifteenth century, ensconced in some dignified but not laborious secretariat, than in any other place or age except his own. The affinity in a temperament so unaesthetic is somewhat surprising: not even Mrs Austin could get him to look at a Primitive with patience; his favourite painter was Correggio, his favourite architecture the palaces of the High Renaissance. But intellectually he homes to Florence and the Early Renaissance as instinctively as he shrinks from the Dark Ages and the North, and his essay is still reprinted in Italy as the best introduction to the study of Machiavelli.

Once this humanism made a mark in history which, for good or evil, has not been, and is never likely to be, effaced. For their celebrity and their consequences, Macaulay's Minutes on Indian Education are the least accessible writings in the language. They were not included in his works: Sir George Trevelyan in the *Life* gave only an abbreviated text: there is no complete copy in the British Museum. Enough is now reprinted to show the spirit in which Macaulay approached the problem, and if the spirit is, in one of its aspects, English of 1835, in all the rest it is Italian of the

Quattrocento, unrestrained by the necessity of paying a decent reverence to the practices of an established religion. The Company, in a remarkable document which office tradition no doubt rightly ascribed to the hand of James Mill, had laid down the principle that, as compensation for the authority they had lost by the Conquest, natives of the higher ranks were to be educated for positions of responsibility in the English services. Neither Mill nor Macaulay had any doubts where the path on which they were entering would lead them. An administration open to all Indians and manned even in the higher branches by Indians of birth was bound in the long run to become an Indian administration. It remained to fit the Indians for their future, which intellectually, meant to detach them from their past and to graft them, if they could be grafted, on to the stock of Western science and culture. The more liberal tradition which, since the days of Warren Hastings, had encouraged English officials to interest themselves in Eastern philosophy and literature, was to be brought to an end. It seems fairly clear that in Macaulay's mind it would be no great loss to India if the philosophy and literature themselves came to an end: the only Eastern writing in which he shows the faintest interest is a Sanskrit translation of Homer reported to be current in the second century. Instruction in Arabic and Sanskrit could produce nothing but a learned native; instruction in English would open to the Indians all the treasures of Western knowledge. So Agricola had civilized the Britons; so Peter had civilized Russia: so Greece had carried her arts and language to the confines of that unknown world which in the revolution of time had become the dominion of the children of the sea. 'The sceptre may pass from us. Victory may be inconstant to our arms. But there are triumphs which are followed by no reverse. There is an empire exempt from all natural cause of decay. Those triumphs are the pacific triumphs of reason over barbarism; that empire is the imperishable empire of our arts and our morals, our literature and our laws.'

Note. Writing of the Education Minute 1835, I forgot that it had been printed by Sir George Trevelyan in that little masterpiece of sense and humour. *The Competition Wallah*.

THE AGE OF TENNYSON

Warton Lecture on English Poetry, British Academy

Read 29 March 1939

SOME thirty years ago, walking in Sussex, I fell into conversation with an innkeeper, very proud of his neighbourhood and of the great men who had honoured it by being born, or coming to live, there. Then, as he ended the list, he suddenly added, 'But there: not one of them could have written *Enoch Arden*. What a beautiful piece that is!'

The volume of *Poems 1842* established Tennyson in the regard of the critical public as the first, after Wordsworth, of living poets; a regard qualified, however, with certain misgivings as to his intellectual grasp, his power to bring under poetic control the turbulent manifold of contemporary life, misgivings which *The Princess* in 1847 certainly did not remove. *In Memoriam* was influential in extending his renown, but within a limited range: many of its earliest readers disliked it, many did not understand it, and those who admired it most were not always the best judges of its poetry. *Maud* in 1855 was a decided set-back: it puzzled, it irritated, it shocked. But with the first four *Idylls of the King* in 1859 the Laureate won the great educated public, and with *Enoch Arden* five years later, the people. Not in his own country only, for, as his German biographer has written, 'with *Enoch Arden* Tennyson took the heart of the German people by storm': a fact well illustrating a truth of which we have constantly to remind ourselves, that our Victorian Age is only the local phase of a cultural period common to all Western Europe and North America. Indeed we need not limit our view to the West, because I am fairly sure that if the last canto of *Evgeny Onegin* in Professor Elton's translation fell anonymously into the hands of one of our younger reviewers, he would unhesitatingly characterize Tatiana's refusal to desert her elderly husband for the man whom she still loves, as a typical example of Victorian smugness, unless, indeed, complacency was the word that week in vogue.

For the rest of his life Tennyson was The Poet: and to the people poetry was the sort of thing that Tennyson wrote. There was, I well remember, a sixpenny encyclopædia of great service to young schoolboys on the eve of examinations, which contained, with other useful matter, a list of the Hundred Greatest Men: 'to know their deeds is to know the history of civilization'; it began of course with Homer, and ended, not less of course, with Tennyson. Lord Morley once, wishing to affirm some idea of social stratification, divided the people of England into those who had a Tennyson at home and those who had not. When I cast my memory back to the bookshops in our more elegant suburbs, or at a seaside resort, the first picture I see is rows and shelves and boxes full of Tennyson; and just as John Stuart Mill used to fret himself with the thought that some day all melodious combinations of sound would be exhausted, and music come to an end, so I used to wonder, what more, when Tennyson had written

> Calm and deep peace on this high wold,
>> And on these dews that drench the furze:
>> And all the silvery gossamers
> That twinkle into green and gold:
>
> Calm and still light on yon great plain
>> That sweeps with all its autumn bowers
>> And crowded farms and lessening towers,
> To mingle with the bounding main:

what more, I say, there was for poetry to do. And, let me add, this was not an inculcated sentiment: no one had told me to admire him: the star of Browning, the star of Meredith were blazing above a landscape all silver with the moonlight of Pater. I must conclude that Tennyson gave me what he gave to the earlier generation which placed him beside Virgil. I cannot conjure up again the enchantment, but I can indicate, I think, the field it covered, and the theme on which I wish to speak this evening is not the poetry of Tennyson by itself or the thought of Tennyson by itself, but the adjustment of both to the world in which he lived, an adjustment so perfect that, as Saintsbury once said, 'no age of poetry can be called the age of one man with such critical accuracy as the later Nineteenth Century is, with us, the Age of Tennyson'.

Take up the faded green Moxon volume with its list of Mr
Tennyson's other works, *Poems,* 16th edition, *The Princess,* 12th
edition, *In Memoriam,* 15th edition, and imagine yourself to be
one of its 60,000 purchasers: or better still, perhaps, sitting in the
village schoolroom to hear it read by the vicar or the squire. What
do you find? An abundance, a vast profusion of poetic learning,
of ornate phrasing and verbal music—which you will recognize
and admire, because it is the familiar accent of Tennyson, though
in detail much of it may be above your head—applied to a tale of
common life lived on the heroic level. Reading it again, I recalled
the story of the French duchess who paid her social and charitable
visits in the same attire, an old shawl and a diamond brooch,
because, as she said, her rich friends only saw the diamonds and
her poor friends only saw the shawl. Listen to the Laureate deploy-
ing all his magnificence of sound and imagery to bring before us
the tropical island and the shipwrecked sailor waiting for a sail:

> No sail from day to day, but every day
> The sunrise broken into scarlet shafts
> Among the ferns and palms and precipices;
> The blaze upon the waters to the east;
> The blaze upon his island overhead;
> The blaze upon the waters to the west;
> Then the great stars that glóbed themselves in Heaven,
> The hollower sounding ocean, and no sail.

But listen also to what, if you are holding hands in the back
row of the schoolroom, will touch you more nearly, the poet's tale
of Enoch's ambition.

> Enoch set
> A purpose evermore before his eyes,
> To hoard all savings to the uttermost,
> To purchase his own boat, and make a home
> For Annie . . .
> And all men looked upon him favourably:
> And ere he touched his one-and-twentieth May
> He purchased his own boat, and made a home
> For Annie, neat and nestlike, halfway up
> The narrow street that clambered towards the mill.

When his child is born, then

> In him woke,
> With his first babe's first cry, the noble wish
> To save all earnings to the uttermost,
> And give his child a better bringing up
> Than his had been or hers.

Accident and competition set him back. So he decides to stock a little shop for Annie, and ship himself on a China barque; meaning to trade and so

> returning rich,
> Become the master of a larger craft,
> With fuller profits lead an easier life,
> Have all his pretty young ones educated,
> And pass his days in peace among his own.

He will in fact become a small employer; in 1867 Liberal speakers will challenge Bob Lowe to justify a law which excludes from the franchise our worthy neighbour Mr Arden: while for the daughter there is evidently reserved the destiny of the young lady in the ballad:

> And now she is the lawyer's wife
> And dearly he does love her:
> And she lives in a happy condition of life,
> And well in the station above her.

To the simple-hearted reader or listener, in fact, Tennyson has done what the critic of 1842 demanded of him. He has brought the living world of shops and ships and going to sea and going to school, under poetic control. It is all there, and it is all poetry. We may object that it is not all there: that this living world is a highly selective composition, this poetry very largely a practised mannerism. I am not concerned to refute either objection, but I will ask you to consider for a little, not the ethical or artistic presumptions —if there be any such—by which poetry ought to be judged, but those which contemporaries actually applied.

'In metaphysical inquiries egoism is the truest modesty', and what little I understand of poetry regarded as an activity of the mind I learnt from a trifling incident in my own youth. The subject set for the Newdigate in my second or third year was King Charles at Oxford. I had no intention of competing, which was perhaps a pity, because the only copy which was submitted contained, I was afterwards told, the passage:

> The Queen from France with admirable tact
> Supplied the money which the Army lacked;
> Grateful the King accepts the proffered boon,
> And gives it to his troops who spend it soon.

But while I was thinking, in an idle and quite disinterested mood, how the theme could be treated, the notion—not the image—of Oxford, with its towers and lawns and trees lying like an island in the sea of civil strife, occurred to me, and with the notion came a line. I wrote it down, and the next line came at once, completing the couplet. In all, I wrote a simile ten lines long, as fast as if I was writing from dictation, and, I wrote each word, not knowing in the least what the next would be. Then the spring failed as suddenly as it had started.

Guided by this experience of my own I have always supposed poetic experience to be a kind of compulsion which has its locus on the boundary between the apprehension of a theme and its rendering in metrical form; and there is this much truth, I believe, in Matthew Arnold's perilous doctrine of the Great Line, that such lines mark, as it were, the moments when the boundary disappears in a sudden intensity of poetic insight so that apprehension and expression become a single act. Such moments are rare, and in the great bulk of every poet's work the two aspects, call them thought and form, are at least critically distinguishable. And corresponding to these two aspects of poetic activity there are, I think, two aspects of reception in the hearer or reader. He wishes to have certain things set before him because they interest him; and every age has its own set of interests. The later eighteenth century, for example, did not want to hear the things that Blake had to say, and so it hardly noticed that Blake was there. The early nineteenth century did most eagerly want something like *Childe Harold*, and having got it, went on to accept from Byron much which a less avid taste would have rejected. But the reader also desires to have these things set before him in a way which is poetically gratifying, and here also his pleasure and satisfaction are very largely conditioned for him by the aesthetic ambient of his time. All which things taken together produce what I have called adjustment; and, if I may ask you to admit one distinction more, within the aesthetic appeal and response itself two elements may be observed. In every work of art there is something which addresses the nerves, a thrill, beside those other things which reach the spirit. It is in virtue of this thrill, very often, that a writer makes his entry and secures his public—Swinburne is as good an example as one can recall—and I believe the curious anger, or detestation, so much beyond any reasonable ground of distaste, with which each age for a time regards the literature of the last, has its cause in this: that it perceives the appeal, but cannot answer it. Nothing is more exasperating to the nerves or the temper than a thrill which has begun to be a bore. You remember Mr Pepys at *Midsummer Night's Dream*: 'Insipid: ridiculous: I shall never see it again!'

I am thinking now of those years between 1840 and 1860 when Tennyson was rising to the throne of poetry, and I ask what was the element in his art which was most stimulating to the nerves, and most satisfying to the taste of his contemporaries, and why. I call upon the memories of that young enthusiast, and without hesitation I answer; in the first instance his descriptive power. I need not tell again a tale which has been told so often, and, to relieve your anxieties at once, I may say I do not intend to mention Lady Winchelsea. But I must pause for moment on a greater name, a more persistent influence. For about a century the repute and vogue of Thomson varied singularly little. 'From 1750 to 1850', one of his biographers wrote,

> Thomson was in England the poet, par excellence, not of the eclectic and literary few, but of the large and increasing cultivated middle class. 'Thomson's *Seasons* looks best (I maintain it) a little torn and dogeared.'

He is quoting Lamb.

> When Coleridge found a dogeared copy of *The Seasons* in an inn, and remarked 'That is fame', Thomson's popularity seemed quite as assured as Milton's. As late as 1855 Robert Bell remarked that it seemed even on the increase. The date may be taken to mark the turning point in his fame, for since about 1850 he has been unmistakably eclipsed on his own ground, in the favour of the class to which he was once dear, by Tennyson.

For a generation or so before the birth of Tennyson English

senses had been brought to a degree of fineness they had never possessed before. The practice of the poets counted for much, of Cowper and those others to whom in this context we need not deny their good old name of the Lake Poets. The new interest in landscape painting, the addiction to sketching in pencil or water-colour, are, as Hazlitt pointed out, influences not to be overlooked in studying the evolution of our literary tastes. I would add the habit of travel, especially of domestic travel imposed by the closure of the Continent and facilitated by the labours of Telford and Macadam. Finally, I would include an influence which I believe to be well worth the attention of some student of the literature of science: I mean the growing devotion to natural history in all its branches, the minute observation of form and colour in leaf and rock and feather and flower. High among those who formed the English aesthetic of the nineteenth century must always be placed the names of White and Gilpin and Bewick: after them of Lyell, and the contributors to the *Cabinet Encyclopaedia*.

This increasing fineness of observation demanded an increasing delicacy and exactitude of record, just as, in another sphere, the metrical practice of the great Romantic poets had created a demand for a richer and more various verbal music than had contented the Augustan ear. But as we go forward into the nineteenth century, this devotion to nature seems to become almost a nervous craving: possibly at the deepest level a biological necessity. The public of which I am speaking, Tennyson's public, was becoming, in spirit, suburban: a country-bred stock, entangled in a way of life which it had not learnt to control, was instinctively fighting for breath. And for sixty years its poet was there, flashing on it, in phrases of faultless precision, pictures of the world from which it was exiled and in which it yearned to keep at least an imaginary footing.

> The ground flame of the crocus breaks the mould.

That is Tennyson at twenty. It might be Tennyson at eighty.

Nothing in Tennyson's art is more admirable than the economy and certainty of his touch when he is on this ground:

> On either side the river lie
> Long fields of barley and of rye,
> That clothe the wold *and meet the sky*.

No wonder the *Quarterly,* whether Croker or his editor, stigmatized that phrase, because, as every one born in the eighteenth century would know, between the top of the world and the bottom of the sky there is in fact a considerable gap. I quote it as one of the earliest and most convincing examples of Tennyson's mastery of the illusionist style, where words have the value of things seen, and the observation seems to go at once into poetry without any pause for reflection, or mental arrangement of the particulars. Think of the spring in *Balin and Balan*:

> the spring, that down
> From underneath a plume of lady-fern
> Sang, and the sand danced at the bottom of it.

It does not matter whether you have ever seen that or not. If you have not, you know now exactly what it looks like. If you have, the words will keep it in your memory far more vividly than any recollection of your own. Here, as Miss Sitwell has said of Smart, 'the natural object is seen with such clarity that for the moment nothing else exists', and in Smart's recently published manuscript *Jubilate Agno* there is a sentence which I must quote because it seems to me exactly to describe the nature of the accomplishment which, after two generations of experiment, Tennyson brought to perfection.

My talent is to give an impression upon words by punching, that when the reader casts his eye upon them, he takes up the image from the mould which I have made.

Tennyson's imagery was studied by men of science, and never once, I think, did they find his observation scientifically at fault. That melancholy achievement was reserved for me. No one who lives in downland and has ever seen a waning moon rising in a windy sky, can fail to respond to the magical aptitude of the lines

> And high in heaven a streaming cloud,
> And on the downs a rising fire.

That fire is a stage illumination: that moon a property moon. I
have it on the authority of the Astronomer Royal, and—

solem quis dicere falsum
Audeat?[1]

that on 10 October 1842, the day of Cecilia Tennyson's wedding
here commemorated, the moon did not rise after supper. It rose
before lunch.

I think it is true to say that Tennyson's accomplishment in this
branch of his art served to constrict for a time the range of our
poetry, and to narrow our critical judgement. After all, images of
external nature are not the only things a poet has to provide: and
in the later part of the century you may sometimes encounter a
naïve habit of criticism, based on the popular notion, as I said,
that poetry was what Tennyson wrote, which assessed the poets by
the number of nature-touches, as they were known in the trade,
to be found in their respective works. But I need not remind you
that it has often been the fate of great poets—and a proof of their
greatness: the fate of Chaucer and Virgil—to impede the progress
of poesy by their very mastery, by the domination they exercised
over their contemporaries and immediate successors.

I have placed this gift of Tennyson's in the forefront of his
equipment, because it is here that we are most conscious—whether
we can still feel it or not—of what I have called the thrill. The
profusion of his natural imagery, domestic or exotic, is—or was
once—as intoxicating as the liquid richness of his verse, and its
ravishing surprises. We are not called upon to be intoxicated, but
to understand those who were, and to follow them as they see their
poet, the poet of *Mariana* and *The Lotos-Eaters,* grow in stature
as a philosophic and religious teacher. Here again, to begin with
what is outward, his mastery of another mode, not less grateful to
an age immersed in anxious moral speculation, is equally conspicuous, not to say obtrusive. I mean the gnomic, hortatory
utterance, the ethical *sententia*. Few lines of Tennyson, for
example, were more admired or more often quoted than these:

[1] 'Who would dare to call the sun a liar?' Virgil: *Georgic* i

> Let knowledge grow from more to more,
>> But more of reverence in us dwell;
>> That mind and soul, according well,
> May make one music as before,
> But vaster.

Perhaps to our less robust and exuberant ethical sense, they are, if anything, too quotable, too suggestive of the birthday book, the calendar, or the chairman of the governors at a prize-giving. They seem, like so much of Tennyson's verse, to be designed for public performance. Indeed I knew a man who, until I convinced him otherwise, had gone through life believing that

> Heated hot with burning fears
> And dipt in baths of hissing tears,
> And battered with the shocks of doom
>> To shape and use:

was the second verse of *Scots wha hae*. We must acknowledge that we have lost the taste for moral declamation, just as the nineteenth century lost the taste for social elegance. But it may come back. In any case I am not defending or assailing Tennyson's manner. I am speaking historically; I am trying to account for what I have called his adjustment. But may I in passing observe that the greatest body of reflective and ethical poetry in European literature actually was designed for public performance? I mean the choruses of the Athenian stage: and it is here, I have often thought, especially among the choruses of Sophocles, that we shall find the nearest analogy to such pieces as *Of Old sat Freedom on the Heights,* many of the lyrics which make up *In Memoriam,* or this, which the Attic Muse herself might not have disdained or disavowed;

> And when no mortal motion jars
>> The blackness round the tombing sod,
> Through silence and the friendly stars,
>> Comes Faith from tracts no feet have trod,
>> And Virtue, like a household god
> Promising Empire; such as those
>> Once heard at dead of night to greet
> Troy's wandering prince, so that he rose
>> With sacrifice, while all the fleet
>> Had rest by stony hills of Crete.

And this gnomic manner was not less pleasing to the ear of a romantic age, when it dissolved, as it often does, into a riddling, oracular style like this:

> Pass not beneath this gateway, but abide
> Without, among the cattle of the field.
> For, an ye heard a music, like enow
> They are building still, seeing the city is built
> To music, therefore never built at all
> And therefore built for ever.

Now are those lines a genuine poetic experience, or merely the application of poetic learning to a promising theme? Is Tennyson expressing himself or exploiting himself? That is the doubt, already audible in the seventies, which grew and culminated in the great revulsion from the Laureate and all his ways which is characteristic of the end of the last century and the beginning of this. There is no need to deny that much of Tennyson's poetry is enveloped in an Alexandrian overgrowth of literary erudition, a kind of Great Exhibitionism not unalluring to an age which loved profusion, as much as it admired invention. He has passages which Callimachus would have approved: others which Ovid might have envied: and Mario Praz has actually called *Enoch Arden* a Hellenistic romance. I do not feel that judgement to be true, but if any one chose to call the *Idylls*, where one can hardly say whether the figures are ancients dressed like moderns, or moderns like ancients, a Hellenistic epic, I am not sure I should greatly differ: and the decorous eroticism which hangs over much—not all—of that performance seems to me to have been finally and adequately characterized by the American schoolboy who observed: 'There is some pretty hot necking in Lord Tennyson, only they never quite make it.'

But in the *Northern Farmer, The Churchwarden*, and the *Entail*, we are far from Alexandria, we are among the oak-woods of Acharnae: and you may think that the spectacle of Tennyson unbending in dialect, and then resuming his poise as Bard to write *The Wreck* or *The Children's Hospital* indicates some weakness in the poetic fibre of the man, or the poetic judgement of his age. If you do, I think you would be right: and I wish to consider rather more closely what that weakness was.

Speaking to an audience like this, I need not remark that the Christian religion and the elements of propriety were not introduced into the United Kingdom by Prince Albert of Saxe-Coburg-Gotha. At the beginning of the century, at least by 1805, the Germans had noticed and named as a national characteristic, or Engländerei, that nervousness and reticence in the sphere of passion which is popularly supposed to be a Victorian characteristic, and which, in passing I may recall, compelled Scott in 1824 to mar the catastrophe of St. Roman's Well. Those who believe in the economic interpretation of everything, including poetry, may find it easier than I do to account for the readiness with which the England of Chaucer and Fielding submitted itself and its literature to this new asceticism. Never I suppose was there a time when people were so willing to be shocked, or when the habit of being shocked was so widespread and so commendable that a man could assert his superior refinement best by being shocked at something which no one else had noticed, like the critic of Enoch Arden, for example, who censured Tennyson for failing to observe that bigamy was not a misfortune but a criminal offence. Now it may be admitted that bigamy is rarer in the upper than in the lower walks of society: and what I think was in the back of the critic's mind was the notion that by taking Annie to himself, without proof of Enoch's death, Philip was descending from the station of a thoroughly respectable man.

I have always thought that the conception of respectability was in its place and time of the greatest moral service to us. To be respectable is to emerge from the anonymous amorphous mass: to be a personality: to live by a standard, actually, perhaps, the standard of the class just above that into which you had been born and in which your fellows were content to live. If we stopped there, we might think of respectability as the characteristic virtue of competitive individualism practised under the eye of an approving gentry. But we cannot stop there, because the respectable man is not only bettering himself, he is bettering his family. Through the family the most powerful of human instincts is harnessed to the secular task of improving the race. So viewed, social progress is a microcosmic section of the evolution of the world under the guidance of that Providence whose purpose, in the great words of Malthus, is ever to bring a mind out of the clod, but a section which has become conscious of itself and therefore capable of a directed effort. As Pitt-Rivers said to a concourse of archaeologists shortly after the appearance of Darwin's *Descent of Man*, 'the thought of our humble origin'—from what I have heard of Pitt-Rivers I think he must have said your humble origin—'may be an incentive to industry and respectability'.

In other words respectability means the continual production and reproduction of distinguished varieties, and to laughter, as George Meredith taught us, the distinguished variety is peculiarly sensitive. In this way we may account for that vicious dichotomy, deep-seated in the Victorian mind, between the idea of comedy and the idea of beauty, which is so observable, for example, in Dickens: beyond question one of the greatest of all comic writers —and yet, how unlovely is much of his satire, how tasteless his sentiment. Seeing that comedy, that wit and humour, are among the most powerful and penetrating instruments that the mind has to work with, we must, I think, acknowledge that this notion of the fenced, secluded area where laughter must not be heard, weakened and hampered the whole intelligence of the age: and in none of its great writers is the mischief more apparent than in Tennyson. Matthew Arnold said he lacked intellectual power. He said much the same of Shelley: and I am not sure that his intense, exclusive, humanism qualified him to judge the intellectual calibre of a poet whose chief interests, apart from poetry, were scientific: I cannot recall any passage in Arnold's writing which suggests that he had ever given a thought to the ichthyosaurus. At all events, contemporaries, not less fitted than he to judge, did not observe the want, partly because they were under the same limitations themselves, but more because they found in Tennyson the most complete statement of the great philosophic issue of the age: if not an answer to its problems, at least an indication of the lines along which the answer was to be sought. What he did lack, and they did not require, was precisely that restraining touch of comedy to save him from becoming, as he can be at times, vapidly pontifical and almost embarrassingly silly.

This issue, the central problem round which the minds of thoughtful men were coming to revolve, can be very simply stated. What was the standing of personality, the finite human personality, in a world which every year was revealing itself more clearly as a process of perpetual flux?

> The hills are shadows and they flow
> From form to form, and nothing stands:
> They melt like mist, the solid lands,
> Like clouds they shape themselves and go.

We may perhaps forget, among our own more pressing concerns, how formidable an attack on human dignity and personal values, the ground of all Western philosophy and religion, was implicit in the new conceptions of geological and biological time. When once you have mastered the thesis that inconceivable ages have gone to make the race, and that after inconceivable ages to come the whole conscious episode may have been nothing more than a brief iridescence on a cooling cinder, what solid ground of conduct is left for you? And Tennyson had mastered the thesis; from his undergraduate days when Darwin was on the high seas in the *Beagle*, he had meditated on the mystery of development and the succession of types.

Thus when he appeared as a philosophic poet with *In Memoriam* he was not only equipped for the great debate which was soon to open; he had anticipated it, had formulated at least a conceivable conclusion; and one based on personal experience: on the mystical, or almost mystical, assurance recorded at the close of *The Holy Grail*.

> Let visions of the night, or of the day,
> Come as they will: and many a time they come,
> Until this earth he walks on seems not earth,
> This light that strikes his eyeball is not light,
> This air that smites his forehead is not air,
> But vision—yea, his very hand and foot—
> In moments when he feels he cannot die,
> And knows himself no vision to himself,
> Nor the high God a vision, nor that One
> Who rose again.

3

That is no borrowed language, no such working up of many possibilities into one plausibility as Victorian theology was so largely engaged in. It is Tennyson's own voice: you hear it again in *The Ancient Sage*.

> The first gray streak of earliest summer-dawn,
> The last long stripe of waning crimson gloom:
> As if the late and early were but one—
> A height, a broken grange, a grove, a flower
> Had murmurs, 'Lost and gone and lost and gone!'
> A breath, a whisper—some divine farewell—
> Desolate sweetness—far and far away—
> What had he loved, what had he lost, the boy?
> I know not and I speak of what has been.
>   And more my son! for more than once when I
> Sat all alone, revolving in myself
> The word that is the symbol of myself,
> The mortal limits of the self were loosed
> And past into the Nameless, as a cloud
> Melts into heaven. I touched my limbs, the limbs
> Were strange not mine—and yet no shade of doubt
> But utter clearness, and thro' loss of self
> The gain of such large life as matched with ours
> Were sun to spark—unshadowable in words
> Themselves but shadows of a shadow world.

It is Tennyson's own voice, telling of what he has known, and as such his age received it. *Perhibet testimonium de his, et scripsit haec: et scimus quia verum est testimonium ejus.*[2]

But what in this vision of the world is the place of Christianity? Or, to put the question as Tennyson and his contemporaries felt it, when the traditional forms of faith have been subjected to the analysis of criticism and science, what will remain? The inerrancy of Scripture had gone, carrying with it both the cosmogony on which the scheme of redemption was founded, and the assurance of immortality. Was there anything left which might serve as a spiritual directive of progress? Now, from Tennyson's early grief over the loss of Hallam, there had emerged a belief in what I may call a hierarchy of types, each realizing possibilities only latent at

2 'He testifies of these things and wrote these things: and we know that his testimony is true.'   John 21, 24

a lower level, and indicating fresh possibilities to be realized at a higher. And here was a creed, or a supposition, reconcilable at once with the monistic or pantheistic trend which science was imposing on our thought, and on the other hand with historic Christianity, and the sublime claims which Christianity makes for personality, and on it. Granted that an initial act of faith is required, because, so far as we can see, progress may be morally downward as well as upward: granted also that the implied metaphysic will be in detail shadowy—a philosophy of Somehow, wavering between a hopeful doubt and a doubtful hope—yet it was open to any Christian to accept the hypothesis, in the assurance that the highest in this human hierarchy is a man, and that man Incarnate God. Thus the argument is rounded off, because, so conceived, personality is not an incident in evolution, but its consummation. Here then was a body of conviction, won from doubt, and even despair, which gave to thousands, in the season of their distress, the guidance and assurance for which they asked.

There is one passage in Tennyson and, so far as I can recall, one only, where he rises to the full poetic height of his argument, to a complete poetic apprehension of his own idea. I mean the close of *In Memoriam*.

> And rise, O moon, from yonder down,
>   Till over down and over dale
>   All night the shining vapour sail
> And pass the silent-lighted town,
> The white-faced halls, the glancing rills,
>   And catch at every mountain head,
>   And o'er the friths that branch and spread
> Their sleeping silver through the hills;
> And touch with shade the bridal doors,
>   With tender gloom the roof, the wall;
>   And breaking let the splendour fall
> To spangle all the happy shores
> By which they rest, and ocean sounds,
>   And, star and system rolling past,
>   A soul shall draw from out the vast
> And strike his being into bounds.

Con quanto di quel salmo e poscia scripto.[3]

3 'With as much of that psalm as is thereafter written.' Dante: *Purgatorio* ii

Here, or so it seems to me, Tennyson has done the utmost that can be asked of a poet, in one act embracing the whole range of his deepest personal thought, and rendering it in the loveliest and most natural imagery that poetry affords, the moonlit sea and the lovers sleeping by its shores.

PURITANS AND VICTORIANS

I HAVE often, in the course of some recent studies, been per-plexed to determine the exact contribution of Puritanism to the middle-class industrial civilization of England in the nine-teenth century. The first difficulty is to decide what Puritanism exactly was: the second, to trace its course through the eigtheenth century: the third, to separate it, in its nineteenth-century form, from other converging or parallel tendencies.

Puritanism, as I conceive it, is a double strand. There is the authoritarian Puritanism of the Presbyterians, and the equalitarian Puritanism of the Independents. The distinction is not perfect, because the Independents tended to assume a certain theocratic authority of their own; the real equalitarian tradition was driven underground; and, when it re-emerged, it was rather in the academic form of Godwin than the proletarian form of Tom Paine. But in the authoritarian brand two main constituents can be observed: Old Testament patriarchy and seclusion. The Saints were an Elect People, and, more specifically, a body of Elect Householders, ruling with divine authority their families, their servants, and their workpeople. So far as they were rulers, they were very much like other householders. It was the sense of election and commission that made them what they were.

It is often said, so often that it is becoming something of a commonplace, that the exclusion of Non-conformists from public life after the Restoration led them to devote themselves with particular assiduity to the pursuit of wealth. There is exaggeration here. Most Anglicans, and most deists, were excluded from politi-cal life, and I cannot suppose that the easy-going borough business of the eighteenth century made so much demand on a man's attention as to leave the Churchman less time than the Dissenter for his own pursuits. It was not the enforced, but the deliberate withdrawal from the world that concentrated the Dissenter's activities. Puritanism was already the creed of the commercial classes, and the most, I think, we can ascribe to it, after the Restoration, is a certain intensification of a money-making impulse already acting strongly.

But this is not what is commonly meant when people speak of the lasting effect of Puritanism. What they do mean comes out, for example, in a sentence I quote from Mr Sitwell's *Dickens*: 'Dickens shared the genuine anti-art bias which has possessed most English people since the triumph of Cromwell and the Puritans.' But the triumph of Cromwell was the triumph of left-wing Puritanism over right-wing Puritanism, of Independency over Presbytery, won at a moment when Presbytery was rapidly coming to terms with Church and King. It was a minority regime which lasted some ten years, and was then swept utterly away. Is it to be supposed that 'most English people' had a pro-art bias in 1640, lost it in 1650 and were unable to recover it in 1660? It is to be remembered that in those ten years there were no profound, or convulsive, social or economic changes. Petty Sessions and Quarter Sessions went on administering the old laws: judges proceeded on assize: freeholders and copyholders met as usual in the manor courts: the Universities flourished: the nobles were respected: landlords collected their rents: tenants paid them: merchants sent their ventures east and west, and, if they were successful, repanelled their mansions in town, bought a new Turkey carpet and a new set of hangings; if very successful, took a little place in the country, and commissioned some builder trained by Inigo or Webb to provide them with a manor house suitable to their new estate. Where so much remained, continuing unbroken from the past, could a little interference with Christmas games and maypoles really have converted 'most English people' from a pro-art to an anti-art bias? To put it another way, can an anti-art bias really be predicated of people who built our eighteenth-century houses and filled them with our eighteenth-century furniture, whose favourite reading in one generation was the poetry of Pope and in another the prose of Johnson, who naturalized Handel and gave Garrick a grave in the Abbey?

The common view, which Mr Sitwell adopts, makes a break in the continuity of our civilization about 1650. Suppose now we went the way of Ur and Mohenjo Daro, and archaeologists had to rediscover our seventeenth century. Would they be forced to suppose a cataclysm to account for the change between 1630 and 1680? I cannot see it. Of music I cannot speak, and our painting has in all ages been subject to waves of influence from the Continent. But in our peculiar and native art of domestic architecture and equipment, decade succeeds to decade without, so far as I can discern, any trace even of a temporary disturbance. On the other hand, an archaeologist who lit upon two sealed sites—the eighteenth-century rooms in the Victoria & Albert Museum, for example, and a room of about 1840, if one were preserved—might very reasonably infer some intervening catastrophe, the conquest of a higher by a lower stock.

'Nothing else', I can see him writing, 'can explain the completeness of the change, not only in the character of the artifacts, but in the attitude of the people to their art. Enough has now been disclosed to demonstrate that the English of 1700 to 1800 were astonishingly gifted not only as craftsmen, but as connoisseurs. Every site reveals a fresh masterpiece, some new ingenuity of planning or delicacy of adornment, in the houses of the priests and the local magistrates. The internal equipment seems to have been directed by the same taste for simplicity, the same unerring sense of balance and proportion that governed their architecture. But at some time between 1800 and 1840 it was replaced by a barbaric and tasteless profusion, an almost aggressive indifference to symmetry and selection. An ingenious attempt has been made to associate this cultural revolution with an invasion from the Continent, the only evidence for which is a medal inscribed in a continental dialect, "Frappé à Londres" (struck at London). But what we know of continental culture in this period harldy justifies the assumption. I am rather inclined to seek the clue in a fragment of the historian Sitwell, in which he speaks of Cromwell and the

Puritans converting the English to an anti-art bias, especially as in other sources Cromwell is associated with a vast destruction of religious edifices. If I am correct, we may perhaps think of Cromwell as the leader—or the symbol—of a great social upheaval, to be dated some time about 1820, in which the art and religion of the ruling classes perished with the destruction of the ruling classes themselves.

'Against this, I must admit, is to be set the fact that there are good grounds for placing the Puritans in the seventeenth century near the beginning of the great artistic period I have been describing. It is very attractive to connect the sudden awakening of the artistic genius of a people with some new religious impulse—such as is observable with Buddhism in the East and the Franciscan revival in the West. And the characteristics of English art in its golden age, its simplicity and the purity of its aesthetic apprehensions, do correspond in a remarkable way with the little we know of Puritanism as a religious movement. With our present knowledge the problem must be declared insoluble. But on the whole it seems most likely that the Sitwell fragment is corrupt and that the passage should read:

Dickens shared the genuine anti-art bias which has possessed most English people since the triumph of Cromwell *over* the Puritans,

the Puritans being the authors and transmitters of the artistic culture of the seventeenth and eighteenth centuries, and Cromwell the general name for a servile revolt not unlike that which destroyed the civilization of Angkor.'

Is there not something to be said for our archaeologist? The gradual fining down and steadying down of Elizabethan architecture and decoration into the exquisite, and yet living, quietness of the later seventeenth century does correspond with the steadying down of temper, and the fining down of prose and manners, which are traceable over the same period, a process of which Puritanism, in its widest sense, is the most complete, the most self-conscious articulation. I really know of no reason for supposing that a Puritan gentleman did not appreciate a good house or a good sideboard as keenly as anyone else, or that his wife and daughters were not as exact as any Cavalier lady in matching tapestries or choosing chairs to go with the table. That his principles may have stirred a special dislike of everything that was splashy or overdone is doubtless very probable. But anyone who has meditated before certain Elizabethan and Jacobean monuments will agree that it was high time someone did protest—on whatever grounds—against the overdone and the splashy.

Specific Puritanism, party Puritanism, was ousted in 1660. It was occluded; led off into a side channel while the main stream flowed on; and it is, I suppose, this deviated Puritanism—cut off from corporate life, from society and from the Universities—which is to be made responsible for so much of the mischief of the nineteenth century. Again I must ask how? My eyes show me that from about 1660 to 1820, with a high tableland between 1720 and 1760, the 'pro-art bias' must have been extraordinarily well diffused among a very large number of ordinary people, so large indeed that one may almost speak of them as 'most English people'. What belated action of 'Cromwell and the Puritans' converted it into the negative or even adverse attitude which created the nineteenth-century town and house?

My diagnosis would be on other lines. Towards the end of the eighteenth century the English eye began to lose its sense of proportion, whether in surface or in mass. The picturesque had come in as an unsettling force. About the same time the middle classes began to get rich, often very quickly. Allusion and profusion between them first blurred, then destroyed, the pure aesthetic feeling for subordination and propriety, for the right handling of a wall-surface or a room. Allusiveness ruined our architecture: profusion our decoration. What makes the first neo-Gothic churches of the nineteenth century so absurd is the complacent designer's voice at our ear, murmuring, like Fanny Price,

A Scottish monarch sleeps below.

And the little houses, once the Augustan instinct for design was lost, could only satisfy their blind craving for distinction by accumulation of ornament, or rather of ornaments, on the traditional lines of the great houses.

In fact, so far from making Puritanism responsible for the anti-art bias of the nineteenth century, I am inclined to look for the secret in a quite un-Puritan delight in unrestrained extravagance, to which the new development of mechanical ingenuity powerfully contributed, the delight of savages free at last to indulge themselves like their betters, and naturally not knowing how to do it. That the readjustment of comparative wealth, which was going on all the time, did raise the occluded Puritanism of the Independents to eminence and self-importance is no doubt true. But, so far as I can see, this Puritanism, though it was, aesthetically, in true descent from the seventeenth century, carried none of its canons forward. It was swallowed up in the stream of competitive expenditure.

> Neat was their house: each table, chair and stool
> Stood in its place, or, moving, moved by rule:
> No lively print or picture graced the room,
> A plain brown paper lent it decent gloom:
>
> But here the eye, in glancing round, surveyed
> A small recess that seemed for china made:
> Such pleasing pictures screened this pencill'd ware,
> That few would search for nobler objects there.

This is an Independent's room as Crabbe knew it in 1812. It would probably strike us as being very attractive. At least it had a good, if quite unconscious, tradition behind it. The owner is a wealthy provincial merchant. The business man's drawing-room of 1850 had no tradition, and usually was all too conscious of itself.

In fact, we can very easily bring the common view to a decisive test. We all know what sort of towns the Victorian middle classes built for themselves and their workpeople. Swindon is a very favourable specimen: it is airy, healthy and soundly built. Go a few miles south and you will see what sort of towns those Puritans built. Marlborough, a Puritan stronghold, was destroyed by fire in 1653 and rebuilt with the help of a national subscription headed by Cromwell. The result is one of the loveliest things in England. It is a little town: it has not the amusing metropolitan air of Cirencester, for example, which always seems to be murmuring,

'Of course, you know, my mother was a Roman colony.' And I do not suggest that Marlborough was rebuilt so, because its people were Puritans. It was the only way they knew how to build. But it was built not on a declining, but on a rising tradition. What religion the burgesses of Blandford professed I do not know. From the pleasure Mr Gibbon took in their society I should infer it was of a mild, accommodating kind. But we do know what sort of town they liked to live in, because Blandford too, very conveniently for historians, was destroyed and rebuilt from the ground in 1731, and it shows the same tradition maturing towards perfection, less homely, more certain, but not yet fixed. One might speculate at length on the probable outcome of an artistic boyhood spent in Blandford or in Birmingham, in the constant, unperceived presence—or absence—of a finished, deliberate, domestic art. But we are not left to speculation. Out of Blandford came Alfred Stevens. Out of Birmingham came Burne-Jones, and he fled from it as far as his art would carry him.

In 1832, the Elect Householder came to his own at last: economically as a manufacturer, politically as a voter, and no one can read the truly astonishing claims made for the middle classes, their wisdom and their virtue, sometimes by themselves, sometimes by their political flatterers, without hearing an echo of the theocratic aspirations of the Saints. But a great part of the Puritan creed, and in particular its moral and intellectual individualism, had been dropped by the way. In this, as in so many ways, New England a hundred years ago was Old England writ large: even more respectable, even less independent: morally more censorious, intellectually more servile. ' "I suppose their best society is like the best society in Manchester?" said Lord Roehampton.' But the Puritanism of New England had kept what the Puritanism of the parent stock had lost, a strong sense of civic responsibility. It struck all English travellers, and the explanation is not far to seek. Insular security had long ago made the walled town unnecessary in England. New England had to start life, as a Greek would have said, 'by cities', because there were always Red Indians waiting outside to scalp the strays. Very rarely in English writing of the nineteenth century do we come upon the idea of a great town as an entity, as a thing in itself. The idea had to be built up by slow degrees. In America it was there from the first. The best society of Philadelphia was trying to improve and glorify Philadelphia. The best society of Manchester was trying to get out of it. Liverpool alone of English towns had, I think, some trace of the civic self-consciousness of a Nuremberg or a Venice, and Liverpool produced, or at least commissioned, in St George's Hall, our solitary masterpiece of civic art. New English Puritanism would never have tolerated the abandonment and neglect of the Lancashire children. Neither, I think, would old English Puritanism. It might have worked their bodies to the bone, but it would have felt bound to do something for their souls. In one of the most powerful of Puritan sermons the preacher bids his hearers ask themselves every night, 'What have I done today for the Public?', for the Respublica, that is, or the Common Weal. When they ceased to ask, the Puritans became a *bourgeoisie,* and the trouble with the English middle classes in the nineteenth century was not that they were Puritan, but that they were not half Puritan enough.

The humanitarianism of the eighteenth century grew out of the reunion of the nobler Puritanism with the parent Anglican stock, blending the responsibility of the one with the cultivated humanity of the other. The last of the great Presbyterian houses, Willoughby of Parham, rejoined the Church about 1750. Granville Sharp was born in 1735: Wilberforce in 1759: Clarkson in 1760. Johnson's plea for the French prisoners of war, one of the earliest manifestos of the new mood, is dated 1758. The word *inhumanity,* used with reference to the animal world, occurs, so far as I can trace it, for the first time in an order of the Borough of Chippenham, 1756, forbidding barbarous sports. This blend came to its flower and fruit with the Tory Evangelicals of the early Victorian years, who did go out to battle with the Devil in the old Puritan way and not infrequently found the Nonconformist conscience in the other camp. For if the ultimate test, the *articulus stantis aut cadentis Puritanismi,* is the question, 'What have I done today for the Public?' there is little doubt which side could have answered it with the clearer conscience.

EYES AND NO EYES

AMONG the changes of the last thirty years the one which strikes me most forcibly, and certainly not most agreeably, is the revolution in transport which has destroyed the mutual seclusion of our villages and smaller towns and is now fast destroying their individuality. I remember that when I was an undergraduate, something in my reading having stirred my fancy, I decided to go over for a day from Oxford and have a look at the country where, in fact, I now live. But having worked out the cross-country trains, and calculated the chances of finding an old horse-bus at the right place, I had to give it up. Not altogether unwillingly, because there remained the pleasant taste of adventure reserved for another time; and as the distance could now, without any gross or obvious violation of the laws designed for our protection, be covered in little more than an hour, it will be seen that adventure was very easily to be had.

Now multiply all that by a hundred: for the road, say, from Oxford to Abingdon or Wantage, put the road from Calais to the Splügen; instead of Malmesbury or Savernake take Genoa or Venice for your objective; and, having fixed these ratios in your mind, read the opening sentence of the Journey from Mestre in *The Stones of Venice*. The 'days of leisurely travel' from one major point to another came to an end, of course, with the railways. But the experience, the sensation, of leisurely travel on a smaller scale was still to be had by anyone who chose, and to be had moreover, not as a calculated indulgence of sentiment, but in the ordinary course of affairs, as soon as he left the station and trusted himself to bicycle, horse, or feet. Add to this, that though 'the base and brickish skirts' were spreading, they had not so much extended the lines or blurred the silhouette of towns as to impair their identity: and still, with some assistance from the fancy, and a rather careful selection of one's approach, one could recover the delight with which, in the olden days, 'from the top of the last hill he had surmounted, the traveller beheld the quiet village where he was to rest, scattered among the meadows beside its valley stream, or, from the long hoped for turn in the dusty causeway, saw for the first time the towers of some famed city, faint in the rays of sunset'.

The reticulation of the English country, with large knots for the market towns and little knots for the villages, was the product of physical causes, among which the pace of an ox and of a horse were not the least important: just as ribbon development and dormitory villages are the product of petrol. And when we look at the knots in detail, analysing them into their component buildings, again we see that Nature has had her say, commanding them to be built of stone or brick or timber or daub, and roofed with whatever material lies to hand. But is this all? Is there not perhaps a metaphysic as well as a physic of domestic architecture, and a certain coherence between the people and their dwelling-places, so that houses are like this or that not only because Nature has ordered that they should be, but because their inhabitants are that way too? And why are the inhabitants so and not otherwise? Must we go back to Nature to find out? Or to history? Or to what?

With these reflections and these queries in his mind, Mr Ruskin, gentleman commoner of Christ Church and just turned eighteen, took up his pen to write on the 'Poetry of Architecture', in the early months of 1837, and he closed his first paragraph with the sounding apophthegm

No man can be an architect who is not a metaphysician. It is this peculiarity of the art which constitutes its nationality; and it will be found as interesting as it is useful, to trace in the distinctive character of this architecture of nations not only its adaptation to the situation and climate in which it has arisen, but its strong similarity to, and connexion with, the prevailing turn of mind by which the nation who first employed it is distinguished.

Nothing could be better, whether our object be the study and preservation of old buildings or the construction of new. In Wiltshire, for example, there are five clearly defined types of construction, determined by the relative accessibility of various materials; and the elegance or solidity with which each type is worked out locally is in pretty close proportion to the value, that is the fertility, of the land. Anyone who had mastered the rules could, from the comparative prevalence of flint, brick, and stone, guess to within a few miles in what part of the county he had been dumped blindfold: and, if he has to build, it will be in a concatenation accordingly, for 'unity of feeling', says the young sage with another dogmatic flourish of his pen, 'is the first principle of goood taste'.

But as soon as we pass from these admirable doctrines to specific observation we become aware that something has gone wrong. First follows a charming description of the lowland cottage of England: it is, of course, thatched and whitewashed, and 'its rough surface catches a side light as brightly as a front one' (that is well observed); the window has diamond panes, and 'a light wooden porch breaks the flat of the cottage face'. Later, Ruskin spreads himself, in an analysis of all possible landscapes into Simple Blue, Picturesque Blue, Green, Brown, and Grey, and concludes, I am sorry to say, that in Simple Blue Country, though the houses may be of red brick, 'no stone quoining or presence of any contrasting colour should be admitted'. Had Ruskin never seen Abingdon?

But there is more in it than a freakish dislike of red and white. How did it come about that a young man, so naturally gifted and so well equipped by travel, could pass some years at Oxford when Oxford was at the peak of her beauty, without apparently noticing that the buildings were rather pretty (he has a word of approval for one of the windows at Brasenose), that there were some nice meadows close at hand, some good views of Simple Blue Country from Elsfield or Boar's Hill (he has instead to quote the view from Richmond Terrace), and a really excellent river? One recalls the magical exactness of some phrase in which he records his observation of a French or Italian landscape, and one asks, if he could see

the flaky veils of the mist of the brooks, spreading low along the pasture lands

betweeen Abbeville and Rouen, why could he not see them

between Eynsham and Iffley? I shall not go to Torcello again, but when I saw it, some years before the war, it was, down to

the door of its ruinous staircase, swinging idly on its hinges,

the Torcello that Ruskin knew; and a few pages would have preserved for us, not less completely and exactly, the Oxford that he knew. They were not written. 'Is there to be no more of Oxford?' Froude asked plaintively, when *Praeterita* was coming out in parts. There was no more.

The truth, and the trouble, was that Ruskin was a Grand Tourist, and below the level of the Grand Tour or the Journey in Pursuit of the Picturesque, in Dovedale or the Lakes, he could not see at all. With the baleful consequences of that insensibility we are struggling today. Suppose it had been otherwise. Imagine Ruskin, not a gentleman commoner accustomed to travel at large and in all the luxury of family coach and courier, but a servitor with nothing but his feet to carry him. Endow him with the same natural gifts, the most observant eye on record and an unrivalled mastery of descriptive prose, and then set him to work, studying, let us say, Holywell and Merton Street with the minute and loving care which he did give to any insanitary back lane in Zug or Verona; or ranging farther afield, not from Milan to Genoa or 'the King of Sardinia's capital' (where he remarks that some of the minor streets are in brick, and really quite commendable), but from Wood to Water Eaton, or from Brill to Burford: his farthest horizon being not

the mighty fragments of peaked light, standing up behind the barred clouds of evening, one after another, countless, the crown of the Adrian sea.

but the Chilterns or the Berkshire Downs; noticing, as he went, how building does cohere with 'situation and climate and turn of mind' and not merely telling us that it does; and discovering that not all lowland cottages are thatched and whitewashed, that not all English landscape is trim, and that the Simple Blue of Otmoor is no more like the Simple Blue of the White Horse than either is like a Blue Cheese or a Blue Moon.

There would have been no *Stones of Venice*, no *Modern*

Painters, and no *Lamps*. Instead, there might have been such an analysis, and such pictures, of the human landscape of England as would have furnished the coming generations with a complete philosophy of planning and design. Excited, dazzled, and overwhelmed by the rapture of travel, Ruskin excited, dazzled, and overwhelmed his age by the splendour of his language: he imposed his standards of appreciation with the united authority of an artist, a critic, and a moralist: and to the business in hand, whether it was building churches or housing the people, those standards were for the most part irrelevant, precisely because his just insistence on 'climate, situation, and turn of mind' had, in England, no backing of historical knowledge or direct observation. It was a conception without perception, and therefore empty. We were left, at the most critical period of our artistic history, without any body of native aesthetic thought to resist the invasion of deceased styles and alien manners, and to preserve the 'unity of feeling which is the first principle of good taste'. In 1936, with the connivance of the Crown, three savages destroyed the Court House at Eltham, in its place and kind one of the loveliest things surviving in England. It had, they said, no historical or architectural interest: it did not belong to any of the styles or periods which are scheduled for admiration. But if it had not been for Ruskin and the Gothic revival, they might have noticed that it was beautiful.

NO SERVILE TENURE[1]

MESSRS DUCKWORTH continue to provide the public with short biographies which maintain an excellent standard of craftsmanship. I must not go on be-rating the Dirty Twenties, a topic to which, I am warned, my pen too frequently recurs. But I own it gives me a great deal of satisfaction to think that there is a growing market for sage and serious biography, and that there should be so many writers capable of meeting the demand.

1 *Charles I*, by Pansy Pakenham; *Peel*, by G. Kitson Clark.

Of the latest volumes in the series, two have interested me particularly. One is Lady Pansy Pakenham's *Charles I,* a book which goes at its subject with a warm and fearless directness which I find admirable. The resulting figure may not be the whole Charles, but it is a very real Charles: and if at times the writer seems to exchange the pen for the shillelagh, I do not know that she is any the worse exponent of an age which ranked Indifference and Neutrality with Heresy and Profaneness, as things equally detestable. Some of my contemporaries may recall the subdued ecstasy with which we used to receive the intimation that once the poet Shakespeare so far forgot his dramatic impartiality as to place in the mouth of John of Gaunt a warm eulogy on the British People. But without imagination neither drama nor history nor biography can be written. And will the imagination ever be neutral? I doubt it. But if it can, then it had better keep clear of the seventeenth century.

And the nineteenth, because there the ashes of old controversy are even hotter to the foot. In Mr Kitson Clark's book I seem to feel a certain straining after impartiality, which at times relieves itself in an ungainly skittishness. It is a pity, because Mr Clark is not a writer who needs to call attention to himself by throwing up his heels: he is only dull when he tries to be bright; and his serious judgements are always worth considering and often most aptly expressed. 'Peel's better qualities', he says, when speaking of his early Irish Secretaryship, 'do not appear in his general conceptions, which were often commonplace. But because, like an able artificer, Peel always thought with his hands, his true quality appears in his administration.' And again: 'He kept tight hold of the ordinary Tory difficulties and arguments, for he took them seriously. But he also took seriously the arguments of his opponents: he was not simply content to parry them: he was sensitive to the moral challenge behind them.' A great deal of Sir Robert is implicit in those well-considered sentences, and I have others marked. But, just from want, I think, of imaginative sympathy, Mr Clark does not quite succeed in building his views into a portrait, and the result is less a book about Peel than a book round about him. We observe by turns his capacity, his unoriginality, his masterful steadiness, his curious and delicate sensibility. But the great Sir Robert Peel does not appear. Mr Clark set me reading again what I have always regarded as a masterpiece of compact narrative— George Peel's article in the *Dictionary of National Biography*. The portrait which there emerges is really clearer, and the reason is that it is drawn with the confidence of a warm and unconcealed regard.

But what surprised me, reading these two books one after the other, was to find myself running parallels between Charles and Peel. Voices seemed to be calling and answering each other out of the centuries. 'No man ever went about to break Parliament, but in the end Parliament broke him.' That is Eliot in 1629, but— substitute Party for Parliament, and it might be Lord George Bentinck in 1845. The explanation, of course, lies not in the character of the King and the statesman—though there again I found myself drawing comparisons—but in their situation. The position of the Sole Person, be it the King in Parliament or the Leader in his Party, must by the nature of things be the focus of analogous relations, and in Charles's day, as in Peel's, they had not been stabilized or regulated by experiment and the process of time. Of the King, a Cavalier wrote: 'He had a greatness of mind not to live precariously by his subjects.' Put followers for subjects and you have Peel. 'I do not desire to be Minister of England; but while I am Minister of England I will hold office by no servile tenure. I will hold office unshackled by any other obligation than that of consulting the public interests and providing for the public safety.' Put King for Minister, and you have Charles. One might go further. In their fine culture, the long love-story of their married lives, their earnest desire for the well-being of the people —a desire in practice found compatible with slitting Prynne's ears and opposing Fielden's Factory Bill—the two men seem constantly to touch and overlap. Both of them were men of the past. Charles was a belated Tudor without the Tudor genius, and Peel, who, as a Harrow boy, had heard Mr Fox replying to Mr Pitt, belonged, as Mr Clark excellently says, to the age of senatorial rather than of representative government.

There is a difference indeed. There have been many abler kings than Charles. But in the whole record of our public life, has there ever been anything to match the magnificent ability of Peel? Ability, not genius. Bagehot called him a second-class man, and Bagehot was not often wrong. There is something missing, which has kept him out of that high place reserved in a nation's memory for those in whom it was not missing—for Fox and both the Pitts, for Gladstone and Disraeli. Above all, he lacked the gift with which both his great assailant and his great disciple were so richly endowed, the gift of long, far-sighted, fertile meditation, and no party, therefore, has taken his memory into its care. In one way his early introduction to office—he was Chief Secretary at twenty-four—was unfortunate. He was cradled in minute-paper, and throughout his life the memorandum was his most natural mode of utterance. Returning from Ireland, he deliberately avoided office for some years, while he was practising himself in the arts of debate, and acquiring that mastery of Parliamentary strategy and tactics which was to make him, in Disraeli's words, 'the greatest member of Parliament that ever lived'. When he returned to office, at the age of thirty-seven, in 1825, he was the Complete Statesman. His party had been in power as long as most people could remember, and there seemed no reason why they should not be there for ever. They had recovered from the panic, and the country had recovered from the depression, which had followed the end of the war. Their legislation and administration were of the first quality; one could hardly wish England a better fortune than to have Peel always at the Home Office, Palmerston at the War Office, and Huskisson at the Board of Trade. Whether to have Canning always at the Foreign Office planting banners on the remembered heights of Lisbon, and calling new worlds into existence to redress the balance of the old, would be a price worth paying, is a question on which opinions may lawfully differ.

Canning once, in a fit of petulance which intelligent Tories can well understand, spoke of 'the stupid old Tory party'. 'To use an odious word,' Peel wrote to a friend, 'the tone of public opinion is more liberal than that of the government.' But if your own side is stupid and the other odious, what course are you to pursue? To a Canning or a Disraeli—and even Gladstone did not always find his followers wholly intelligent or sympathetic—the answer is clear: you must educate your party. You must see to it that, when an issue emerges and a conflict is inevitable, they meet it with a programme, a policy, a philosophy: with the ideas of today or to-morrow, not those of the day before yesterday. This was what Peel could not do. He accepted the Tory position, which implied the permanent subjection of the Catholics in Ireland, the exclusion of the Nonconformists in England from municipal office, the maintenance of an unreformed representation. Within limits, he made it his own. But it was for him and not the party to say what those limits were. When, therefore, convinced by the logic of facts, he conceded Catholic Emancipation and the repeal of the Test Act, he surrounded his name with a volume of party obloquy which to a man of his temperament must have been an agony. Nearly twenty years later, admittedly the first man in England, as England, thanks in no small measure to his good sense and good faith, was the first country in the world, he would whiten at the ill-conditioned yell from his own back-benchers: 'Who killed Mr Canning?'

He recovered his credit with his party by the steady opposition he offered to the Reform Bill, and nearly lost it again by his tran-quil acceptance of the Reform Act as the definite solution of a great constitutional problem. This is the Peel of the thirties, dis-trusted by all those 'stern, unbending Tories who follow, mutinously and reluctantly, a leader whose experience and eloquence are indispensable to them, but whose cautious temper and moderate opinions they abhor'. This is the Peel whose advent to office the young Queen contemplated with something like terror. And this is the Peel whom the country demanded in 1841, as emphatically as it had, in even darker days, called on Pitt, and on his son, to end the disorders of the State. In ten years, a leader whose relations with his party were very largely governed by mutual aversion, disdain on one side answering suspicion on the other, had rebuilt that party and re-established it in power. Five years later, it broke in his hands. But, pass over not five years but nine; think not of the Repeal of the Corn Laws or the triumphant audacity of the great Budgets, but of the day when a sudden hush, as of all men speaking in whispers, fell on London; and a journalist, going about his business, saw working men and women sobbing at their doors because the great Sir Robert Peel was dead. 'People', he once wrote, 'like to feel that they are being governed', and the people of England knew that they had never been governed by a man more resolute or more sincere in all that concerned the public interest and the public safety.

THACKERAY[1]

IN the good old times, examinations in the Classics usually included what was known as a Taste Paper, and the paper a question, 'Which of the lost authors of antiquity would you most like to recover, and why?' The correct answer was Menander. But it was not my answer, because of a strong suspicion I had that if he were recovered he would turn out to be one of those writers who are best known by their fragments. And the sands of Egypt have given up enough of him to convince me that my suspicion was justified. Exquisite Greek: admirable pictures of middle-class life in the Hellenistic age. And I am reminded, that is exactly what I said about Thackeray in a sixty-word biography composed for a picture postcard. Is there anything more to say?

'Mr Thackeray', according to the old lady quoted by Bagehot, 'is such an uncomfortable writer.' He was—he meant to be—and in a letter quoted by Mr Dodds he proclaims his intention without concealment. That there is something wrong with the world of which I am a part is a discovery that most people have at some time or other made, and so far as I can see there are three ways of dealing with it. You may blame it on the world, or on yourself, or you may placidly remark, 'Well, that is so: and, being so, though there may be much to be done, there is no more to be said.' And all the discourse, in which today we so much abound, discourse about frustration and adjustment and what not, comes round to

1 *Thackeray: A Critical Portrait*. By J. Dodds. (Oxford University Press.)

this: some people are comfortable, others uncomfortable, and if they are writers they will tend to paint their world accordingly, and project their mood on their readers.

The age in which Thackeray grew up was intensely uncomfortable. William Ward, Ideal Ward of the Oxford Movement, has left on record the opinion of a doctor known to him. 'The chief causes of insanity in England', said this sage, 'are the pressure of the commercial system and the uncertainty of religious opinion.' Doctors are sometimes wrong, but that a highly intelligent man like Ward should have thought this diagnosis worth noting down has always appeared to me one of the most illuminating incidents of his time. If 'the pressure of the commercial system' could drive people mad, we may be sure that it brought many more pretty near the edge, and that the uneasiness and distraction made themselves felt over a still wider range.

What was the doctor thinking of? Mr Leonard Woolf once wrote a most ingenious analysis on Marxian principles of the world of Jane Austen. It is a world in which nobody comes to grief: they may rise—the Westons had risen into 'gentility and property' though it had taken them two or three generations to do it—but they never fall. In the novels of the next age, the question is not whether the local bank will fail or the fortune of the family be lost in Anglo-Mexicans, but only at what point in the story the catastrophe will occur, and how the heroine will be restored to her due place in society. Families do not rise and decline: they shoot up and down, and every neighbouring atom feels the thrill, the anticipation, the hope, and the alarm.

But these movements had to work themselves out in a society very toughly and formidably organized; and the internal strains and stresses were proportionately great and painful. It would be hard to say (Lytton, I think, has made this remark somewhere) which was the more uncomfortable: the gentleman compelled to treat the tradesman as an Insider because he wanted his influence at the county election, or the tradesman who realized when the election was over that he was an Outsider still. Now all this is fair game for the Comic Spirit: and the *vis comica* was possessed by Thackeray in full and noble measure. But it is not the only game on the heath: and with Thackeray one feels—at least, I feel, and contemporaries, writing when his fame was in full glow, felt before me—that his preoccupation with one mode of the social movement is exorbitant. It narrows the working ambit of his other gifts, his ironic power, his mastery of incident and character. A scene, a character, a conversation, yes—like the immortal dialogue on Blood between Hamlet's aunt and the young man with weak legs. But—take it in your stride, and don't nag. And if the sufferer answers: 'I am so uncomfortable that I can't help nagging,' for my own part I can only reply, 'Well, that being so, I suppose there is no more to be said.'

I took up Mr Dodds's book with interest to see how far his conception of Thackeray coincided with mine. American writers on English themes have an advantage over us, in that they see their subject from a greater distance, while it is not so familiar as to drive them into a forced originality. They look their subject square in the eyes, while the Englishman, too often, must be looking up or looking down. I have often noticed in American biography a sedate and workmanlike habit which I wish was rather more commonly cultivated among ourselves. And I think Mr Dodds's portrait is true. Thackeray, to me, is not an interesting man: and it struck me as curious, considering how exact and faithful his pictures are, that I so rarely have had occasion to cite him as an authority on Victorian ways of thought and feeling. The reason, I think, is an instinctive distrust of his proportions. In saying that I may be revealing a personal limitation, and I am not suggesting that a novelist must be ranked by his utility as a source book, or *Alton Locke* would come somewhere near the top of Victorian fiction. But I never mind sharing a limitation with Walter Bagehot, and another saying of his, 'This endless accumulation of detail to prove that tenth-rate people are always endeavouring to behave like ninth-rate people', does seem to me to reveal the black drop at the bottom of the cup. Does it matter if they do? It mattered to Thackeray. It mattered far too much. The Railway is the great Victorian symbol, and I often picture the people of that age as a railway crowd, all pushing, scrambling, and shoving—backwards or forwards—at once. And what a journey lies before them, what mountains those tunnels will pierce, what valleys those airy viaducts will span, what novelties, what adventures, what delight! And among them I see a passenger whose joy is darkened by one anxiety——he is not quite sure if his ticket entitles him to travel first class.

MR AND MRS DICKENS[1]

IN themselves these letters are good reading, and Mr Dexter's editorial work has been performed without fuss and with an excellent economy of notes, chronology, and index. If they had appeared anonymously, an acute reader would very soon have found himself observing that this man writes like Dickens, on page 72 that he must be Dickens, and on page 192 that he is Dickens.

An old lady who had been outside all day and came in towards dinner time, turned out to be the mistress of a Yorkshire school returning from the holiday-stay in London. She was a very queer old lady, and showed us a long letter she was carrying to one of the boys from his father, containing a severe lecture (enforced and aided by many texts from scripture) on his refusing to eat boiled meat. She was very communicative, drank a great deal of brandy and water, and towards evening became insensible.

The only travellers we have encountered have been two English maiden ladies, whom we found sitting on a rock (with parasols), in the most magnificent part of the Gorge of Gondo, the most awful portion of the Simplon, there awaiting their travelling chariot, in which, with their money, their parasols, and a perfect shop of baskets, they were carefully locked up by an English servant in sky-blue and silver buttons.

After dark last night, a landlord where we changed horses, discovered that the baggage would certainly be stolen unless cords were attached to each of the trunks, which cords were to hang down so that we might hold them in our hands all the way, and feel any tug that might be made at our treasures. You will imagine the absurdity of our jolting along some twenty miles in this way, exactly as if we were in three shower baths and afraid to pull the string.

1 *Mr and Mrs Charles Dickens*: His Letters to her: with notes, etc., by Walter Dexter.

Dickens at his ease, no doubt; neither his observation nor his fancy is working at full power, and, on the other hand, he is neither declaiming nor posturing. If we can suppose all other records to have been lost, our judgement based on these letters only would undoubtedly be that the writer was a man of great natural aptitude for prose, a well-bred, considerate man, addressing a wife to whom he was obviously devoted and who shared his interests and his friends. The letter preparing her for the death of their infant daughter is a touching example of the native delicacy which Bagehot singled out as one of Dickens's most attractive characteristics as a writer. There has not been a word to forewarn us of the announcement—'Mr and Mrs Dickens have agreed to separate'—or of the explanation: 'I suppose that no two people, not vicious in themselves, ever were joined together, who had a greater difficulty in understanding one another, or who had less in common.'

Of course, he was a natural author; he always found it easier to write than not to write. Even Byron, when he could forget that he was addressing Lady Byron, could run into most agreeable gossip about his journeys and the history of Ferrara; and letters came as easy to Dickens as diaries to Macaulay. Still, the whole tone of the correspondence is so unforced and intimate as to leave upon our minds the impression either that, when the crisis came, Dickens imagined the part to have been far more difficult than in truth it had been, or else that he had played for years a part imposed upon him by a sense of duty, and discharged with the self-control of a great actor determined to make the play succeed. Nothing will make of Dickens a simple character to understand. But those critics who believe that every work of art is the artist's substitute for going to bed with someone, or his excuse for going to bed with someone else, will find singularly little in these letters to substantiate their lunes.

Of an ordinary man, one would say that, having found he had married the wrong woman, he made the best of the situation till the children were growing up and then resolved to end it by an amicable parting. But then, the ordinary man has an office to go to, a shop to manage, a ship or a battalion to command: in any

case, an area of work, where the most incompatible wife, even if
she neglects his children and makes his home uncomfortable, can
work no serious disturbance. Dickens's work was done in his
imagination, and after *David Copperfield* his imagination was
beginning to flag. The effort was greater, the returns less. He felt
it: we can feel it. His sap had gone into *David Copperfield*, and
he needed a season of refreshment and quiet before it would run
again. The right wife would have provided it, and Catherine
could not. In *Bleak House* we are aware that the wheels are grind-
ing; in *Hard Times* they can hardly move the machine. If *Little
Dorrit* were an Elizabethan play, critics would have been ready
to prove that it was the work of an imitator with some incomparable scenes, the Marshalsea, the arrival at the Hospice, the
death of Merdle, by the master's hand. The *Tale of Two Cities* is
so far removed from Dickens's way that it hardly belongs to the
Canon. A valuation of the Dickens concern in the fifties shows a
steady depreciation of all the assets. The business man would cut
his losses and reorganize. Dickens separated from his wife. To
judge by the results, it was the wisest thing he could do: and if it
was done with a shocking want of dignity, it was done cleanly,
firmly, and generously. Having done it, he recovered control of
his genius: he found his way back to the world where he was
sovereign. He wrote *Great Expectations*: he ended on *Edwin
Drood*: a serene evening after a splendid morning and a baleful
afternoon.

Without these two, and without the dark magnificence of the
River theme in *Our Mutual Friend,* we should have to think of
him as exhausted by *David Copperfield* and going on mechanic-
ally when he had little or nothing more to say. 'In *Bleak House*',
he wrote, 'I have purposely dealt on the romantic side of familiar
things.' Purposely: there is the weakness. The spontaneous irradia-
tion of a created world with a natural and unsought beauty, which
makes *David Copperfield* the wonder which it is, has been
checked at its source. And yet, if ever we put to ourselves the
question whether Dickens is great enough to carry his colossal
faults, it is surely in this power that we must look for the answer.
In *Great Expectations* it re-emerges, fainter perhaps, or mellower,

but still authentic; and, for my own part, I feel it still working, with a grave, a delicate, a final perfection, in *Edwin Drood*.

A few strange faces in the streets: a few other faces, half-strange and half-familiar, once the faces of Cloisterham children, now the faces of men and women who come back from the outer world. To these, the striking of the cathedral clock, and the cawing of the rooks from the cathedral tower, are like voices of their nursery time. To such as these, it has happened in their dying hours afar off, that they have imagined their chamber-floor to be strewn with the autumnal leaves fallen from the elm trees in the Close: so have the rustling sounds and fresh scents of their earliest impressions revived when the circle of their lives was very nearly traced, and the beginning and the end were drawing close together.

Sunset, but the sunset of Homer.

THE SCHOOLMAN IN DOWNING STREET[1]

ONCE upon a time, two examiners were setting a paper on the Napoleonic Period. One of them produced: '(7) How many nations were engaged in the Battle of Leipzig, and what were the losses of each in killed, wounded, and prisoners?' 'Oh come,' said the other (and I need not indicate, I hope, to which University he belonged), 'you can't ask them that.' 'Why not?' said the first, with some surprise, 'I'm sure they won't know the answer.'

If I wanted to trip up an examinee who offered the nineteenth century, I should ask him to say what Mr Gladstone's political position was on Christmas Day in each of the ten years following the death of Peel. If my object was the more humane one of giving him a chance to show what he knew, I should put the question thus: What was Gladstonian Liberalism, and how did Mr Gladstone get there? But the candidate who wishes to be prepared

1 *The Two Mr Gladstones*, by G. T. Garratt.

for either event, will find in Mr Garratt's book competent guidance through the material intricacies, and many suggestive judgements on the spiritual convolutions, of an exceedingly tortuous career.

The theme of his book is the duality in Mr Gladstone's nature: Liverpool below, Oxford on top; or, the Highlander handcuffed to a Lowlander; not, by any means, as will be seen, an original topic, but worked out in an original way, with much confirming detail. I do not mean to follow Mr Garratt over the whole course, but I should like to dwell a little on the Mr Oxford of his portrait: 'an ascetic scholar, a High Churchman with celibate leanings and a deep love of recondite theological arguments. He looked upon human beings as souls to be saved, and distrusted the economic theorizings of laymen. He longed for a definite mission, one which involved self-sacrifice, and found it in Ireland.' There is certainly much truth in this analysis, but it leaves out, I think, one of the most important elements in the make-up of Mr Oxford, and that is Oxford.

About the year 1830 a visitor to Christ Church, who had pushed open the door of the lecture room next to the hall staircase, would have seen assembled two head masters to be; three bishops; three Regius professors; three viceroys, Canning, Dalhousie, and Elgin; Gladstone, Newcastle, and Cornewall Lewis. Lowe sometimes looked in, and Sidney Herbert regularly came across from Oriel. They sat there translating Aristotle's *Rhetoric* in turn at the feet of Mr Biscoe. He is little known to fame, but what villatic fowl ever hatched such a brood of eaglets? Among them was Martin Tupper, to whom we owe the roll of names.

Take now a young man of genius, trained at home in habits of friendly disputation and regular piety, always bracing himself to the evangelical standards of personal holiness; in all his social and intellectual relations of a most vivid and energetic disposition; subject him, in the most congenial surroundings, among contemporaries of the governing class, to a persistent discipline in scholarship, logic, and history; and above all, make him translate Aristotle aloud. What will be the result? To my recollection, Aristotle imposes himself on a young reader first by his determination to settle his meanings before he starts reasoning from them: and then by the resoluteness, often ungainly, often long-winded, often involved, with which he pursues his argument to the end: the parentheses, admissions, and qualifications into which he is always dropping being so many safeguards against interruption or misconception by the way. But our young man has also brought with him, from home or Eton, a gift or habit of words, vast, nebulous and resonant, recalling the Biscayan roll of the younger Pitt. Allow for that: and then tell me, have I not described the regular movement of Mr Gladstone's mind, on the platform, in Committee, or in those analytic and deductive memoranda which the poor Queen had to have translated before she could make head or tail of them? Morley permits himself a distant smile over the fervour with which the Peelites debated where they ought to sit. 'Taking a seat,' Mr Gladstone said, 'is an external sign and pledge that ought to follow upon full conviction of the thing it was understood to betoken.' That is not the language of this world. But it is the phraseology of the Schools, and in particular, of the Divinity Schools: in the great Eucharistic controversy which sprang up when Pusey was silenced by the Heads of Houses in 1843, the contrast of 'external sign and pledge' and 'that which it betokens', was part of the staple of the argument. But dazzled by excess of light, and perplexed by excess of definition, the baffled mind grows suspicious, and, when dreamer and fanatic no longer meet the case, the mutter of Sophist is heard. To no two figures in our history, I suppose, has the name been so persistently applied as to Gladstone and Newman: potent and mysterious figures, their outlines obscured by the very brilliance of their dialectic.

Often when I am reading Newman, an unholy analogy presents itself, and, as he would have said, 'stains my imagination'. I cannot help thinking of those African virgins who in Gibbon's language, 'admitted priests and deacons to their bed, and gloried amidst the flames in their unsullied purity'. He is always skimming along the verge of a logical catastrophe, and always relying on his dialectic agility to save himself from falling: always exposing what seems to be an unguarded spot, and always revealing a new line of defence when the unwary assailant has reached it. I am not

sure it is not a general characteristic of Oxford: we are not the
children of Ockham for nothing: and we are all, I think, more
ready to take intellectual risks than they are at 'the less ancient
and splendid' place, trusting to Aristotle to inspire us with the
right mood and figure when needed, and so to preserve 'the
unsullied purity' of our reasoning.

The content was very different, but in what may be called the
articulation of their minds, their routes from point to point,
Gladstone and Newman were not at all unlike. Morley admitted
that Gladstone had a habit of using words in a sense they could
be grammatically made to carry, knowing all the time that his
hearers would take them in another; but if I wanted to illustrate
this habit, or this gift, it is to Newman that I should first turn.

'What are the humble monk, and the holy nun, but Christians after
the very pattern given us in Scripture? Did our Saviour come on earth
suddenly, in whom would He see the features of the Christians He
and His Apostles left behind them, but in them?'

It is provocative. It is meant to make Mr Bull put his head
down and charge,

Charge for the hearth of Vesta!

and the holiness of the domestic affections. Newman sidesteps.
'What I said was: "If He does not find pattern Christians among
monks and nuns, He will find them nowhere." But He will find
them among monks and nuns. Therefore, obviously, He may find
them elsewhere: in Mrs Bull, for example, and in some (I hope)
of the little Bulls. Really, my poor Cambridge friend, there is
nothing to make such a noise about.'

Meeting last year in the gay and congenial air of Blackpool, the
British Association discussed the popularity of Giant Racers, and
concluded that they gratify the Fear-Escape Propensity (this is
their English:

For God's sake, reader, take it not for mine)

giving their devotees the sensations of acute peril and perfect
security at once. The man who is endowed, over-endowed it may
be, with dialectic astuteness is very apt to keep himself in practice

by taking up indefensible positions for the fun of defending them: practice makes perfect, and without some restraining sense of responsibility—well, Mr Bernard Shaw's dialogues on the Abdication point the moral. Gladstone had a strong and carefully cultivated sense of responsibility—its cultivation being at times even more obtrusive than its natural strength—but every now and then the sophist has to have his run on the Racer, in the matter of the Ewelme Rectory for example, for which really one can find no other explanation than that he wanted to see how fast he could take a corner without crashing. Parliament had said that the Rector of Ewelme must be an Oxford man—dark blue, you know, and that sort of thing. But any Cambridge man can become a member of the other University by incorporation. So Gladstone picked a Cambridge man, saw that he was incorporated, made him Rector of Ewelme, and presented him to Parliament and the world as an Oxford man. Even the faithful Morley has to wish that he hadn't.

Yet in the end both men won their way to honour and even reverence. Newman in the *Apologia* took the whole of educated England into his confidence. Gladstone threw himself on the warm-hearted, close-thinking, hard-fighting Liberalism of the North, and told it what it wanted to hear in the accents of a great actor who has found his part at last. But the instrument with which he worked had been forged and tempered in the Schools of Oxford. It was a dangerous instrument, especially for a man in whose mind the boundaries of self-conviction and self-deception were so feebly guarded. No one has wielded it since: no one today rises from such subtle and laborious argument to such majestic denunciation or appeal:

> nec rapit immensos orbes per humun, neque tantam
> squameus in spiram surgens se colligit anguis.[2]

He carried it with him into history, and perhaps it is as well for us that he did.

---

[2] 'Nor does the snake dart in so huge curves across the ground, nor with reared head gather its scaly body into so great a coil.'   Virgil: *Georgic* ii

MR GLADSTONE

The Romanes Lecture

Delivered in the Sheldonian Theatre, 2 June 1944

WHEN I was honoured with a summons to read a lecture on this Foundation, my first thought was a doubt whether I had anything to say which was worthy to be said in the Schools of Oxford. Then I reflected that for a good many years most of my reading had been concerned with a topic almost inexhaustible, the history of Victorian England, and in particular of Victorian opinion; and in that almost illimitable field I thought I might put together some sheaves which should be worth the carrying. And as I looked along the ground for a more particular theme I remembered that the first of these lectures was read in 1892, the year in which as a boy of ten, an ardent Tory, and a convinced supporter of the Union, I had my one sight of the lecturer, and the face I saw that day, half eagle, half lion, is still my picture of Mr Gladstone. It was, I think, some three years later that I was given Macaulay's *Essays* as a Christmas prize, and I can still recall the shock of reading the words *Gladstone on Church and State* 1839 and realizing that the man whom I had seen driving back to Downing Street that afternoon was as much a part of history as Chatham or Warren Hastings.

When Harcourt heard that Morley was appointed to write the *Life of Gladstone*, he is reported to have said: 'You cannot write about his religion, because you don't believe it: his finance, because you don't understand it: his Irish policy, because you know too much.' Possibly for that reason, or for others which might be thought of (Morley was not one of the First Companions but a late, and, in the beginning, a somewhat distrustful adherent), it failed to be a completely satisfying book: judicious and well-proportioned, charged with devotion and regard, but without the penetration, and without the real sympathy, of a book which it is a special pleasure to mention in this place, Dr Hammond's *Gladstone and the Irish Nation*. Looking back, I should now say that Morley's *Life* is to be taken rather as a biographical commentary on a period of history which must be mastered before the biography can be understood, and Victorian history then—the *Life* appeared at the beginning of my fourth year here—was already falling into that trough of deep obscurity and ignorant contempt which always separates the contemporary from the historic.

Then, in the darker months of the last war, I took to studying, for my private comfort, the history of the great Napoleonic conflict. From Waterloo and Vienna, I went on with Castlereagh and Canning, through the years of wretchedness and gloom which followed so swiftly on the victory: years which impressed on men's minds the picture of the social order as a Beleaguered City, and government as a defensive instrument against subversion: then the slow recovery, and then again the financial catastrophe of 1825, the Reform Bill and the New Poor Law. And in this pilgrimage of mine, in that pause of thankfulness and relief which followed the convulsion of 1831, I came up with Mr Gladstone, much as Christian overtook Faithful when both had passed through the Valley of the Shadow; Mr Gladstone at twenty-five, but already thought worthy of a place, a minor place, in the brief administration of Sir Robert Peel, and, in the words of Macaulay's famous afterthought, almost too famous ever to be quoted again, the rising hope of the stern unbending Tories.

How will he strike us on a first encounter? A most vivid presence, in an age when manners were at once more courtly and emphatic, when young men were not ashamed of clustering locks and flashing eyes, of righteous sentiment and flaming indignation, the chosen phrase and the improving word: and Privilege walked the streets, possibly hated but surely admired. A voice of extraordinary range and charm, and an elevation of speech which already recalls the Biscayan roll of the younger Pitt. This he has brought with him from the Debating Society at Eton, or the home in Liverpool where friendly disputation reigned from morn to eve and Canning was a household deity. But on it Oxford, and Butler, and 'the splendid integrity of Aristotle' have imposed a discipline in statement and inquiry; in definition, sometimes over-laboured;

in distinction, sometimes too finely drawn. What they have not
given him, because they had it not to give, is any idea, any constant
and active idea, of intellectual progress, of the process of science.
Of Tennyson, Jowett once observed, mysteriously, that he was a
good scholar in the Oxford sense of the word. Of Mr Gladstone's
scholarship, his criticism, and his philosophy, it would be equally
true to say that he remained to the end a Christ Church man of
the 1830's.

But ah! what days were those, Parmenides!

when, if we had entered the room next to the great staircase, that
last glory of the Gothic world, we should have found Gladstone,
Sidney Herbert, Robert Lowe, Dalhousie, Elgin, and the younger
Canning, translating the *Rhetoric* by turn at the feet of Mr Biscoe.

The conjunction of a grand reverberating copiousness and a
vehement mathematical exactitude was, throughout, the characterizing note of his oratory, his writing, and, when his mind was
charged with some public theme and not relaxing itself in play-
fulness and triviality, of his conversation also. *Censoria oratio
erat.*[1] And the passage between the two was effected by a dialectical faculty of almost dizzying, and, at times, of wholly unscrupulous agility. An example: *instar mille.*[2] In one of the great debates
on the extension of the franchise in 1866, the most splendid
banquet of oratory, I suppose, that was ever set before even a
Victorian Parliament, when hexameters sped like arrows, and the
Trojan Horse fairly pranced on the floor of the Commons, Mr
Gladstone startled the world with these words:

> Every man who is not presumably incapacitated by some considera-
> tion of personal unfitness or political danger is morally entitled to come
> within the pale of the Constitution.[3]

Well might the world be startled, because to the plain man those
words could mean nothing less than manhood suffrage, with the
exclusion of half-wits and persons politically dangerous: British

---

1 'His style was in the Censor's tradition.'

2 'Let it stand for a thousand.'

3 The quotation is from Gladstone's speech on Baines' Bill for lowering the
borough franchise, 11 May 1864 [Ed.].

subjects, for example, owning allegiance to a foreign centre, Popish priests or Irish Fenians. But, though there can hardly have been one adjective expressive of devotion or dislike that was not at some time or other applied to Mr Gladstone, there *was* one: no one ever called him a plain man. He issued an interpretation from which it appeared that nothing was farther from his thoughts than manhood suffrage.

[The franchise] should exclude those with respect to whom it might appear that though no personal unfitness can be alleged against them, yet political danger might arise from their admission, as for example through the disturbance of the equilibrium of the constituent body, or through virtual monopoly of power in a single class.

An interpretation which leaves the speaker free to vote, not only against manhood suffrage, which would clearly create a mono-poly of power in the working class, but against any extension whatever which in his view amounted to a disturbance of equili-brium. Now, microscopically examined, the statement can be made to bear the gloss. But though the canons of intellectual integrity are doubtless everywhere the same, yet surely the mode of application should vary when you are debating a high constitu-tional issue in the hearing of the people, or doing a logic paper for Mr Biscoe.

But if, this barrier once passed (and it was and remained a formidable barrier, edged and spiked with suspicion and distrust), we are admitted to a more intimate view, such as was had by Arthur Hallam, by Hope-Scott or Manning, we become aware that to this young man, so richly and uncommonly endowed, the world is foremost a field wherein to exercise the tense athletic holiness of the Evangelical, but an Evangelical fired with the glow of the Anglican revival and its vision of a Church renewed, and drawing back its errant sheep once more into the fold. Holiness before Peace: and certainly we may think that a man so fastidious and censorious (his own confession), and we may add so conten-tious, so self-centred, so self-distrustful, will hardly find the world a peaceful place or make it a place of peace for others. In the horoscope which Bulwer playfully cast for him, it is written:

At heart a solitary man . . . and, though he has pleasure in all things peaceful, yet a friend with a real soldier's nature would understand and love him heartily.

There was something of the soldier's nature in Mrs Gladstone: there was much in the close-fighting Radicalism of the North. But we need not go to others for a portrait which, perhaps unconsciously, perhaps not quite unconsciously, Mr Gladstone has drawn for us himself. Speaking of the grandeur and intensity of Homer's Achilles—and grandeur and intensity are the words which come most naturally when we reflect on the achievements of those sixty years and the fire which sustained them—he says:

Its self-government is indeed only partial. But any degree of self-government is a wonder when exercised over such volcanic forces. It is a constantly recurring effort at rule over a constantly recurring rebellion . . . and there is a noble contrast between the strain put upon his strength to suppress his own passion and the masterful ease with which

—let us end the sentence for him—

on that famous midnight in 1852 he bounded on to the floor of the House of Commons, and tore Disraeli's budget into shreds.

But this discipline, this ascesis, does not exclude the fullest and most grateful enjoyment of all the privileges of rank, of wealth, of education—leisure and travel, good books and good cheer. I said grateful: I might almost have said most reverent. Because all these things and the social order by which they are provided and maintained are part of a God-given heritage: a national treasure consecrated by the living and active presence of a national, and apostolic, Church. That so stated the conception was an anachronism was one of things which Mr Gladstone was to learn on his long, slow journey back from Oxford to Liverpool. But to the conception itself he was always true. In the spring of 1869, a few days after the division which sentenced the Irish Church to Disestablishment and proclaimed him to the world as a Liberal beyond recall, we find him writing to Matthew Arnold:

Of the narrowness which you ascribe to Non-Conformity I find the root in what I may call non-veneration of the past, or incapacity from whatever source to claim and appropriate our full share of our heritage.

Few words will be found to occur more often in his writings than these two, reverence and veneration. At the heart of his labyrinthine character he was a worshipping man: one of those who in his own words 'tread the floor of the earth with an upward and not a downward eye': fearful of judgement, in awe of the Nemesis that waits on excess of power, or the wantonness of prosperity: and, for such a one, to labour in, and for, the heritage, whether as a Minister of the Church or as a servant of the Crown, was itself a kind of worship. There were times when one sentence of Mr Gladstone's would have shaken the monarchy to its foundations. He never uttered it. He never dreamed of uttering it.

I have indeed sometimes thought that if, like Bright and Cobden and Disraeli, he had been born and reared wholly without, or like Herbert and Newcastle wholly within, the governing circle of his young days, he might have contemplated the social hierarchy which fenced and framed the heritage, with a less serious or more familiar regard. But he stood at the right distance to perceive its charm, to respond to its attraction, to respect its high—might one not say its Homeric?—qualities of dignity, purity, and courage; and at the same time to appropriate its habits, its standards, and its ruling idea of a State

holding by descent, by the intellectual superiority of its governing class, and the good will of the people, a position of underived and original authority,

by Divine Right, we might paraphrase, put into commission among Zeus-born kings.

But if Church and State are to be joined in a hypostatic union, two natures spiritual and material in one 'personal society' (and that, we may remember, is the doctrine of Hooker), it would seem to follow that the governors of that society, the nation, are bound to direct themselves by the truths which the Church is commissioned to impart, whether the governed are willing to receive them as truths or not. In other words, every government is a theocracy, and in 1839 a theocracy based on the £10 franchise and directed by Lord Melbourne, Lord Palmerston, and Lord John Russell, with Peel in reserve if ever the Radicals were obstreperous, and the Duke of Wellington to see that the Peers behaved, was a conception which plain men might pardonably decline to entertain. Mr Gladstone published his book: there was applause, polite but puzzled. But his voice sent back no echo. Ruefully he found himself alone.

But let us for theocratic substitute paternal, and so bring ourselves nearer to earth, to practical politics (which Mr Gladstone more than once defined as the politics of the next election) and the application of the Tory faith to circumstance. And here we can cite a document of high authority, a letter of 1845 in which Mr Gladstone writing to Newman seems to have caught a lucidity not his own.

According to the old European and Christian civilization, the State was a family, and the rulers had the position and duties of parents. According to the modern notion the State is a club, the Government is the organ of the influences predominating in the body. Where its spirit is hard, what has been called the tyranny of the majority rules with a high hand. Where its spirit is more gentle, as it can scarcely fail to be in every State founded on the ancient basis, other sentiments entertained by bodies of sensible magnitude besides those of the mere majority find their way into, and are represented in, the action of the State. With us the State is neither a family nor a club: but it is on its path of transition from the former to the latter. It is less like a club than America or than France: it is less like a family (I mean as to duties, not as to their fulfilment) than Austria or than Russia. The public men of the present day are—I must not conceal it from myself— engaged in regulating and qualifying, and some of them in retarding this transition. But the work proceeds: and as to that work regarded as a whole, and its results, I view them with great alarm. The ancient principle of reverence of truth, the supreme law of the State in its higher condition, is crossed and intercepted by the law of representation, and equality of claims according to number and will—the supreme law of the State in its lower condition when the hand of death is palsying it by however slow degrees.

I have read that passage at length, not only for the light it throws on the movement of Mr Gladstone's mind—and when he wrote it he had had some twelve years' experience of Parliament and some five of office—but for its accuracy as a diagnosis of our political state and as a forecast of our political development. In the course of the nineteenth century our theory, or one might say, our philosophy, of Representation was entirely transformed, and the history of the transformation is written in the words democracy and democratic, words which Canning—the unwavering opponent of parliamentary reform—did not shrink from using at the high point of Tory ascendancy, the year of Salamanca. But Canning, of course, was thinking within the framework of that famous doctrine which ascends, I suppose, to Polybius or even higher, the doctrine of a constitution mixed of monarchical, aristocratic, and democratic elements. Adjusted to the medieval practice of representation, the outcome of the doctrine will be Government by Estates, and a Parliament which is the gathering and debating place of Interests. Here, under the old constitution, through the open boroughs, the freemen, and the scot-and-lot men, the Labouring Interest had at least a token representation, which the Reform Act undoubtedly depressed. What was more, such representation as the Act did accord to the skilled artificer tended, over the course of a generation, to shrink. But any attempt to restore the balance, even to give the Labouring Interest a representation such as the improvement of the labouring classes probably warranted, was an inroad on the principle of the mixed constitution: an inroad only, not an occupation, until the democratic element could find, and find in abundance, representatives, and therefore candidates, of its own way of thinking—if indeed it had a way of thinking different from the other two.

I have often thought that there is no better way of bringing a decade or a generation into focus than to ask—what were they most afraid of and what did they do about it? Sometimes it is pestilence: and our Health Services have their deepest root in the fear of cholera. Sometimes it is Foreign Competition, and of that alarm our technical schools are the memorials. In the years through which we were then passing there can be little doubt of the answer. The Reform had indeed demonstrated that the people of England still preferred to have their political experiments timed and directed for them by noblemen and gentlemen enjoying the confidence of the respectable classes. But it had divulged the arcanum of party government that the franchise could be indefinitely extended. It had left almost unimpaired the influence and even the authority of the aristocracy, the gentry, the landed interest, great and small, the Universities, the Church. But how long they could withstand the new principle of a purely numerical representation, and whether in their fall they might not pull down Parliament and Crown together, these were questions to which even hopeful men in their darker hours could see only dark answers.

Because, those 'bodies of sensible magnitude' whose function it was to regulate, to qualify, and to retard the advance—let us call it by its new name, the advance of democracy—were involved in the prosperity of the Land. But if that prosperity rested on protection—if protection in its turn brought with it, perhaps dearness of bread, certainly limitation of markets and scarcity of employment, then it was not easy to deny the position—common to middle-class Free Traders and working-class Chartists—that the whole constitution in Church and State was grounded upon an injustice, that at the very heart of the heritage there was an evil which might some day demand a fierce evacuation. Many years later Mr Gladstone was receiving a deputation of trade unionists. In the course of conversation he remarked: 'You are not, I think, so much interested in Parliament Reform as you were when I was young.' 'No,' they replied, 'when we got Free Trade we gave up agitation. We have every confidence in Parliament and so we now spend our evenings in improving our minds.' In that homely acknowledgement you have the history not only of what happened but of what might have happened, of what Peel set himself to avert.

It was given out that on the 10th of April issue would be taken between the loyal inhabitants of London and the enemies of order. But when the day arrived it appeared that order had no enemies. The people were all on one side.

And Mr Gladstone, swinging an idle truncheon, patrolled the parish of St James from 3 to 4.15 p.m., while his grateful friends, the coalwhippers of Wapping, marched west to defend Whitehall.

Peel, who always seems to have handled his young colleague

like a headmaster dealing with a promising but difficult Fifth
Form boy, had been careful not to give him Cabinet office until
he had proved himself in the most laborious of all government
posts. He was hurt. I am not sure he ever quite forgave. He was
not a forgiving man. But the discipline—or the doubt it implied
—worked wonders. At the Board of Trade he learnt that whether
or no

in moral science government occupies the place of $\tau\grave{o}$ $\pi\hat{a}\nu$[4] in physical
science

—a dictum which Macaulay had pronounced to be elevated but
indistinct — government in Whitehall meant business. Mr
Gladstone at thirty and in Opposition is unquestionably an able
man, industrious and eloquent, but withal a little vague, perhaps
even, to borrow the wicked epithet which a later Prime Minister
once applied to a predecessor, a little flocculent. Of Mr Gladstone
at thirty-five, and in office, the Gladstone of the great Budgets, of
the Irish Church Bill and the Irish Land Bills, what strikes us,
what struck Parliament, what as much as anything was the secret
of his hold on Lancashire and the North, is that he is an extraordinarily competent man, as Pelham was and Chatham was not,
Pitt was and Fox was not, as Huskisson and Canning were, as
beyond all men Peel was himself: at times, one might say, too
competent, racing so far ahead that his followers could see neither
where he was going nor, always, where he was.

But this revelation of his powers as a governing man brought
him little satisfaction because it showed how different government
was from anything which the austere young innocence of the
worshipping man had pictured, and very slowly, very reluctantly,
did he abandon the fabric of his dreams:

> A bird still crouching in its nest,
> A sword that will not leave the sheath.

Few men have ever been so unwilling—he acknowledged it himself—to quit one field of ideas for another, and not many men
have had such a power of excluding from their minds all notions,

4 'the All' or 'the Universe'

all questionings, and even all facts, which might disturb an established system of opinion.

The range of Mr Gladstone's interests was legendary: and he was at all times only too ready to discharge his copiousness on matters which had better have been left to those who understood them. But his limitations are equally remarkable and historically more important. Out from the classic and well-charted waters of Free Trade, Free Contract, and Free Competition he never pushed an adventurous prow. He was a late, half-hearted convert to the ballot: to free education he was never wholly converted. With those two movements which were gathering force through all the second half of his life, Socialism and Imperialism, movements over which the far less stable genius of Disraeli shot rays of fantastic light, he was utterly out of sympathy. He never understood why Chamberlain should spend the money of the Birmingham ratepayers on 'fine schools' for the children of the poor: he never understood why England worshipped Gordon. Strangest of all is this. He must have known, in all likelihood he had heard, how Macaulay in 1833, speaking for the Whig party, had defied O'Connell to give one reason why there should be a Parliament in Dublin and not in Londonderry. He must have remembered, he had good reason to remember, the hammer-strokes with which John Bright had shattered the Liberal party in defence of the Loyal Protestants of Ulster against the rebels who had insulted the Queen. But in the volume of his collected writings on Ireland (a book of 370 pages) Ulster receives two passing mentions—one a quotation from Castlereagh. And this self-willed conservatism of the intelligence was reinforced by a singular insensitiveness to personal and party claims, even to personal and party obligations.

Thus when, in 1845, Delane, at Aberdeen's bidding, disclosed the secret of Peel's resolve to open the ports to foreign grain, it is not at all surprising that his first emotion was one of consternation. A fortnight later, when the failure of the Whigs to form a Government had reinstated Sir Robert in office, we find him writing in a letter which, very excusably, he afterwards forgot:

My principle by which (under God) I hope to decide is that I am not free to take away the Corn Law unless the facts of the Irish [situation] can on examination prove to be so great and special as to put the question altogether beyond ordinary rules.

Two days later, 'with a clear conscience but a heavy heart', he made his decision, the great decision of his life, because the rock on which his Liberalism was founded was his unshakeable belief in Free Trade and in his own capacity as the financier of Free Trade, proved against Disraeli in 1852, triumphantly established in his own first Budget of 1853, and matured from 1859 to 1865 under the shadow, the somewhat chilly and unfriendly shadow, cast by the European splendour of Palmerston. Yet it is plain that something had held him back—a secret distrust, an unconfessed distaste. The auguries were not good. Once more Peel was changing sides: once more the Tory party was breaking in his hands. And he had seen Peel frozen into helplessness by the icy blast of Disraeli's invective, he had seen Peel whiten at the cry from his own back benches, 'Who killed Mr Canning?': Mr Canning, who had taken notice of him when he really was a Fifth Form boy: whose memory he cherished with a devotion he showed to no other man: whose true successor on the European stage he felt himself, not Palmerston, to be. Yet if something held him back, a force still stronger drove him forward. Mr Gladstone's mind, 'fastidious and censorious', was more easily moved by repulsion than attraction: like that other pilgrim, called Mr Talkative, he was very apt to persuade himself that in crying out against sin, of policy, he was moved by a godly antipathy; and I cannot help asking myself whether with his prayers that December there did not mingle the petition that Disraeli might be withdrawn to a more appropriate sphere of usefulness, and the reins of a United Tory party placed in more Catholic hands. But the seat was filled. And if he left Peel, where was he to go?

From the accession of Pitt in 1784 there has never, I suppose, been a time when the course of politics is so wayward and bewildering as in the years which run from the fall of Peel in 1846 to the appointment of Aberdeen in 1852, years when, as Mr Gladstone said in one of happiest images, the Peelites drifted in the political sea like an iceberg on which no man can safely land but which can easily sink a ship. And on this crowded, exciting

scene there is no one whose movements seem more wayward and
bewildering or more distrustfully watched than this extraordinary
man, who cannot rid his mind of the conviction that the only true
work of government is 'moral and paternal' and yet who shows
hardly the faintest interest in the new social legislation which is
pressing into the Statute Book; a man who, in the England of
Factory Acts and Housing Acts and Baths and Washhouse Acts
and Smoke Abatement Acts, seems to bear a closer affinity with
Clarendon than with any later statesman; a man whose conscience
is burdened with the fear that if he remains in Parliament (where
everybody knows he will remain) it will be as the helpless witness,
if in office (and everybody knows he can be Prime Minister when
he likes) as the helpless agent, of a tragic transformation—the
replacement of the religious, the Catholic conception of government by one which is at once 'mechanical and infidel'.

But, as he once wrote, 'logical continuity and moral causation
are stronger than the conscious thought of man: they mock it,
and play with it, and constrain it even without its knowledge to
suit their purposes'. More plainly stated, there was no reason why
he should not be Chancellor of the Exchequer in Lord Aberdeen's
government and every reason why he should; there to defend and
consolidate the work of Sir Robert, the magnificent simplicity of
which had really come to occupy in his mind 'the place of $\tau\grave{o}$ $\pi\hat{a}\nu$
in physical science'. Peel's finance, and Gladstone's, was grounded
on a conviction that with an expanding market it would be
possible to raise the real wages of labour, and therefore its capacity
for self-improvement, without reducing the revenues of the landed
interest, and therefore its capacity for government. Establish that
by a strict frugality, which means peace, and by a due balance of
direct and indirect taxation, and the social structure will return
to equilibrium, vibrating in harmony with the social tradition. So
the heritage is saved.

Plainly this Chancellor of the Exchequer is a very different man
from the writer of that despairing letter to Newman eight years
earlier. The truth is that he, like everybody else, is living in a
different age. Of Oxford, Mark Pattison said that a man who had
gone to sleep in 1846 and woken up in 1850 would have found

himself in another world: and the difference, I have often thought, between the England of the last Chartist demonstration in 1848 and the Great Exhibition of 1851, is like the difference in one's own feelings at the beginning and end of a voyage in wartime through waters beset by enemy ships, or like the opening of the city gates after a long wintry siege: *hiems transiit, imber recessit*.[5] Delivered from the noise of archers in the places of drawing water, then shall the people of the Lord go down to the gates, and those gates stood open to the world and all its traffic. It was in that Maytime of youth recaptured that Gladstonian Liberalism was conceived. It was the only atmosphere in which it could have been conceived, an atmosphere composed in equal measure of progress, confidence, and social union: from which the image of the Beleaguered City had faded—out of sight, and almost out of memory. And the man has changed too. By shaking off his antique doctrine of Church and State, and the Church as the conscience of the State, he has released his energy, full-powered and whole-hearted, for his real business of secular statesmanship. Neither now nor at any time would he have subscribed to the Eleventh Point of Oxford Liberalism as professed at Oriel and set forth by Newman: 'There is no such thing as a National Conscience.' But he has begun to listen for it elsewhere than in the official utterances of the Anglican body; in public opinion, in the uncorrupted judgement of the people, in 'that sentiment of nationality which almost assumes in, and for, a nation, the office which conscience discharges for the individual, as the tribune of ultimate appeal'. And he has remembered, too, that 'the Reformation had thrown on every individual Christian the responsibility of being his own spiritual director'. In these avowals we hear shaping themselves the terms of that alliance between the great High Churchman and Nonconformity which though sorely strained at times was never quite dissolved.

Finally, he has been to Naples. At some time or other, I suppose, it has happened to all of us—or will happen—to find some carefully cherished scheme of thought or feeling suddenly collapsing on a practical application. The highest functions of government,

5 'The winter is past, the rain has gone.'   Song of Solomon 2, 11

we have just heard, are moral and paternal, and at Naples he
had seen in what paternalism might issue: he had observed 'the
religious and Catholic conception of government' in operation,
and he had pronounced it to be the negation of God. I do not
doubt that other incidents befalling at the same time, the shock
of the Gorham Judgement and its sequel, the sad parting from
Hope-Scott, the bitter separation—behind which lies a mystery
still—from Manning, impelled him in the same direction, kind-
ling what was to be the fiercest passion of his later years, hatred of
Ultramontanism. But what he had seen—his friends observed it
on his return—took possession of his whole mind and imagination and left it, we may say, a different imagination and a different
mind, charged with a horror of all coercive powers, great or small
—Empires, Papacies, Parliaments, Sultans, Colonial Offices,
Trade Unions—which do not rest their authority on consent,
habitual or expressed: and *habitual* saves the phenomenon of
deference to a native aristocracy so long as it submits to govern,
that is, to apply its superior knowledge, in accordance with the
finer and less corrupted judgements of public opinion. And with
that the evolution of his own opinion is complete. His political
mind is fully formed and closed. The rest is application only:
application and extension, because in the foreign field his objective
is the same—the bringing of separate national interests to
acknowledge the sovereignty of a European opinion. The pilgrimage is over: and Faithful, you will remember, though his end was
glorious, never in this life got farther than Vanity Fair: never
trod the Delectable Mountains whence Ruskin and Kingsley and
William Morris had their sight of the City of God. Perhaps it was
just as well. He might have found Disraeli there.

But of men, as of revolutions, the old saying is true, that you
cannot get more out of them than you put into them, and this
Liberalism is wholly misconceived if it is thought of as a mitigated
Radicalism or a modernized Whiggery. Indeed with another
backward glance at Canning, we might almost call it a Tory
heresy. Because, starting from that common doctrine of the ideal
polity mixed of monarchical, aristocratic, and democratic elements,
it was Canning who had brought in as a fourth element

that public opinion which, embodied in a free press, pervades, checks, and in the last resort nearly governs the whole,

a theme, you will remember, which at Liverpool he had illustrated in one of the most splendid, most Asiatic, images, drawn from that other invention which had given

to the fickleness of winds and the faithlessness of waves the security and tranquillity of a highway on the land.

There are times when Mr Gladstone seems to be treading on the verge at least of Rousseau's doctrine: *la volonté générale est toujours droite*. With reservations of his own I think he would have accepted it. Again and again he recites his catena of instances to show that public opinion—or the people—were right when the governing classes, or the educated classes, or the Conservatives, or the West End—they appear under all these names according to the exigencies of the platform—were wrong. They were right with Huskisson in 1825, with the Whigs in 1830, with Peel in 1846, with Mr Gladstone himself in 1868, and when they were wrong, as they were over the Ecclesiastical Titles Bill, the whole governing class went wrong with them. But the reservations are part of the creed. The general will is true, public opinion is right, if it is informed, elicited, and directed by men trained from youth in the business of government by the 'invisible education' of home, of school, of the Universities, and by the open conflicts of the House. You might, he once said, as soon start training for the ballet at forty-five as start training for the Cabinet.

It is strange at times—Matthew Arnold seems to have found it diverting—to note with what rich fervour Mr Gladstone, 'an out and out inequalitarian' as he once avowed himself to be, reiterates his belief in aristocracy, in 'that great safeguard, the love of inequality which has made safe the changes past and will make safe the changes yet to come', 'the religion of inequality', the 'shadow which the love of freedom casts or the reverberation of its voice in the halls of the Constitution'. The chain of proof and instance might be lengthened indefinitely. One can think, for example, of many reasons why close scholarships should be abolished at the Universities, and patronage in Whitehall. It is characteristic of Mr Gladstone that his own reasons are the least popular, the least democratic, that could well be conceived. One measure he thought would strengthen the ascendancy of Eton and Harrow here and at Cambridge. The other would attract the aristocracy into the Civil Service, just as Home Rule would restore the Irish nobility to their proper place as leaders of the Irish people. In his controversy with Lowe over the extension of the County Franchise, which of course he supported, he neverthe-less admits the fear that enlarged constituencies, uninfluenced by family connexions, would tend to elect old men who had made their fortune rather than young men who had their way to make, thus enfeebling government into a Gerontocracy and degrading it into a Plutocracy. Has time shown that he was altogether wrong? And his final judgement is pronounced in a paper which he republished in the year when he became Prime Minister for the last time.

The natural condition of a healthy society is that governing functions should be discharged in the main by a leisured class. In matters where the narrow interests of that class seem to be concerned, it has its beset-ting sins and dangers. But for the general business of government it has peculiar capacities; and whatever control a good system may impose, by popular suffrage, by gathering representation from all classes, by tradition, or opinion, or the press, yet, when the leisured class is depressed, that fact indicates that a rot has found its way into the structure of society.

Let us leave these matters to settle themselves, some day, and ask, rather more exactly, what are the relations between the statesman, however he may be selected, and that public opinion which it is his business to inform, to elicit, and to direct. There is no theme on which Mr Gladestone is more copious, or instructive, or on which he has a better right to be heard. In the office of Prime Minister he was not altogether successful (Dilke said that, of the two, Asquith was the greater Parliamentarian). His Cabinets had a persistent trick of coming to pieces: and he was far from success-ful as a Party Leader. 'It is in the nature of Liberalism', he once mused, 'to be subject to diversities' (in 1874 there were twenty-five constituencies where Liberals stood against each other and gave the seat to the Conservatives), diversities which he was at once too vehement, too subtle, and too remote to reconcile. Of one of his successors it was said that he knew what you were thinking before you had begun to think it. But of those roving explorations of other men's minds; the undirected exchange of hypothesis, suggestion, and proposition; the advances and withdrawals out of which a common opinion is educed, Mr Gladstone was by temperament incapable.

Until I am prepared with a plan and see public opinion reaching such a point that I can make myself responsible for the proposal and support of that plan, I decline to raise false expectation by committing myself to an abstract resolution. . . It is impossible to say what law ought or ought not to be passed at any given time in a country like this. . . Subjects ripe for action supply a Minister with abundant materials for communication with his colleagues, and to make a rule of mixing with them matters still contingent and remote, would confuse and retard business instead of aiding it.

And this is always his defence against the twin charges of reticence and precipitancy brought against him by colleagues who found that, till his mind was made up, he could not be moved, when it was made up he could not be restrained, but who were never admitted within those mountainous ramparts where the old man sat immured, self-absorbed and self-absorbing, self-convincing and self-convinced, but always listening for the gathering of the waters and the rising of the tide.

Ripeness is all. It is not the bell that takes me to church, he once said: my duty takes me: the bell only warns me that the time has come. In Mr Gladstone's political philosophy the doctrine of Right Timing takes the place of Burke's doctrine of the Higher Expediency. Indeed, they are the same, transposed from the senatorial to the representative mode of government. It was not the murder of two policemen in Manchester that disestablished the Irish Church, but the sudden attraction of attention to an Ireland which since the famine had almost been forgotten and which, while Mr Gladstone lived, was not to be forgotten again. It was not obstruction, or the Land League, or the murder of Lord Frederick Cavendish, that begot Home Rule, but the proof they furnished that Parliament could not govern Ireland. Ripeness is all:

but all men do not perceive, all men do not appreciate, ripeness, with the same degree of readiness or aptitude, and the slow must ever suffer inconvenience in the race of life.

True, but it was the slow man Hartington who won the last race of all.

That young Tory of whom I told you, who in September 1893 could not wait for the paper, but went out to meet it, to learn by what majority the Lords had thrown out the Home Rule Bill and saved the State, found, as he grew older, that he never cared to think much of the last years of Mr Gladstone's public life, of that heroic squandering of heroic endowments on a problem which (we may now say) the intellectual equipment of the age was not capable of solving—in a world which was passing beyond his comprehension, the world of Empire, of Science, of wealth without tradition, of armed power acknowledging no restraint. An old friend of mine, then a young bride, was with him at the opening of the Kiel Canal. She used to tell us of the wrath that darkened the old man's face when he saw the assembled fleets, and she heard him muttering: 'They told me it was a purely commercial enterprise. And the armaments of the world are gathered together.' A world where strange and terrifying forces were stirring in the depths, and fears forgotten for a generation were raising their heads once more. I remember being taken to see the Thames crowded reach after reach with shipping that could not be unloaded, while the gaslight in the streets and houses sank to a tiny blue flame. A Beleaguered City: where, by the strangest of all strange reversals, it was not to Gladstone, but to Manning, that men turned.

I would rather think of Midlothian. Political oratory is the most evanescent of all arts, and Mr Gladstone's eloquence is gone with Chatham's, and the old Greek music:

οἷον μὲν γὰρ κλέος οἷον ἀκούομεν, οὐδέ τι ἴομεν.[6]

They used to tell us, 'You cannot understand Mr Gladstone

6 'Of that we hear only a rumour: we have no direct knowledge.'
Homer: *Iliad* ii

unless you have heard him in the House', and someone else would say, 'No, you must have heard him on a public platform'. We are told that people came from all parts of Greece to hear Demosthenes replying to Aeschines. They came almost as far, they came from the Outer Hebrides, to hear Mr Gladstone.

The Bulgarian horrors rekindled the flame which had consumed him when he wrote of what he had seen at Naples. But his pamphlet had lighted no answering fire. In London, the excitement had soon died down: in Parliament, friends grew restless, alarmed, and angry: it was not the sufferings of Bulgaria and the hideous iniquities of the Turk of which the people were thinking, but of Russia stretching out to Constantinople, aflank of our own highway to the East: of fleets and armies in motion: of England an Empire among the Powers, and the Queen an Empress among Emperors. Here and there, some sober men might have begun to count the cost, in money—and bad trade was following on bad harvests, and neither in India nor in South Africa was there peace; the cost in honour and moral weight when we came to reckon our acquisitions and how they had been made, against our obligations and how they were to be met. But resounding majorities made Disraeli's Government impregnable in Parliament, and if they were to be assailed it must be in another and a larger field; if they were to be brought to judgement it must be before the tribunal of public opinion. Parliament had some time to run and the danger was that the misdoings of the Government would be forgotten, so short is the memory of the crowd, before the Liberals had time to rally, so inveterate were the diversities in that unhappy flock. But, ripeness is all, and there was just enough weariness, just enough distrust, just enough anxiety about the future, and the Income Tax, to furnish fuel for a conflagration, if the torch was set to at the right moment.

But what is memorable in that amazing feat of eloquence and bodily endurance is its revelation of what might otherwise have remained concealed from us, the grand, intense simplicity of Mr Gladstone's mind. Strike out certain local or topical issues, such things as every political speaker has to treat with becoming seriousness and disproportionate respect; and the themes will be found to reduce themselves to two or three. But each of them is developed with such abundance of detail, drawn from such rich stores of knowledge and experience set out with such limpid clarity, that taken together the Midlothian speeches make a hand-book of political instruction, of constitutional, of Parliamentary, of diplomatic, of financial lore: and if to inform opinion be the statesman's first duty, no other man has ever equalled or approached him in its discharge. And the lucidity is not the artificial lucidity of a man constraining himself to make things clear. They *are* clear. The intensity of his own feelings seems to have consumed that overgrowth of alembication and refinement which so often encumbers his Parliamentary speeches: and to have fused into a single and sustained utterance the abstract and concrete, the ideal and the practical, without any effort, or necessity, of dialectic or enforced conjunction. Whether he is speaking of the treaty-making powers of the Crown, of the proper duration of Parliament, or the nature of a realized surplus; of the strategic insignificance of Cyprus, or the relations between the Indian Government and the ruler of Afghanistan; or setting forth the elements of foreign policy, peace, and good faith and the Concert of Europe abroad, just laws at home to maintain the unity, and foster, for worthy occasions, the might of the Empire, every sentence is stamped with the unmistakable precision of a master's hand, and every word has the ring of an entire sincerity.

He was a great man: let us take our leave of him at his greatest hour.

THE LIBERAL MIND IN VICTORIAN ENGLAND[1]

BEFORE we think for a while about the liberal mind in Victorian England, may I remind you of something which we are all apt to forget—I mean that the Victorian age, as we call it, is the insular phase of a movement common to the whole of

1 A broadcast delivered on 5 May 1948, and reprinted the same year in *Ideas and Beliefs of the Victorians*. (Sylvan Press.)

western Europe and its offshoots beyond the seas. When we lift our eyes from our own country, our own ancestors, and look across the Channel, or across the Atlantic, constantly we find that ways and habits, fashions and prejudices, doctrines, ideas, and even phrases which we think of as typically Victorian, are really part of a general European pattern. Let me give you one instance. You know how hotly our Victorian moralists and satirists inveigh against the shortcomings of women's education, the silliness and shallowness of the boarding school, the time wasted on trivial accomplishments. Which of them wrote this passage?

She had been brought up in one of the most exclusive establishments, where three objects are regarded as of the highest importance. First comes French, then the piano, that she shall be able to amuse and soothe her husband, and lastly a thorough acquaintance with the principles of household economy in its highest and most aesthetic sense, including the art of knitting purses.

Is it Thackeray, or Dickens, or George Eliot? It is none of them: it is not English. It comes from Gogol's *Dead Souls*, I suppose the most intensely Russian book ever written. But written in an age when thoughtful men and women were deeply concerned with this question of women's education, and so you find Gogol at the far end of Europe writing a sentence which you would not be surprised to meet in any English book of the time, while if you searched I have no doubt you would encounter the same ideas, in much the same language, in Swedish books and Portuguese books. It is part of what I have called the European pattern: just as Gothic architecture was part of the pattern before the Renaissance, and classical architecture after the Renaissance. But as we travel about Europe we soon learn to distinguish French Gothic from English Gothic, or Spanish baroque from German baroque. They are the same, but with a difference, and you might perhaps say that the difference is more interesting than the identity, and the identity is more significant than the difference. That I think is the right way to look at any of these great European patterns, and I shall try to show what I believe to be the fundamental unity of liberal thought in the Victorian age, and to set off against it the English variations from the common type, and the English contributions to the common stock.

Take that word 'liberal'. In England, before the French Revolution, it meant magnanimous, open-handed, open-hearted, and—just note the change which is setting in—open-minded, free from prejudice, ready to judge things on their merits. What things? Everything! The State and its institutions, the Church and its doctrines. You see there is something rather explosive in that word 'liberal', because if the State is oppressive or the Church corrupt, if the laws of the State are unreasonable or the teaching of the Church incredible, then your liberal man will tend to be a revolutionary and a free thinker. So you may understand why Sir Robert Peel called 'liberal' an odious word, and why some people in speaking of Liberals were careful to call them by their French name, *les libéraux*, or their Spanish name, *los liberales*, just to show that Liberalism was one of those hateful foreign doctrines, immoral and irreligious, which had brought about one Revolution in France, and might bring about another, perhaps in England.

The liberals were in fact the disappointed heirs of the Revolution, and when after Waterloo the dynasts returned to their thrones, the liberals in Spain and Italy and in France were the opposition, the resistance, ready to overthrow the restored order of things whenever occasion offered, and if necessary by force. In this sense Byron and Shelley were liberals—in Italy. But in England the word lost its subversive sense, partly because we had a much more expressive word of our own, 'radical', and partly because with our long political experience and education, our reformers knew very much better than the foreign *liberales* what they wanted and how to get it. So in England, the wide-sweeping liberalism of Europe was canalized, so to speak, towards one object, the reform of the House of Commons and an extended franchise. And when that was achieved, and the decision loyally accepted by the Tory opposition, liberalism in England became respectable. If a man called himself a Liberal in 1837, no one imagined that he wanted to dethrone the Queen or plunder the bishops. He was certainly a loyal subject and very likely a devout churchman—as Mr Gladstone was, and Mr Gladstone, destined as we know to become the greatest liberal of all time, never for a moment abated his reverence for monarchy, aristocracy, and the Church.

You see how difficult it is to pin the liberal mind within the four corners of a definition. But I think we can get a little nearer if we consider this. Before the French Revolution, even intelligent men seem to have taken if for granted that the world would always be very much what it was. It would improve, no doubt: civilization would spread to the Pacific Islands, superstition would make way for reason, science would be cultivated in Siberia and the Far West of America, and the nations, if they were wise, would live in harmony under free constitutions like that which had made England so great and so happy. That was about as far as the most far-sighted man could look. Then came the French Revolution, which showed that institutions which had lasted for generations might be destroyed in a few months, and that Europe, so far from being stable, could, if revolutionary principles prevailed, be turned upside-down. The nations might, indeed, defend themselves against the French armies. But could they defend themselves against French ideas?

But that is only one half of the story, because even if there had been no French Revolution, a great change in men's ways of thinking would have come about, simply from the development of science, or, as they called it, natural philosophy. And to that there was no end in sight. If a train could run 30 miles in an hour, why not 300? If a Lancashire mill could turn out 10,000 yards a day, why not 100,000? If science could master smallpox, why not all other diseases? And so in place of the old notion of society as something static and gently improving itself, you get the new notion of society as something dynamic and constantly transforming itself, by processes to which no limit could be assigned.

Bring these two ideas together, the French idea of Liberty, Fraternity, and Equality, and the English idea of progress by means of science. What shape will the compound take? Something like this, I think: 'Frame your institutions so as to give the utmost scope to these new pioneers and this new power. Throw down everything that may obstruct the progress of industry and the march of mind. And that means, bring your laws and your administration by means of free discussion into accordance with the findings of public opinion. Then there will be no subversion, no revolution, because the people will be on the side of the law; the Government will govern with their consent: and the process of improvement will be working everywhere and all the time, because political freedom and material progress are two sides of the same medal.' That, one may say, is standard mid-Victorian liberalism. But here we must remember that in England public opinion and discussion were bound by conventions—moral, social, and religious—stricter, I should reckon, than in any European country enjoying the same amount of political freedom. The liberal, we remember, is the man who claims the right to judge everything on its merits, without prejudice or dogma, and English society was, we may say, dogmatic all through. A man did take a risk if he discussed too freely certain religious questions or certain social questions, if he criticized our divorce laws or asked whether God really commanded the Israelites to put the people of Canaan to the sword. Mill's *Essay on Liberty* is really a plea for freer discussion of serious matters, and no wonder thoughtful men looked wistfully to the Continent—to the universities of France and Germany and Holland where you could believe what you liked and the only question was 'What reason have you for believing it?' And the breaking down of these conventions in England was one of the greatest services, and most lasting, of the liberal mind.

But whether here or abroad the central conception of liberalism is political, it means government in accordance with opinion elicited by discussion, and so it was possible to divide the nations of the world quite simply into the liberal, who were our natural friends, and the despotic, who were our natural enemies. 'There are two parties in Europe,' Palmerston once said, 'one party considers nations to be the property of their governors, the other holds that governments are established for the good of the many, and that is the principle on which our government was founded in 1688.' And the good of the many, means that they think good for themselves, not what someone else, however wise and benevolent, thinks good for them. Hence comes the liberal watchword, 'Self-government is better than good government'. But notice once more how the concept has to be adapted to fit our island circumstances, and our long tradition of government by a parliamentary aristocracy which the Continent did not possess. What, for example, is the essence of Gladstonian liberalism? I should say, a detestation of all authority, from empires to trade unions, not omitting parliaments, which does not rest on the consent of the governed, habitual or expressed, and note that word 'habitual' because it is the dividing line between the Liberal and the Radical, between, say, Gladstone and Bright. The Liberal makes allowance for the fact that the people still respect, admire, and trust the old governing class, so long as it acknowledges the power and final judgement of public opinion. And so in the mid-Victorian years, we settled down into an easy genial compromise between progress and tradition—years when a candidate, being asked about his political opinions might reply, and very often did reply, 'Sir, I am a liberal Conservative', which meant 'our old institutions have served us well, and I see no reason to change them. But I have an open mind and if there are any improvements which public opinion demands then I am ready to consider them.'

What are the improvements which public opinion demands, and the liberal will support? I think you can bring them under one head and say, the removal of any unfair advantage, social, political, national, or racial. To introduce competitive examination for the Civil Service; to disestablish the Irish Church; to abolish the purchase of commissions in the Army; to admit dissenters to the Universities and Jews to Parliament; to give self-government to the South African States after the Peace of 1902—these are all typically liberal measures. But when you come to economic inequality, to the advantage which the rich man has over the poor man, then you feel that liberalism, political liberalism, is coming to the end of its programme: it is passing the torch on to a new competitor in the race for power. Socialism in late-Victorian England has not begun to make itself felt. But it has begun to make itself heard. And what it is saying is that neither party, Liberal nor Conservative, has any answer to the great problem of modern life—poverty in the midst of plenty. You tell us, these new-comers say, that our old institutions have served us well. We reply that they are serving us very ill today. You tell us that you are prepared to improve them. We reply that your Education Acts, your Trade Union Acts, your County Council Acts, none of them goes to the root of things. We do not want improvements. We want change.

And now you see the tide turning. Throughout the Victorian age, our political ideas were ascendant: it was to England that all political reformers looked, while from foreigners we had nothing to learn. But when we come to social and economic ideas, the influence is the other way. It is we who look abroad, to America, to Germany, to France. And as European liberalism evolves towards socialism, so does ours. But always with that difference, which we have noticed so often, when European ideas have to be fitted into the island framework.

But will the framework hold them, or will the explosive elements in the new doctrines shatter it to pieces? Are socialism and parliamentary methods really compatible? Are you in your heart convinced that self-government *is* better than good government? Can you make the welfare of the people your aim without sacrificing their liberty? Can you bring progress under control and not take the heart out of the pioneer, so damping initiative and responsibility together? It is in questions like this that you hear late-Victorian liberalism—the liberalism of men who had grown up under the influence of Mill and Morley—taking its stand, measuring itself against the new ideas: questions which they have left us to answer.

THE HAPPY FAMILY[1]

SUPPOSE you fell asleep tonight and woke up in 1860. What is the first thing you would notice? It depends, of course, where you woke up. But if it was in a town there can be little doubt as to the answer. The noise—the noise of the traffic, of

---

[1] A broadcast delivered on 20 May 1946

wheels on granite setts. There is a patch of road near King's Cross which gives you some idea of what a Victorian street sounded like. But only half an idea, because in 1860 all the wheels had iron tyres. And when you had got used to this noise, the next thing you would observe would be the murkiness of the atmosphere everywhere, and, as you went on your way, every now and then a sudden puff of tainted air. Compared with the London of 1860, London today is sweet, clean, and quiet. Hoarse voices, shouting to make themselves heard; smudgy faces; eyes bleared with fog; bare-footed ragamuffins dashing in and out under the horses' heads; and a traffic jam at every corner; that is what you would encounter. That is what Tennyson had in mind when he spoke of 'streaming London's central roar'. And if you woke up in one of the great industrial regions, on Tyneside or in the Black Country, you would find things so much worse, so much dirtier, fouler, and noisier, that you might ask to be put to sleep again and carried back to 1946.

But suppose you decide to face it, and see for yourself what England in 1860 is really like, how people live and what they think about it all. We shall need a guide, a typical average man. But where are you to find him in a country which shows such endless variety of life and such violent contrasts of condition? The extremes of wealth and poverty, civilization and savagery, jostling each other—literally jostling each other—in the streets. However, a guide we must have, and we will take a printer, a skilled man in good employ—fifty-eight hours a week and a half-holiday on Saturday. He lives at Kennington or Islington. He travels to his work by a horse-drawn bus, wearing a morning coat and a tall hat. He takes his midday meal at a chop house—a plate of veal and ham and a pint of good beer, one shilling. When he married, and he was careful not to marry too young, he was getting forty-eight shillings a week, and they rented a six-roomed house for about thirty pounds a year. In those days they took a lodger to help with the rent. Now at three pounds a week, they have the whole house to themselves and their three children. Meat is sixpence a pound; they can dress themselves in good cloth and sound leather, the father for nine or ten pounds a year, the mother for six or seven pounds, and the children perhaps for two pounds each. He and his wife are really very comfortable. The father has a vote, and on election day he will march up to the polling place and give his vote in ringing tones, whereat half the crowd will cheer and the other half throw cabbage stalks at him. The children, you may be sure, go regularly to school; on Saturday afternoon the family take a steamer to Greenwich or Gravesend; on Sunday morning they all go to church or chapel while the joint is cooking at the baker's shop, and in the afternoon they walk in the Park, and have their friends to tea. After which they will practice hymns on the harmonium. On a whole holiday, they may give themselves a day at Brighton, three and sixpence there and back. Their annual fortnight will be spent at Margate, if they want to be jolly; Herne Bay or Littlehampton if they prefer to be quiet. You can pick them out for yourself in Frith's famous picture of Ramsgate sands.

So, you see, when statesmen stand up on the platform and talk of our unrivalled prosperity, when *The Times* writes of a state of contentment such as no other country in the world has ever known, this is what was in their mind: cheap food and regular work, the skilled man well fed and well housed; the farmer in the country; the village craftsman, the blacksmith or wheelwright: the grocer or the innkeeper in the country town. In fact, one writer was so bold as to prophesy that soon we should all be so well fed and well employed, and well housed, that we should have to import Negroes and Chinese to do the dirty work. And do not forget, if a young man found himself cramped at home, there was always Australia, New Zealand, or Canada, calling for settlers and pioneers.

Our printer has a vote and always reads the debates in Parliament over his veal and ham. But politics do not trouble him very much; do not trouble anybody very much in 1860. On the main principles of policy Whigs and Tories agree with one another, and the printer agrees with both—Free Trade and peace, but a strong Navy in case the French get above themselves, as they are apt to do, but strict economy and low taxation: above all, leave the people alone. They know what is good for them and how to get it, by working hard and saving up. And where in the world will you find such workers, where will you find so many workers who own their houses and have money in the Savings Bank? Where are people so vigorous in mind and body? And as you went about with our printer and talked to his friends—the three-pounds-a-week families in a house of their own—what you would notice, the general tone of their conversation, would be pride, pride in one another, in the doings of Lancashire and Clydeside and the West Riding: the bridges built all over the world by our engineers, the railways laid and the mountains pierced by our labourers. And we had done it all ourselves, the printer will tell you, without any help from government.

We were, in fact, very well pleased with ourselves. And with good reason. There had been times, in the thirty years after Waterloo, when it looked as if we might collapse, times when sober-minded people thought that insurrection and even civil war were not far off. But all that was ancient history now. And the people who had profited most by the change were, I should say, the three-pound-a-week families. If you want a name for them, they are the respectable classes, and that word 'respectable' covers a great many virtues and one or two shortcomings. A Frenchman visiting our shores would probably think the printer's life unutterably dreary compared with life in a French town with its cafés and music and well-behaved crowds of working people strolling up and down. But in England people like the printer keep themselves to themselves: they know little of the world outside: they have not much sympathy with the class below, or with the swarming, drinking, fighting multitude, who never go to church or chapel and do not send their children to school.

They are rather self-righteous: they are severe in their judgement on other people, especially those who have fallen behind in the race of life: like Tennyson's farmer, they are inclined to think 'the poor in a loomp is bad', and perhaps a little too much disposed to rate people by their success in making a good income. But being proud of themselves and conscious of their superiority to the mob, they are not jealous of those above them in rank and fortune. They enjoy the scenes of splendour when the Queen, for instance, goes to open Parliament and the streets are crowded with state carriages and powdered coachmen. They have a great regard for the Royal Family, which, after all, does its work and takes its holidays and brings up its children very much as they do themselves. The differences of wealth do not trouble them greatly. It is part of the magnificence of England that there should be families with £20,000, £50,000, £100,000 a year. When the printer and his family take a holiday, as likely as not they will visit Blenheim or Longleat or one of the great houses, they will be shown round the picture galleries, glass-houses, stables; and come away feeling what a great country England is, and what a fine thing it is to have a real aristocracy, and not be governed by greedy officials or politicians on the make.

We keep coming round to that sense of pride, and it is not only pride in our material achievements, our domestic comfort, and the industry which sustains them. Very likely our printer is a reading man: before he married he went to the Polytechnic and belonged to a Young Men's Mutual Improvement Society. He keeps up the habit of going to lectures, and the whole family will take part in a Penny Reading got up by the vicar in aid of the new ragged school for the children of the really poor. There Alice will recite Mr Tennyson's 'May Queen', William will declaim Lord Macaulay's 'Relief of Londonderry', and the doctor will say something about Mr Faraday's discoveries in electricity, or the new book everybody is talking about, Mr Darwin's *Origin of Species,* followed by a few straight words on cleanliness and fresh air and the importance of good cooking. And we go home once more feeling that, whether it is science or poetry or history, our people lead the world. To be so small on the map, and yet count for so much among the nations—it really was rather wonderful. And, once more, we had done it all ourselves. We had a right to be proud. England was the greatest country in the world—no one doubted that: the richest, the most powerful, the most enlightened. But we were still on the upgrade, and every year we were getting richer and more powerful, more enlightened and more humane.

More enlightened and more humane?—I wonder. I know there has been a great burst of social legislation, the Factory Act and the Health Act and the famous Education Minute of 1846; and the Metropolitan Board of Works has splendid plans for a Thames Embankment, and broad streets sweeping away the pestilential old rookeries. But still, one fine morning your business might take you into the City, and you would find the streets blocked by an enormous crowd, some fighting, more of them already drunk. They have come to see a man hanged in front of Newgate Prison, almost under the shadow of St Paul's. Try Westminster: within sight of the Houses of Parliament, there are streets where no decent person, except a doctor perhaps, or a Sister of Mercy, would venture. Even if no one threw a dead cat at you, or tried to tear the clothes off your back, the sights and the sounds and above all the smells would be enough to send you hurrying back. Try Deptford on a Saturday night. Under the glare of a gin palace a ring has formed to watch two women, stripped to the waist, fighting with broken bottles. Or take two villages within a mile or two of each other. One is a delight to the traveller, all spick and span and friendly. In another all is gaping walls and torn thatch, and if the people trouble to notice you at all, it is probably to call out a few bad words and send a rotten turnip after you.

Contrast everywhere, you see. Suppose, for instance, having seen the great house and its treasures, they charter a fly at the station and take a drive through the villages. All about them they will see fields and cattle which are the admiration of the world. Never had there been such harvests, such sheep, or such cows. The most jealous foreigner had to own that English agriculture was the first in the world, and still improving. There was not much machinery yet: labour was abundant and cheap, and on the road you might encounter a strange sight, a gang of Irishmen in rags and tatters, each with his sickle wrapped up in straw, who came over for the harvest and kept wages down. The wages *were* low. In Dorset, for example, thousands of families were living on a wage of eight or ten shillings a week, or even less. Of course, they had their garden and their harvest money, their cottage rent was only one shilling or one and sixpence a week: there was always help from the manor house when a baby was coming, and beef and blankets at Christmas time. And if the landowner lived on his estate and took a pride in it, the cottages were well built and comfortable, there was good water, and a school close at hand. The people may be poor, they are poor: but they are certainly respectable. If the landowner was an absentee, or a gambler, or if he was in debt, then the village was a dreary sight. No wonder the younger people are drifting away, some to the towns, the more venturesome to the Colonies. And if they go to the towns, what awaits them there? How long will they remain respectable? It really depends on three things—what work they get, what company they fall into, what lodgings they find. This is where the friendly society and the trade union are so useful, passing a man from lodge to lodge and helping him to find his feet. But if he does not find his feet, it is only too easy for him to go under altogether.

The great dividing line in 1860 is not rich and poor, but the respectable and the others. You may be rich, but if you are not respectable you will not pass muster in the eyes of society. The Queen will not have you at Court. Mothers will not let their daughters dance with you. On the other hand, you may be poor, but if you are respectable the world will think well of you. And what are the outward and visible signs of respectability? Well, by now I think you know: cleanliness—the children at school—sobriety (a pint of beer may pass, but the respectable man never enters a gin shop)—the benefit club—the family walk on a Sunday afternoon—the weekly magazine, like the *Weekly Welcome* or the *British Workman*. You can complete the tale yourselves.

And so, human nature being what it is, there is a certain amount of hypocrisy about it all. I expect the printer would rather slip off to a quiet game of bowls on a Sunday morning than be marched off to church: and I am not sure that what he heard on Sunday he lived up to on week-days. But he has ambitions for himself and his children, and he cannot afford to lose the reputation of being a thoroughly respectable man. It makes it easier to get the boys into a good trade, or for the girl perhaps to become a school-teacher. And at the printer's level, the family counts for everything. If there is one text in the Bible which they firmly believe, it is the one which says:

But if any provide not for his own, and specially for those of his own house, he hath denied the faith, and is worse than an infidel.

As you go downwards, the family, the home, counts for less and less, until it breaks up altogether. And when you got really familiar with England in 1860 and could find your way about yourself, the most lasting impression on your mind would be, I think, this division, this contrast, between the households where the children are cared for and those where they are left to shift for themselves: the ragamuffins we saw darting about under the horses' heads in a torn shirt and a pair of trousers worn down to the right length. They were the children of the underworld and will be the fathers and mothers of the underworld. Our printer is no politician, but he cannot help asking himself sometimes whether this is a sight to be proud of: whether something ought not to be done. Yes but what? This is a question to which 1860 had not found the answer.

THE GREATEST VICTORIAN

*T*HOSE who have had occasion to adjudicate at some country festival are aware of an embarrassing difficulty which comes upon them half-way through. The first arrangement of red, white and blue strikes one as very pretty and apt to the occasion. But is the fiftieth better or worse than the tenth? Are there no colours in the world but red, white and blue? And, by the hundredth, one is in a mood to award the prize, with a hearty ejaculation of relief, to anyone who had the originality to display the Swastika or the Hammer and Sickle. I have been turning over in my mind the names of some who might be candidates for the title of the Greatest Victorian. One needs a man, or woman, who is typical of a large and important class: rich in the abilities which the age fostered: one who made a difference, and under whose influence or direction we are still living. These being the notes by which posterity, looking back, recognizes the really great men of a former time, in whom, among the remembered figures of the

5

Victorian Age are they best exemplified? And I wondered if I might include Karl Marx. He had two of the qualifications which, perhaps unfairly, one associates with eminence in that time. He once had to pawn his spoons, and he was buried in Highgate Cemetery.

Fifty years ago a large body of intelligent persons, headed by Lord Acton, would have adjudged the place to George Eliot. She had genius of the blend, humorous, observant, didactic, which that age most appreciated: she had raised herself to the head of the literary profession: her gnomic wisdom was a light to thousands who had learnt from her that, in the darkness deepening over all ancient faiths, the star of Duty shone clearer than ever. Grave and wise men thought that George Eliot had, single-handed, by her ethical teaching, saved us from the moral catastrophe which might have been expected to follow upon the waning of religious conviction. They were not altogether wrong. George Eliot did give body, and expression, to a great volume of moral thought necessary to her time. In so doing she shaped a generation, and through that generation something of her influence is still at work in an age which knows as much of her writings as it may catch sight of displayed on the Wayside Pulpit.

Tennyson, 'illustrious and consummate', is a strong candidate. We have outgrown the days when it was possible to pretend that he was not a great poet: but what strikes me now, and what explains the hold he had upon his age, is the dexterity, the almost journalistic address, with which his poetry follows and records its intellectual moment, putting all the questions which the advance of science was forcing it to ask, and indicating answers with which, in the general confusion of faith, it might, with some allowance, be contented. But on the test of lasting direction, the claim must be disallowed.

To be typically great, a man must be, as Tennyson was, profoundly in sympathy with the chief preoccupations of his time; and the preoccupations of the Victorian mind, the points to which it swung most constantly and anxiously, were on the one side theological and moral, on the other social. Something therefore might be said for Matthew Arnold, in whose admirably clear intelligence both were in due subordination to the higher and more permanent rights of culture: much more for Ruskin, and on Ruskin's claims one must pause carefully and long. If the test of influence were solely to be applied, then the title would go beyond doubt to Darwin. His work, however, belongs to the isolated and timeless world of pure scientific speculation; he only happened to be a subject of Victoria as Pasteur happened to be a subject of Napoleon III. But what other age or country could have fostered the genius of Ruskin or given it such a field to work in? And of Ruskin it may, I think, with truth be said that, using no doubt the reflections of other men and their experience, absorbing for example all of Carlyle that is really Victorian, and taking not a little of Maurice and Kingsley, he evolved, and forced his world to accept, a new set of axioms as the basis of all future political science in England.

If anyone reckons this claim too bold, I would ask him to consider it thus. Let him first call up the world of political and social thought in 1837; the atomism, the individualism, the economic determinism from which the young intelligence of Disraeli so violently recoiled. Let him compare it with the common assumptions of our own time as they disclose themselves in our legislation and administration. Then, taking his stand almost midway, let him read the address of the economists to Ruskin in 1885: and their acknowledgement that the world of thought in which they now moved, 'where Political Economy can furnish sound laws of life and work only when it respects the dignity and moral destiny of man: and the wise use of wealth, in developing a complete human life, is of incomparably greater moment both to men and actions than its production or accumulation, and can alone give these any vital significance', was a world of his making.

But Ruskin is too fantastic, too childlike, too incoherent, to be typical of an age which loved solidity and efficiency—in politics, for example, the efficiency of Peel and Gladstone, in science of Faraday, in controversy of Huxley: and was always a little dubious and distrustful of genius, like that of Browning, or Newman, not precisely to be specified. And I am not sure that the great and world-known figures are before us to be judged: they are at the

Coronation, we are holding our village feast. We are looking for a man who was in and of his age, and who could have been of no other: a man with sympathy to share, and genius to judge, its sentiments and movements: a man not too illustrious or too consummate to be companionable, but one, nevertheless, whose ideas took root and are still bearing; whose influence, passing from one fit mind to another, could transmit, and can still impart, the most precious element in Victorian civilization, its robust and masculine sanity. Such a man there was: and I award the place to Walter Bagehot.

I do not assert that Bagehot was the greatest man alive and working between 1837 and 1901: I am not sure that the statement would mean anything: and I agree that the landscape of that age is a range of varied eminences with no dominating peak. Indeed, in a footnote to my *Portrait*, which somehow got lost in the proofs, I suggested that anyone who wished to understand the Victorian mind should turn away from the remembered names and survey the careers of three men: Whitwell Elwin, Alderman Thomasson of Bolton, and Charles Adderley, first Lord Norton: reflecting, as he went, on the breadth of their interests, from sound prose to sound religion, and from town planning to Imperial policy, and the quiet and substantial permanence of what they did. It is along this level that we must look, to find 'if not the greatest, at least the truest' Victorian. As I looked, my eye fell on Walter Bagehot and there it has stayed. *Victorianorum maximus*, no. But *Victorianum maxime*[1] I still aver him to be.

Of the Victorian mind, by which I mean the kind of intelligence that one learns to look for and recognize in the years of his maturity, say, from 1846 when he was twenty to 1877 when he died, the characteristics that most impress me are capaciousness and energy. It had room for so many ideas, and it threw them about as lustily as a giant baby playing skittles. The breadth and vigour of Bagehot's mind appear on every page he has left, and they were, we know, not less conspicuous in his conversation and the conduct of affairs. But what was peculiarly his own was the perfect management of all this energy and all these resources. He

[1] 'Greatest of the Victorians.' 'Most Victorian of the Victorians.'

was as well aware of his superiority in intelligence as Matthew
Arnold of his superiority in culture. But he carried it with such
genial and ironic delight, that his influence—and he was through
the *Economist* and the Reviews a very influential man—encountered no resistance. His paradoxes became axioms: and there are
thousands of people thinking and even speaking Bagehot today
who might be hard put to it to say when exactly he lived and what
exactly he did. Let me give an illustration:

If one makes a close study of a society different from one's own, one
finds that institutions the very opposite of one's own are defended by
the people to whom they belong with as much fervour as that with
which we defend ours. They do not seek to be delivered from them
and endowed with something better. Self-government, in fact, does
not mean responsible government: it means government by the
authority you have been brought up to respect, whom you obey readily
because you as well as he take the obedience for granted, who is
hallowed by all the dignity of tradition and religious belief and is a
symbol of national pride and achievement. Above all in a period of
rapid change such as is confronting men today, the preservation of
such continuity with the past, with the standards they are used to, and
the social world where they can find their way about, is essential if
the transition is to be effected without producing mere confusion and
chaos.

That is pure Bagehot. Observe the psychological realism which
is concerned only to discover how men in societies actually do
behave, and the unpretentious colloquialism of the style. No one
ever thought or wrote quite like that before: and it contains the
gist of the famous doctrine, which he first propounded, with
much youthful flippancy, after observing the *coup d'état* of 1851,
and restated more gravely in *Physics and Politics,* that the surest
guarantee of stability and freedom in a state is 'stupidity', or the
general habit of identical response. And today, will anyone deny
it? But the odd thing, to use a common phrase of his, is that the
passage I have quoted is not Bagehot at all. It is Dr Lucy Mair,
speaking in the later Thirties on the administration of Tanganyika.

But Bagehot was no lonely thinker, anticipating the common-
places of another age. He was as thoroughly immersed in the
Victorian matter as the most pugnacious, self-satisfied, dogmatic

business man of his day. In his profession as banker, economist and editor he was highly successful, his word carried equal weight in Threadneedle Street and Downing Street. He could even write verses, beginning (or ending, I forget which)

Thou Church of Rome!

and it was his affectionate and humorous interest in all the doings of his time that furnished him with the material of his philosophy. Of Macaulay he acutely says that he lacked 'the experiencing mind'. Bagehot's mind was always experiencing, and always working its observation into pattern, into system, but—and here we touch on his central excellence or virtue—into a system open towards the future. He distrusted swift, unreflecting action. Equally he distrusted all closed, dogmatic combinations: here picking up the true English tradition which the Radicals had done their best to sever, the tradition of Burke:

> When he forewarns, denounces, launches forth
> Against all systems built on abstract rights
> Keen ridicule: the majesty proclaims
> Of Institutes and Laws, hallowed by time:
> Declares the vital power of social ties
> Endeared by Custom; and with high disdain
> Exploding upstart Theory, insists
> Upon the allegiance to which men are born,

—which laborious flight of Wordsworthian eloquence Bagehot would probably have countered with his favourite 'How much?' Uncorrected, this insistence on habit leads to an unthinking Liverpudlian conservatism, and Bagehot was a Liberal. What, then, is the correction? In his answer, I confess I see no flaw, and I think that the experience of sixty years has established its truth and disclosed its profundity. People do like splendour, distinction, and authority in their rulers. This is their natural allegiance. Very well; then see to it that the allegiance of the rulers themselves is rightly directed. And to what? You will find the answer in a brief paper published in 1871, and called 'The Emotion of Conviction'. And if there be in English a more 'wholesome doctrine or necessary for these times' than is contained in the last pages of that essay, I must own it has escaped me.

THE MERCIAN SIBYL[1]

TWENTY years ago, in a chapter on the Political and Social Novel, A. W. Ward asked what it was that gave *Scenes of Clerical Life* its instant success with the public of 1857. 'In the first place', he wrote, 'its gnomic wisdom, which generally takes the form of wit, is as striking as it is pregnant', and he proceeds to illustrate its lucid directness, its lambent humour, its poetic power; and to give one example where 'it rises to the height of a prophetic saying, or a maxim for all time'.

> Trust and resignation fill up the margin of ignorance.

That is not really a good sentence; the image lacks precision. But it is the sort of sentence which the contemporary reader liked to encounter, to underline, and to copy out. It is not surprising that, with the author's full approval, a volume of *The Wise, Witty and Tender Sayings of George Eliot* was published in 1872.

Great successes in literature are most often gained by a fresh and powerful handling of some recognized theme, or some established form. From Bulwer's earliest novels the fiction-reading public had been taught to watch for the *sententia*; and, of maxims which could be extended into compact and impressive discourses, George Eliot was a master. Her dismissal of Dorothea, for example, is a fine specimen of a manner perfectly adapted to the ear of a generation which desired to be instructed, whose interests were predominantly ethical, and which expected art to be, if not subordinate, at all events directed, to some earnest purpose.

> The effect of her being on those around her was incalculably diffusive: for the growing good of the world is partly dependent on unhistoric acts; and that things are not so ill with you and me as they might have been is half owing to the number who lived faithfully a hidden life, and rest in unvisited graves.

How easily this passage could be cast into blank verse, and set down, unremarked, in *The Excursion*! The native seat of the maxim, the traditional vehicle of gnomic wisdom, was didactic or

1 *George Eliot: a Biography*, by Blanche Colton Williams.

dramatic poetry: George Eliot, first among writers of prose fiction, was searched, as the poets had always been searched, for the brief, memorable, instructive Text.

Her affinity with Wordsworth is manifest: a Wordsworth brought down from the mountains to the wide landscapes and slow streams of the East Midlands, a land of unhurried business and placid, Protestant belief. It is in this setting, physical and spiritual, that George Eliot is first to be apprehended. Some people will not like it, and it may be acknowledged that to be habitually slow and sententious is at times to come very near to being a bore. But Miss Williams's book, the fruit of an ardent enthusiasm, is evidence that, with others, the enchantment is still as strong as when George Eliot's first critics spoke of that other Midlander from the Avon, and Lord Acton compared her, not altogether to their advantage, with Sophocles, Cervantes, and Dante as well. It is interesting in an age which probably regards her very much as a family might regard an aunt in the Cabinet, of whose eminence they are proud but whose visits they do not encourage, to find that the enchantment can be revived, and that after fifty years and more George Eliot can still inspire a genuine affection as well as a generous admiration.

After the Midland childhood and youth, over which Miss Williams lingers with all possible care and precision of place and date, came the rigorous intellectual discipline of London and the *Westminster Review*; and this it was that set upon her genius its identifying mark. She was an intellectual woman by birth. So was Miss Martineau. But she came before the world as a woman of finely trained intellect, which Miss Martineau was not. She was really learned: she had proved her brain by hard work on craggy themes: comparing *Romola* with *Rienzi,* one's first observation is: how much better George Eliot knows her subject than Bulwer does. She shows at times the ungainliness of humour, the labour to be entertaining, which often betrays the scholar condescending to a less serious audience. But she always has the scholar's mastery of his topic. Never could she have exposed herself to Croker's coarse, but not unjustified, advice to Miss Martineau, to ask Mamma before she wrote on Population.

What would have become of this finely balanced blend of natural genius, pondered observation and intellectual training, if she had not joined Lewes, is not a very profitable speculation. Her passionate nature, which Miss Williams does right to emphasize, would sooner or later have carried her to some man; and if her lofty standards, old Evangelical standards surviving the loss of a formal faith, had stood in the way, she might have been wrecked in the conflict between Love and Duty. The union with Lewes preserved the balance, and made manifest her genius by releasing the creative spring. She struck into the current at exactly the right moment. A taste was forming for a wholesome and homely naturalism, restrained in its humour, not effusive in its pathos. Bulwer, always quick to catch a shift of the breeze, had opened a new line in domestic fiction with *The Caxtons*, and neither *Tamerton Church Tower* nor *The Heir of Redclyffe* is to be ignored if we are to recover the scent and temper of the years when Trollope was at work on *The Warden* and George Eliot on *Scenes of Clerical Life*. It appeared in 1857, along with *Barchester Towers*. Then Trollope went ahead with *Dr. Thorne,* and George Eliot followed with *Adam Bede*. She had won her public; but she did not have to make it. It was waiting for her.

By drawing deeply on her early memories she had, with a kind of instinctive strategy, placed herself in a commanding position. A famous jurist of the last generation once remarked: 'The sort of novels my wife likes are what I call village gossip with a dash of religion.' Piety and the Pastoral were notes to which the Victorian heart readily vibrated, and simply the placing of Dinah Morris in Mrs Poyser's farm was enough to admit those early readers into one of the most favoured regions of their fancy. But, once admitted, what held them there? Partly that gnomic wisdom, of which Ward spoke; partly the humour—it was not only all so true but all so amusing as well: and neither the humour nor the wisdom is quite in the key of our age. In her comedy, the traces of mental fabrication are sometimes too obtrusive, and a habit of self-conscious vivacity grew with time into the osseous gambollings which make her latest manner unreadable. But her character drawing remains; and, if we could pursue it to the recesses where

the secret of genius lurks, we might find that her distinguishing
excellence in her command of progressive psychology, not merely
revealing in successive episodes a character which was there all
the while, but setting it, on a crowded stage and in leisurely time,
to develop itself: to change, as most characters do change, under
the pressure of relationships and the assimilation of experiences;
some do not. Celia is a perfect darling from start to finish, and no
one would wish her to be anything else. Her uncle is an ass, whose
pedigree runs back to the humorous figures of the Elizabethan
stage, or Fanny Burney. Such stationary characters are needed to
keep a story ready. But Dorothea is moving, is growing, all the
time. So is Lydgate, though his motion is steadily downwards,
and his growth is only from material failure to material success.

This movement, this growth, is subject to a clear, inexorable
and yet compassionate law: operating, one might say, within a
Scheme of Subjective Retribution. Miss Williams quotes a once-
famous passage of Frederick Myers describing a conversation with
George Eliot; when 'taking as her text the words God, Immortality, Duty, she pronounced, with terrible earnestness, how
inconceivable was the first, how incredible the second, and yet
how peremptory and absolute the third'. To many of her contemporaries she was the Sibyl who had restated the moral law, and
the processes of soul-making, in terms acceptable to the rationalist,
agnostic conscience. Of Righteousness and Temperance and
Judgement to come she seemed to them to reason with the weight,
the fire and the conviction of a prophetess standing in the full
light of scientific day. She spoke, in an age distracted between
new knowledge and old belief, as Delphi might have spoken; and
who, indeed, can follow the life of Bulstrode to its stricken end,
'in that sad refuge of indifferent faces', without hearing an echo
of the oracle once given to Glaucus, son of Epicydes?

> Do as you like today—swear and keep the money.
> Let a man tell truth all his life, yet Death will get him.
> But there is Something, without hand or foot or name,
> Something that comes with vengeance and brings utter
>   destruction
> The whole house and race of the man who swears falsely.

THE VICTORIAN NOON-TIME

THE notion of a century we owe, it seems, to religious contro-
vertists of the Reformation time, who found it a convenient
framework within which to set the results of their researches into
the history of the Early Church. The word gradually found its
way into secular speech, but not until the eighteenth century was
some way advanced did its inhabitants commonly think of it by
number. The nineteenth, which began with a hot debate, renewed
in 1900, as to which was its opening year, was from the first very
conscious of its standing in the scale of time. Looking back, we
may think of it as coming to birth, in literature with *Lyrical
Ballads* 1798, in economic science with Malthus's *Principle of
Population* of the same year and, politically, with the Union in
1800. If we consider how much of English thought was absorbed,
in the next hundred years, by the successive stages of the Romantic
movement, by the rights and wrongs of Ireland and the pressure
of population on subsistence, we must acknowledge that, for once,
history had consented to raise the curtain with a truly dramatic
flourish.

But the rapid extinction or slow waning of the earlier lights—
Byron, Shelley, and Keats; Coleridge, Wordsworth, and Scott—
sets a bar of twilight across the years about 1830; and the accident
of a long reign, beginning shortly afterwards, has given an illusory
show of unity to a tract of time in which men and manners
changed more swiftly than at any other epoch of our history. The
ferment of the thirties produced a literature which in twenty years
had attained almost classic rank. Young men in 1850, reading
with the proper avidity of youth, could have found most of their
tastes, and most of their curiosities, satisfied by masterpieces
published, since their birth, by men who had been pointed out to
them in the streets. To watch Mr Macaulay threading his way
through the Piccadilly traffic, book in hand: to see Mr Dickens
running up the steps of the Athenæum: to recognize the Laureate
by his cloak and Mr Carlyle by his shawl, were the peculiar joys
of that time. The stonecutter by the Tiber, chipping out 'Carmen

composuit Q. Horatius Flaccus'[1] on the memorial of the Secular
Games, must have had the same feeling that he too was living in a
great age, peopled with Immortals.

Who were these young men? It is a question always worth
asking, because what sixteen to twenty-four is talking about,
twenty-four to sixty-four will usually write, or think, or do. Those
are the charging years. The admirable *Annals of English literature*[2] which Dr Ghosh has prepared for the Clarendon Press make
such cross-sections easy to draw at any point we may choose. In
1850, Huxley is twenty-five; Bagehot twenty-four; Rossetti and
Meredith twenty-two. Christina Rossetti is just twenty; Mark
Rutherford a year younger; Lewis Carroll and Leslie Stephen are
eighteen; Morris, Acton, and Du Maurier are sixteen. Behind
them as the schoolboys, Swinburne, Morley, Pater; Hardy is
just ten; and over them all droops the fading youth of Matthew
Arnold, in the full decrepitude of twenty-eight. Those who are
fortunate enough to have memories of a Dissolving View will
recall the excitement of watching the Norwegian Bride fade away
while the Sogne Fjord gradually affirmed itself on the screen. It
is so at the mid-century. There is no twilight, but a swift replacement, and, for a while, a bewildering shift of lights and forms.

In *The World's Great Age,*[3] a book written with the generous
gusto which its title promises, Mr Buck selects Matthew Arnold
as the representative of the New Humanism, and prefixes to his
chapter Arnold's lines:

> And life ran gaily as the sparkling Thames,
>   Before this strange disease of modern life,
> With its sick hurry, its divided aims,
>   Its heads o'ertaxed, its palsied hearts, was rife.

Bagehot, more tersely and less querulously, spoke of the ragged-
ness of contemporary thought. 'Whatever may be thought',
Macaulay wrote in 1859, 'of the theology, the metaphysics, the
political theories of out time, boldness and novelty is not what
they want.' The truth was that the co-ordinates of the past age, by

1 'Q. Horatius Flaccus composed this Ode.'
2 *Annals of English Literature*, 1475-1925.
3 *The World's Great Age*, by Philo M. Buck, junr.

which the intellectual position of a man could be reckoned, and by which he could set his own opinions, were no longer applicable. In the early thirties he could range himself promptly at the call, as a Reformer, a Radical, or a Tory. He was either for the Tractarians or against them: for or against the New Poor Law, and the Repeal of the Corn Laws: for the Charter or its determined foe: issues important enough to tax the head and make the heart beat strongly. But from about 1846 the storm of controversy dies rapidly down into a pleasantly exciting breeze, before which the country drives, 'sails filled and streamers waving', past the dangerous reefs of India and the Crimea, into the halcyon weather of Palmerston's old age. Of the years from 1830 to 1850 Mr Mottram has written: 'There are times when we catch our breath to see the risks we were running.' It is very true. With no less truth could *The Times* in 1861 speak of 'a degree of general contentment to which neither we, nor any other nation we know of, ever attained before'. It was in this season of national euphoria that the mind of the next age was formed: and divided aims, sick hurry, o'er-taxed heads and palsied hearts are hardly now the faults we should specially assign to the decade which was crowned with *The Origin of Species,* which bred or shaped Meredith and Hardy, Huxley, Stephen, and John Morley, or disclosed the genius of George Eliot. There is a sparkle, an intoxication in the air; released from its gnawing fear of social subversion, the general mind seems to give itself up to holiday. It is the sparkle of spring: the intoxication of a renewed youth. *Hiems transiit, imber recessit, flores apparuerunt in terra nostra.*[4]

In a curious fragment of spiritual autobiography dating from that time a young man records his relief at escaping, with Kingsley's aid, from the Devil-and-Human-Corruption to God's Earth. The successive prefaces to *Alton Locke,* which appeared in 1850, are documents of the first value for the inner history of the mid-century: for the change, partly of social circumstance, but more of social feeling, which brought about the 'general contentment' of 1861. *Hypatia* (1853) and *Westward Ho!* (1855)

---

4 'The winter is past, the rain has gone, the flowers have appeared in our land.'
Song of Solomon 2, 11

are landmarks not less significant in its spiritual journey. Mr Buck remarks, with great truth, that Victorian prose seems to go much deeper than Victorian verse. He is writing from the memories of a late Victorian boyhood, when the heartiness of Browning was beginning to sound a little hollow and the Philosophy of Somehow, as set forth by Tennyson, seemed rather thin. No one will set Kingsley by the side of either of them. Of the great Victorian art of word-painting he is indeed a master, but it is not an art of the first consequence in literature. He has become, and will remain, a secondary figure. Yet how much of the late Victorian mind is embryonic in his writings: its Imperialism in *Westward Ho!*: its feminism, its socialism everywhere. The frank and glowing sensuousness of *Hypatia* added a rainbow of new colours to the palette of fiction. 'I have a certain artistic knack of utterance (nothing but a knack),' he said. It was the knack of uttering what the new age wanted to hear. A Royal Commission in 1860 asked an undergraduate what books he read at school. 'Scott, Dickens, Macaulay, Tennyson; Kingsley of course.'

The religious catastrophe of the mid-century was not a sudden or a universal deluge. Whole tracts of society stood above its reach for another thirty years. Mr Kellett,[5] whose thoughtful and entertaining recollections of cultured Nonconformity in late mid-Victorian times admit us into a world not very accessible, but very important, dates it a generation later. But catastrophes are long preparing, and the fifties are such a time of preparation: of deep-seated folding, straining, and faulting: old strata and new shifting against each other into fantastic and precarious poises. Francis Newman's *Phases of Faith* and Browning's *Christmas Eve and Easter Day* are of the same year, 1850, the year of *In Memoriam*. *The Scholar Gipsy* and *Hypatia* are of the same year, 1853. But this season of speculative adventure, and not unevenly matched debate, was brief. *The Origin of Species* converted a private, if widely held, doubt into a public issue. 'I don't see,' said an old clergyman, 'what there is to make a book about. God created them.' The Darwinian theorem imported an alternative revelation. It created a new framework of reference for ideas. It breached

[5] *As I Remember*, by E. E. Kellett.

the cosmogony of the old faith, and, with it, the whole metaphysic of Redemption; and through the gap surged wave upon wave of criticism gathering for years in the vast receptacle of German learning. 'Fifteen cubits upwards did the waters prevail; and the mountains were covered.'

Nothing is harder to determine than the exact degree of conviction with which a widespread creed is actually and individually held: of the current Protestantism of 1830 to 1850, as of every other religion, we shall probably be right in saying that it was preached more earnestly than it was practised, and professed more stoutly than it was believed. But a decent, if formal, respect for the confessions and observances of the Churches had for a long while past been imposed by social sanctions. Of *religio,* Macaulay, for example, had much. Of religion he had as little as might be expected of a Protestant who had escaped from Clapham; and when he pays his reverence 'to Him that raises up and pulls down nations at His pleasure', we must take the words as an act of respect to English society rather than to Almighty God. When Lyell came forward in defence of *The Origin of Species*, Darwin wrote, with that quiet simplicity which he shared with Faraday: 'Considering his age, his former views, and his position in society, I think his conduct has been heroic.' The phrase is worth pondering. The battle was fought not for the destruction of old beliefs or the affirmation of new hypotheses, but for social recognition of the right to follow the argument wherever it goes. 'Never mind the mistakes of Moses, Sir; where were you last night?' was one of the most formidable arguments in the dialectics of true belief. Wilberforce thought he could crush Huxley with the condescending sarcasm of a platform bully accustomed to the applause of curates. No one ever tried it again. When Pusey set out to organize the forces of the faith against *Essays and Reviews,* even curates turned.

Thus the young men of the fifties grew up in an emancipated world, free, within the limits of a widening decency, to think, to speak, to write, very much as they pleased; and, being young, they availed themselves of the privilege by writing, speaking, and thinking a great deal of nonsense. The drastic revision to which

Meredith afterwards subjected the text of his early works is the
verdict of a cooler time on the high spirits of youth.

> 'Twas gladsome, but often
>   Foolish forsooth;
> But gladsome, gladsome!

Like the young mischief of the *Saturday Review* and the young
roarings of the *Daily Telegraph,* which leapt together into the
world in 1855. And what is *Maud* but the Laureate's proof that
he, too, was abreast of the times? There is in Tennyson's literary
character a well-marked strain of journalistic adaptability. From
the rick-burners of 1830 to the Krakatoa sunsets of 1883, all was
copy that came to his muse. In *Maud,* the hero learns 'to feel with
his native land'; and Tennyson had learnt to feel about Company
Promoting and Industrial Insurance as the Christian Socialists
felt: about the Northern Anarch and John Bright as a warlike
electorate felt.

   Mr Buck says, with reason, of the age which Arnold found 'not
ungrand, not unmoving, but unpoetical', that seldom in any age
of the world's history were there so many poets. But how many of
them, and how much even in the best of them, must we silence to
hear the true Muse singing.

> And rise, O moon, from yonder down,
>   Till over down and over dale
>   All night the shining vapour sail
> And pass the silent-lighted town,
> The white-faced halls, the glancing rills,
>   And catch at every mountain head,
>   And o'er the friths that branch and spread
> Their sleeping silver thro' the hills.
>
> When, from far Parnassus' side,
> Young Apollo, all the pride
> Of the Phrygian flutes to tame,
> To the Phrygian highlands came;
> Where the long green reed-beds sway
> In the rippled waters grey
> Of that solitary lake
> Where Maeander's springs are born;

Whence the ridged pinewooded roots
Of Messogis westward break,
Mounting westward, high and higher.
There was held the famous strife;
There the Phrygian brought his flutes,
And Apollo brought his lyre.

Golden head by golden head,
They lay down in their curtained bed:
Like two blossoms on one stem,
Like two flakes of new fall'n snow,
Like two wands of ivory,
Tipped with gold for awful kings.
Moon and stars gazed in at them,
Wind sang to them lullaby,
Lumbering owls forbore to fly,
Not a bat flapped to and fro
Round their nest:
Cheek to cheek and breast to breast
Locked together in one nest.

That is how the poetry of the fifties comes back to the memory
best: in fragments, like the Greek lyric, and, whenever it can forget
its ethical or doctrinal formalities, with not a little of the fresh,
instinctive perfection of Greek lyric. In the urbane and fluid prose
of the time—the prose, for example of Thackeray and Froude in
contrast with that of Dickens and Macaulay—the same clear note
is heard. The truculent, the pompous, the gushing are no longer
the mode; and if, out of the whole record of our public oratory,
we had to choose one passage to show what the Attic manner was,
what could it be but this?

I met him a short time before he went out, at Mr Westerton's the
bookseller, near Hyde Park Corner. I asked him whether he was
going out. He answered, he was afraid he was; not afraid in the sense
of personal fear—he knew not that; but he said, with a look and a
tone I shall never forget: 'It is no light matter for a man who has a wife
and five little children.' The stormy Euxine is his grave; his wife is a
widow, his children fatherless.

Politically, the halcyon days ended in an unseemly shuffle out
of Schleswig-Holstein under the grim, contemptuous eyes of
Bismarck. 'Those who were young', Green wrote, 'in the weary

days of Palmerstonian rule will remember the disgust at purely political life which was produced by the bureaucratic inaction of the time.' The tacit agreement to leave things as they were so long as the old man lived imposed a general silence, which burst into a deafening volubility as soon as the old man was laid to his rest. But, both in literature and in manners, the stirring and good-humoured fifties had left a grace and brightness behind them across which the Early Victorian time appeared as a season of construction, heaviness, and gloom. Let anyone make the experiment of reading in succession a good popular novel of the forties and seventies—say, Mrs Gore's *Cecil a Coxcomb* and Black's *Madcap Violet,* where, incidentally, he will encounter Swinburne's favourite heroine—and gauge for himself the change in the social atmosphere. The use of fictional sources for social history is a practice to be followed, doubtless, with caution. But on one point their evidence is almost infallible. They show us what types were biologically attractive to a particular generation, and by natural law those types will be ascendant in the evolution of the next. They are documents for the Origin of Social Species by Sexual Selection.

Malthus had glimpses, which Darwin enlarged into a steady view, of evolution as a cosmic process, 'bringing a mind out of the clod'. Reduced to a plan of society, the Malthusian doctrine seemed to have established self-aggrandizement and self-restraint as the balancing forces behind all progress. Regarded as a scheme of creation, does the Darwinian hypothesis establish competition as heaven's first law, or does it point to the emergence of a moral order above itself? Evolving—yes, but evolving what? Must we look forward to a progressive segregation of finer types, a biological aristocracy; and will the political democracy ever allow it to come into existence? Or to a general raising of society; and will that democracy possess either the brain or the resolution for the task? May we trust the deep and irresistible appetences and recoils of instinct, which forbid Clara to mate with Willoughby and carry her as swiftly and directly to Vernon as Nature bore Haidée into the arms of Juan? But consider, then, what impoverished, constrained, conventional material our social discipline has made for Nature to work upon. Vast are the powers of Evolution to create, but vast, too, are the ages which it needs to create in; and, if it cannot make a better individual without a better ambient, neither can it make a better society without better components. We see the new co-ordinates drawing and the Late Victorian intelligence aligning itself between self-realization and self-sacrifice, the improvement of the individual or the race, self-culture or self-subordination to the welfare of some immediate or remote society: or tracing that strange diagonal which Morris was to follow from *The Earthly Paradise* to Trafalgar Square.

The *Annals of English Literature* gives us a watershed from which to survey two landscapes.

> 1852 Thomas Moore died.
> George Moore born.

Thomas Moore lived long enough to read Macaulay's Third Chapter and its exultant close:

> We too shall, in our turn, be outstripped, and in our turn be envied. It may well be, in the twentieth century, that the peasant of Dorsetshire may think himself miserably paid with twenty shillings a week; that the carpenter at Greenwich may receive ten shillings a day; that labouring men may be as little used to dine without meat as they now are to eat rye bread; that sanitary police and medical discoveries may have added several more years to the average length of human life; that numerous comforts and luxuries which are now unknown, or confined to a few, may be within the reach of every diligent and thrifty working man. And yet it may then be the mode to assert that the increase of wealth and the progress of science have benefited the few at the expense of the many, and to talk of the reign of Queen Victoria as the time when England was truly merry England, when all classes were bound together by brotherly sympathy, when the richer did not grind the faces of the poor, and when the poor did not envy the splendour of the rich.

This is the confident and solid humanism of the past, with its near objectives and measured advance: in that faith the earlier Victorians went out to win for their children the triumphant peace of the mid-century.

George Moore lived long enough to read, if he could have borne to read it, Hardy's summing of the whole matter:

Pain to all upon earth, tongued or dumb, shall be kept down to a minimum by loving kindness, operating through scientific knowledge, and actuated by the modicum of free will conjecturally possessed by organic life when the mighty necessitating forces—unconscious or other—that have 'the balancings of the clouds' happen to be in equilibrium, which may or may not be often.

The rustic, Cyclopean, phrasing is all Hardy. But the thought is the thought of one who had grown to manhood in the rich golden noon of nineteenth-century England and, through a long afternoon, had watched the horizon receding as the light faded and the colours paled.

NEWMAN AGAIN

ONCE for some dreary and self-denying purpose I read many books on education—not method, which is not my concern, or the psychology of childhood, which interests me deeply, but Education with a big and gloomy E. I came to the conclusion that if two were kept, the rest might, with no loss to humanity and possibly some advantage, be pulped. Because these two go to the point and stay there: the point being, what are you after with all this teaching, and preaching, and training? With your rewards and punishments, your social pressure and economic inducements, your praise and blame? What are you trying to do, or, better still, to make? What product does your art profess to deliver? Is it attractive? Is it estimable? Is it useful to society as it is, or likely by influence, or direction, or example, to improve society? Above all, is it worth while to the product's self? And unless you can answer that question, it seems to me you had better hold your tongue.

One of these books is Aristotle's *Ethics,* and the other is Newman's nine discourses on *The Idea of a University.* In the first four he is in the cell, speaking, we may say, confessionally;

and though they contain passages which—like the descant on the Papacy in the First Discourse, on the attributes of the Creator in the Third, and on the Fine Arts in the Fourth—are unrivalled in English for the simplicity of their means and the majesty of their effect, yet, their doctrine being based on an assumption which must either be taken as of faith or set aside as unproved, many readers may find them unattractive and in places repellent. They are addressed to fellow Catholics, and addressed, it must be borne in mind, by an alien, a recent convert, an already suspected man. Reading them again against the biographical background depicted in Dr Tardivel's full and well-documented study,[1] I understood better than before the peculiar vehemence and urgency of those opening discourses on the place of Theology in a University. Newman is not only pleading a cause: he is pleading his own right to be heard. And even if there had been anyone to listen to him, the Irish Bishops were determined that he should not. In Ireland, I gather, he is still denounced as an enemy of the Irish race: and there are passages in the Discourses, like the panegyric on the English public schools and the men they bred,

heroes and statesmen, literary men and philosophers, men conspicuous for great natural virtues, for habits of business, for knowledge of life, for practical judgement, for cultivated tastes, for accomplishments, who have made England what it is—able to subdue the earth,

which must make us, if we remember they were delivered in Dublin within a few years of the great famine and while the great migration was in progress, admire the self-restraint of the audience as much as the eloquence of the speaker. Tact was not Newman's strong suit.

But in the Fifth Discourse he steps into the daylight and speaks to the world. And the sum of what he has to say is this: There are all the special sciences which advance knowledge; there are all the arts and professions which, by applying knowledge, make things. But above these is the Science of Sciences, or Philosophy, which, because it is the peculiar possession of the educated man, it is the peculiar function of a University to impart.

An assemblage of learned men, zealous for their own sciences, and rivals of each other, are brought, by familiar intercourse and for the sake of intellectual peace, to adjust together the claims and relations of their respective subjects of investigation. They learn to respect, to consult, to aid each other.

(As a description of Oxford during the heat of the Tractarian controversy, this benign picture is not without its humour.)

Thus is created a pure and clear atmosphere of thought, which the student also breathes, though in his own case he only pursues a few sciences out of the multitude. He profits by an intellectual tradition, which is independent of particular teachers, which guides him in his choice of subjects, and duly interprets for him those which he chooses. He apprehends the great outlines of knowledge, the principles on which it rests, the scale of its parts, its lights and shades, its great points and its little, as he otherwise cannot apprehend them. Hence it is that his education is called 'Liberal'. A habit of mind is formed which lasts through life, of which the attributes are, freedom, equitableness, calmness, moderation, and wisdom—

(the speaker cannot be charged with drawing his own intellectual portrait)

—or what I have ventured to call a philosophical habit. . . And now the question is asked me, What is the *use* of it?

Let us leave the answer for a moment, and, without stopping to inquire whether any University ever did, does, or will come up to these requirements, let us remember that Newman has all the time in view the practical object of raising the Catholic upper classes, in Ireland, but not in Ireland only—his imagination ranged over the whole English-speaking world to which Dublin was to be what Athens had been to Greece—to the intellectual level of the English Protestant upper classes: to fit them for their duties as 'men of the world, statesmen, landowners, and opulent gentlemen' (the innuendo, that they were not fit, being, no doubt, vastly agreeable to their ears). In other words, he is laying down the form of mind proper to an aristocracy. He is trying to *make* something, to determine an idea, and create an institution with which to realize it.

But observe next the limits within which the idea is elaborated.

Sharply and emphatically, he distinguishes this philosophy from the pervading habit of 'viewiness', engendered and encouraged by journalism, or the trick of propounding bright generalizations on every topic, of which Brougham, 'half knowing everything from the cedar in Lebanon to the hyssop that groweth out of the wall', was the most conspicuous exemplar. On the other side, he holds out no hopes that it will do more than it promises: it is a form of mind, and cannot affect the quality of mind as given by Nature. But it is the form common to all men who have once grasped the difference between knowledge and not-knowledge, and have thoroughly mastered the methods of reasoning, of getting from point to point, in their own branch of study, making their communications with each other prompt, easy, and certain: unencumbered by the misunderstandings and ambiguities, and unobstructed by the kinks and opacities, of the untrained mind.

I hold very strongly that the first step in intellectual training is to impress on a boy's mind the idea of science, method, order, principle, and system: of rule and exception: of richness and harmony. Let him once gain this habit of method, of starting from fixed points, of making his ground sure as he goes, of distinguishing what he knows from what he does not know, and I conceive he will be gradually initiated into the largest and truest philosophy. . . Moreover, such knowledge is not a mere extrinsic or accidental advantage, which is ours today and another's tomorrow, which may be got up from a book, and easily forgotten again, which we can command or communicate at our pleasure, which we can borrow for the occasion, carry about in our hand, and take into the market; it is an acquired illumination, it is a habit, a personal possession, and an inward endowment.

All which, and the form of mind that contains them, Newman holds—thus answering his own question—to be a good in itself: just as, for example, health and a clear enunciation are good in themselves, quite apart from their utility if a sentence of hard labour had to be served, or a position is being sought where B.B.C. vowels are, as the advertisements say, essential. And in the following discourses he employs all his magic to enlarge and refine and exalt this conception of intellectual cultivation as a good in itself, worth while for itself, to be prized and esteemed for itself beyond all knowledge and all professional skill; while, all the time, so earnestly does he affirm its inadequacy, its shortcomings on the moral side, its need to be steadied and purified by religion, that at the end we feel that what we have heard is the final utterance, never to be repeated or needing to be supplemented, of Christian Humanism: as if the spirit evoked by Erasmus had found its voice at last.

SOPHIST AND SWASHBUCKLER

WHEN Kingsley, in a review of Froude's *History,* gave a passing flick at Newman, neither he nor any of his readers could have guessed the results that were to follow. Newman in 1860 was no great figure: out of the world, and almost out of memory. It was supposed that he was uncomfortable in the Church of Rome: he was not, or at any rate the Church was the more uncomfortable of the two. He was regarded, so far as anyone regarded him at all, with some pity, some suspicion and some contempt. He had been badly treated by Rome, but why had he ever left Oxford? He wrote fine English, but the meaning was sometimes doubtful and sometimes repellent. What had an Englishman, an Oxford man, with taste and judgement refined by the classics and philosophy of the Schools, to do with the glories of Mary, and the healing oil that flowed from the bones of St Walburga?

Dislike and fear of Popery is a Victorian datum. The educated eighteenth century took its Catholics very coolly. Plans could be discussed for a union of the Anglican and Gallican churches. French privateers were ordered to spare the Manx fishermen out of respect for the apostolic virtues of Bishop Wilson: emigrant French priests were welcomed, cared for, found employment. If Pitt had carried Catholic Emancipation with the Union, there would have been no line left on which the opposing creeds could array themselves. The division, which he was compelled to make between Protestant and Catholic citizens, crystallized the distinction between Protestant and Catholic believers. If we ask, what harm could Rome do to England? the answer was that it might make Ireland rebel.

Emancipation was granted, as we all know, too late. In that interval of lost opportunity, English religion, the religion of the ascendant class, had taken one of its periodic turns. It had been sacramental in the seventeenth century, ethical in the eighteenth; it was becoming evangelical: and the essence of the evangelical faith was the effort to ensure salvation by the deliberate perform-ance of actions which had an individual moral worth, and the calculated avoidance of all others. It left no neutral ground: and the canon of moral worth was simple. Not the practice of society, nor the impulses of the wayward heart: not even, as the Bentha-mites vainly talked, the greatest good of the greatest number. Scripture, and the deductions therefrom of the most scripturally-minded persons.

In one of her stories, Harriet Newman, who had a distinct touch of her brother's ironic humour, gives the conversation of three or four young people on the question of manners. Should a young man, for example, open a door for a young woman? Mary Anne demands an instance of Abraham being polite to a girl. Ellen counters with the presents he sent to Rebecca. 'That,' says Mary Anne, 'is no precedent for personal attentions.' 'Then what,' says the persevering Ellen, 'do you say to Jacob's rolling the stone away for Rachel at the well?' Constance, as usual, had her Poly-glot Bible with her: they turn up the passage and the verdict is for Ellen.

Now nothing can be plainer than that many of the observances, rites, and tenets of the Church of Rome are quite as unscriptural as the practice of setting chairs for ladies. Therefore they were sinful. Therefore those who enjoined them were anti-Christ, frustrators of the scheme of salvation: those who followed them, unless they could be excused by helpless ignorance, were lost. Certainly, this conclusion is no part of the authentic Anglican tradition. The Caroline divines would have rejected it with disgust, and indeed one biting phrase of Hooker's, 'the mystery of a gospel-like behaviour', seems by anticipation to dismiss the whole apparatus of evangelical morality. But it was, over a large part of

English society, the accepted doctrine a hundred years ago. Rome was a danger to the State. Not less, Rome was a danger to each individual soul.

Given the premises and the equipment of the average middle-class mind of the time, is there any answer? I confess I can see none. We cannot say the issue was unimportant: it was all-important—Ireland a French province barring the western outlet of our trade: hell, increasingly tenanted with lost English souls. It really was rather serious. And of those who did not take either the French or the Devil quite so much to heart, on the great mass of church- or chapel-going voters, serious, regular men, the authority, uniformity, beauty, and history, which make up three-fourths of the appeal of Rome, operated with exactly a reverse effect. They were individuals and men of the present: they would tolerate little interference by the State and its officials: none by a foreign church and its ministers. Even in worship, they must feel their own weight, whether they were criticizing the sermon or joining in the hymns. They would not have the management of their affairs, their families or their souls, taken out of their hands. They disliked ritual as much as they disliked the sight of Gold Stick walking backwards before the Queen, and for very nearly the same reason. There was no historic or aesthetic fibre in their composition to respond, and it made them feel outsiders.

Thus the antipathy to Rome was in part political, in part religious and, in part, what we can only call temperamental. The England which the Tractarians came to startle was solidly and actively Protestant: the Wesleyans had not quite withdrawn themselves from the Church, and the Evangelical movement had brought the Church nearer to the old established sects, the Independents and the Baptists. Froude looking back on it all blamed the Oxford leaders for not leaving well alone. He thought of the twenties and early thirties as a golden age of good feeling and harmonious activity which they had ruined. But it is often forgotten that the Oxford Movement, in its inception, was a defensive measure against a positive danger. The Whigs had shown that in Ireland they were as ready to rearrange the dioceses as if they had been so many Government departments, even to appropriate Church funds for other than Church purposes. What if they, of their own volition or by the urging of the Radical and Irish left wings, tried their hand on the Church at home? There was a promising field for reform, and popular agitation: tithes, sinecures, pluralities. Round what could the ministers of an impoverished and discredited communion rally, if they were to continue their work, and not become, like the non-jurors, levites and chaplains, patronized where they had once ruled and dependent for their living on the tone of their sermons? There was, as we know, no real danger, and the alarm soon quieted down. But there was a danger of another, more insidious kind. Suppose the Whigs used their patronage to liberalize the Church?

One of Newman's rarest gifts was his capacity for stating the other side of the case: his Eighteen Propositions of Liberalism, as it was professed in Oxford in his young days, could have been signed by Grote, Mill, Macaulay, or Palmerston, with hardly more delay than was necessary to express their surprise at such sound doctrine coming from such an unsound quarter. What is more surprising, Huxley and the agnostics of the late nineteenth century would have proclaimed, and constantly did proclaim, their adherence with gusto. What could be more to the Late Victorian taste or more in the Late Victorian manner than Propositions 4 and 5?

(4) It is dishonest in a man to make an act of faith in what he has not had brought home to him by actual proof.

(5) It is immoral in a man to believe more than he can spontaneously receive as being congenial to his mental and moral nature.

Indeed why should he? Or indeed, how can he?

We are approaching a chasm which the modern mind cannot easily cross. Somewhere about 1860 a rift opens in the English intelligence. To us it seems the most obvious thing in the world that, in logical jargon, every judgement must be in the form: I being what I am, and the evidence being what it is, am disposed more or less strongly to think so and so. The force may be so great that I am unable to think otherwise. Today: but it may not be so tomorrow. Psychologists say that one of the characteristics of the child mind is the capacity for holding contradictory ideas simultaneously. Another, I think, and one that lasts longer, is the craving for certainty. The child loves speculation, but when his meditations have issued in a question he wants a definite answer. We do not often think of the early Victorian age as primitive. But in many ways it was. It could hold with undisturbed conviction a religious and an economic faith which were incompatible, and it wanted to be sure. Certitude came naturally to an age which still had a Sacred Book. But a Sacred Book is a precarious basis of assurance: it may always turn out to be wrong. Much Early Victorian thought was given to widening the basis, and principally, on two lines. One which runs from Carlyle and Arnold through Kingsley and Froude would make the Book co-extensive with history. The other would make it co-extensive with natural science. In Kingsley they meet and blend.

In dealing with a past age we constantly need a central man to refer to, and naturally he will not be one of its greatest men in the eyes of later generations. Kingsley is very nearly the central man of that period of swift change which sets in soon after 1845 and was consummated about twenty years later. In the main it was a period of liberation and conservatism. Kingsley was with equal sincerity and heartiness on the side of knowledge and the State, religion, and the family: and he realized, while believing in them all equally, that religion must allow for science, and the family for sex. Inevitably therefore he passed for a revolutionary, a heretic, and a propagator of impurity. When Newman wrote, in his own defence, 'I have long thought that the Protestant system leads to a lax observance of the rule of purity' the stroke went home. *Yeast* had been attacked on that very ground, and Kingsley had been reduced to calling his critic—the first Lord Coleridge— a liar. But if we put ourselves at the point of view of 1848 when the book appeared, I am not so sure that Coleridge was wrong. Kingsley was, perhaps without quite knowing it, assailing the Evangelical ascesis at its most delicate point, and not putting anything in its place. We may agree that Tom Brown is on the whole a better sort of man than Pitt Crawley. But Pitt Crawley's religion made it much easier for him to keep away from the girls.

But this was only half of him. The other half exemplifies one of the most elusive and puzzling cross currents of the mid-Victorian times. Nordicism: *Furor Teutonicus*: aristocracy: muscular Christianity. One can interpret it in many ways. Mr Sitwell might say that it was the last struggle of the fair-haired stock to maintain its ascendancy in an urbanized world which is naturally inimical to the type. The time was favourable. The triumphant *bourgeoisie* of 1830 was looking rather small in 1850: the gentry, who, in 1846, seemed to be down and out for ever, were in fact just entering on their golden age. There was a great deal of day-dreaming in it all. But the fundamental facts fitted with the dream: on the whole, with the inevitable reservations, the gentry knew that they ought to treat their underlings well, the *bourgeoisie* did not: it was becoming every year clearer that what England needed was active authority somewhere: and where could a better model be found than in the active authoritative country gentleman? Tory men and Benthamite measures was a promising combination. And in fact it worked. It is working still.

The classics of this tendency are Froude's *History* and *Westward Ho!*

> Froude thinks Kingsley a divine,
> And Kingsley goes to Froude for history;

and the passage in which Kingsley attacked Newman might indeed have been written by either of them. They had their eyes on the Jesuit invasion of Elizabeth's time which more than anything else stabilized the English attitude towards Rome. It has often been pointed out that the ordinary theatre-going public of Shakespeare's time evidently expected Catholic observances to be treated with respect. But Jesuits and their Pope neither the Elizabethan nor any other generation of Englishmen would endure. In 1850 the Oxford Movement had run its course and been re-absorbed with the main stream of religious tendency. Papal aggression drove the public into hysteria and raised a dark cloud of suspicion both against those who had left the Church and those who remained. It rested most heavily on Newman.

But when we turn to the passage itself and the sentence of Newman on which it was founded, it is difficult not to feel that in their clumsy way Kingsley and the public were right. It was a very clumsy way, certainly. But if the public, or the modern reader said, 'Never mind all that: what we want to know is, when Dr Newman or one of his pupils tells us a thing, can we believe it as we should believe it if the old-fashioned parson said it?' I am afraid the upshot of the *Apologia* and its appendices is No. And what is one to make of a man, especially of a preacher, whose every sentence must be put under a logical microscope if its full sense is to be revealed? In the end one is as sorry for Kingsley as one is for the Jesuits to whom Pascal replied. In controversy, it is important to begin by understanding the size of your opponent: and Kingsley, it is plain, had no conception, when he drew his broadsword, of the dexterity of his opponent's rapier play. It was the bowling of the village champion with a Blue at the wicket, and what did not go wide went to the boundary. Yet I think the judgement must be, if we take the controversy seriously and not as a game, that Newman is after all only operating with incomparable marksmanship from a position of invincible credulity. But it is in a flank position: he does not face his opponent. When the day ends, Newman is still there with colours flying, but the enemy is miles ahead.

Because it produced the *Apologia,* the onslaught of Kingsley keeps its place in the history of thought. Entirely forgotten is an earlier and far more skilful assault. Newman's fatal defect was want of historic learning: he had enough for Kingsley: but in the hands of Milman he was helpless. The *Essay on Development,* is, as its title declares, nothing if not historical: and of historical evidence, as of the methods of historical inquiry, it may be safely affirmed Newman knew nothing. Firmly handled, the Essay simply crumbles to pieces, and what is left—let us call it by its right name—is nothing but a compost of sophistry and superstition. Milman came too soon to be affected by the Nordic fancies of Christian Socialism: he was an Anglican of the centre, of the generation which had grown up in the glow of Evangelical enthusiasm, but had abandoned neither the learning nor the authority of the *Clerus Anglicanus*. Entirely forgotten: yet as a statement of the Anglican philosophy, insular but not parochial, Protestant but with no rejection of the common tradition of all

Western churches, soundly historic, soberly aesthetic, observing always the practical balance of the moral and mystical elements in its faith, I know nothing more wisely reasoned, or—speaking within the mind of the age—more convincing, than Milman's review of the *Essay on Development*.

THE FAITH OF THE GRANDFATHERS[1]

IN 1800 that Bishop of Rochester whom Gibbon called 'the mighty Horsley', and Wilberforce 'a dirty scoundrel', complained that in matters of religion 'the vicious ignorance' of the poor was balanced by 'the presumptuous apostasy' of the aristocracy. Eighty years later, John Bright got into hot water—a favourite and familiar element with him—by saying that the working classes cared as little for the dogmas of Christianity as the upper classes for its practice. Yet anyone could have confuted the bishop or the statesman by pointing to thousands of working men who were deeply studious of the Bible and its commentators, and scores of upper-class families whose life was a model of Christian decorum. The rejoinder, I suppose, would be that they were only thousands among millions, and scores out of hundreds. In other words, when we speak of Religion in the Victorian Age we mean, primarily, the movement of religious thought and practice in the Middle Class, among the people whose writings and conversations made opinion.

Where, then, did these people, clergy and laity, stand at the opening of the Victorian age—an age which may be reckoned from Catholic Emancipation in 1829, the Reform Act of 1832, Keble's Assize Sermon in 1833, or the New Poor Law of 1834? Now that the Victorian era has begun to rise again above the ignorant contempt of the last decade, there is a tendency to push the Dark Ages one generation farther back. Anglo-Catholics, in

---

1 *Religion in the Victorian Era,* by L. E. Elliott Binns, D.D.

particular, seem disposed to borrow the old Whig dodge, of forgetting Huskisson and Peel, and pretending that every good law and every perfect law was passed by the friends and followers of Charles Earl Grey. Anyone who is disposed to think of the pre-thirties as an age of arid prelates and boozing parsons, should study as a corrective Daniel Wilson's Introduction, dated 1829, to Wilberforce's *Practical View,* then in its fifteenth edition. Incidentally, he will make a curious discovery. Jeffrey would not have wondered where Macaulay picked up that style, if he had heard Wilson preach, and know that every Sunday the Macaulay family sat under him in Bedford Row. The short, swift sentences sound like trumpets blowing for victory:

A spirit of inquiry into the great principles of Christianity has been more and more excited. The importance of Vital Religion has been more generally felt. The distinction between the form and power of godliness has been better recognized. The idea of a purer Christianity has prevailed. The general tone and character of religion has been elevated. The details of Christian duty, the doctrine of morals, the obligation of the holy law, are all in progress. At the Universities, the higher standard of preaching, the vigilance exercised over the morals of the students, the strictness of the divinity examinations, are so many pledges of good. The pious parish priest is the guide, the comforter, the pastor of his flock. One point remains, without which all other criteria would be fallacious. It is the diffusion of personal and family piety, which denotes the abiding mercy of God with us, and prepares for every future blessing.

Including the Oxford Movement? Unquestionably, because it was only in this seed-plot of 'personal and family piety' that the Movement could have taken root and flourished. 'Our brethren of the Establishment', Hall, the great Baptist preacher, wrote, 'hold with us that without holiness none shall see the Lord.' 'I hung on the lips of Daniel Wilson,' Newman said, 'when he gave the history of Thomas Scott's life and death, and for years I used almost as a proverb what I considered to be the issue of Scott's doctrine, "Holiness before Peace".' To say, that 'the Oxford Movement derived some measure of quickening power from the Evangelical Revival' is an understatement almost amounting to a mis-statement. The power came from the moral atmosphere which the revival had created. That the atmosphere was now charged with elements for which the Revival had not allowed; with the corporate philosophy learned from Coleridge, the historic understanding imparted by Scott, is very true: in Newman's admirable phrase, they had interested the genius of their age in Catholic truth. The time was ripe for a supplementary and corrective revival: 'for a better understanding of the foundations and proportions of the Church's polity, and the nature and value of her discipline'. These are the words of Bishop Blomfield, judging the Movement in 1842, and they are both generous and exact. There is something to be said for Greek-play bishops. They could usually write English.

But the self-protective instincts of English Protestantism felt, whether rightly or not, that the Oxford Malignants—the title supplied by Napier to Arnold's article in the *Edinburgh*—were doing more than revive ideas or observances neglected since the Reformation. They were undermining the national defence against Popery, and of all the Thirty-nine Articles the only one that Englishmen at large could ever be got to take any interest in, is that which asserts that the Bishop of Rome hath no jurisdiction in this Realm of England. In 1903 a Dorset farmer was summoned for not paying his education rate. His objection to that impost was unambiguous. 'I wean't,' he said, 'pay money to set up the Pope over we for to rule we.' Of the No-Popery panic in 1850 Dr Elliott Binns writes that 'it is simply inexplicable to the present day'. The present day must be singularly dense or have a singularly short memory. That the Ecclesiastical Titles Bill in itself was as foolish as the agitation which compelled the renaming of the *Leviathan* as the *Great Eastern* may be admitted. Was the rejection of the New Prayer Book by the House of Commons a few years ago so much wiser? Behind the No-Popery uproar there was a great body of ancestral prejudice, no doubt, but also of reasoned conviction. Many wise, pious and tolerant men believed, out of Scripture, that the Pope was anti-Christ. At home they saw in Catholic Ireland the gravest menace to the stability of the Empire. Abroad, they compared the Lothians with the Campagna. Little more than thirty years ago an educated Dissenter assured me that the view commonly held by older members of his denomination was that no Roman Catholic would be saved. In 1866, Bickersteth, who died Bishop of Exeter in 1906, published an immensely successful epic on the Four Last Things, which is well worth the attention of anyone who is not satisfied to find his ancestors inexplicable and leave them so. In the last book the beauties of a regenerated earth are described. From its face rises one solitary volcano. It marks the spot where Rome had stood.

But a philosophic eye, contrasting, let us say, the year of Catholic Emancipation with the year of No Popery and the Great Exhibition, would have noticed three or four significant changes. The institutions of religion are much more vigorous: churches are fuller, services more frequent and moving, the auxiliary societies more flourishing. The tide which set in some fifty years earlier shows no signs of ebbing. On the other side, he would observe that controversy is angrier and more spiteful; that there is a new tension and distress in many thoughtful minds, and a growing indifference to the whole matter in many more. And if he could return again at the end of the century, he would find the tide running out fast. Somewhere between those years we must put the decisive secularization of English society and thought, a process the origins and stages of which it would be interesting to have traced for us. Perhaps one might put it thus. The conception of a Church transmitting a tradition and interpreting it by authority had no place in the general English mind or imagination. The faith of Protestantism in its various modes was a documentary faith, and the documents were losing their validity. When Hale White was a young student for the ministry, he and his companions were suspected of loose views, or doubts, of Scripture, and the question was tendered to them: 'Do you believe a thing because it is in the Bible or because it is true?' What the answer to this Lady-and-Tiger dilemma may be, I do not know. Neither did they. So they were expelled.

Could the documents, when analysed by the new criticism, and read in the light of the new biology and archaeology, justify the philosophy that in the course of ages had been raised on them, or developed out of them? To a Catholic the question does not present itself quite in this way, but England was Protestant. And to an ever-increasing number the answer was definitely no. They were making the discovery which Ruskin made, that the religion in which they had been brought up was simply not true. To a smaller group the answer was yes, in so far as that philosophy explains the world to me, or explains me to myself. In other words, the only alternatives open to a sincere and thoughtful mind were agnosticism, often a reverent and almost pious agnosticism, and a religion of personal acceptance. The social atmosphere was on the whole decidedly adverse to belief. 'People suppose,' Creighton said, 'that a man who takes orders must be a knave or a fool, and they know I am not a fool.' Our natural talent for compromise gave for a time a certain standing to thinkers who, like Seeley, Arnold, and Hutton, seemed to have found a possible Via Media—

Correcting 'I believe' to 'One does feel'.

One might call it by great and solemn names, 'the stream of tendency making for righteousness', or the *testimonium Spiritus Sancti*. But that was what it meant. Nothing was left of which you could say, 'It is true, because it is in the Bible.'

But if, at the same time, you are keenly aware, in Coleridge's phrase, that the Bible 'finds you', that the Hebrew prophets, the person and teaching of Christ, the experiences of St Paul do, in a very remarkable and unique way, interpret to you your own problems and those of the world, and perhaps—perhaps— indicate a solution for another age to discover, then surely it is the path both of wisdom and of duty, to hold fast to the old forms of observance and devotion, and compel them, if they can be com- pelled, to yield what once they had yielded, assurance of the saving and regenerating impulse imparted to mankind by Christ through his Church, and renewable, whether morally or mysti- cally, in the Sacraments.

I am trying to describe what I believe to be the central area of the higher religious thought in Late-Victorian England; out of which issued the movements, common to the Anglican and the

Free Churches, towards a more profound and liberal interpretation of the Scriptures, a less forensic and more philosophical reading of the Creeds, a more concrete and vigorous sense of coherence and continuity, of the personal origin and historical transmission of the Faith. On the other side, the creed and programme of its secularist thought need not to be set out anew.

Without denying that in the matter of religion some things are true and some things false, still we certainly are not in a position to determine one from the other. And, as it would be absurd to dogmatize about the weather, and say that 1860 will be a wet season or a dry season, a time of peace or war, so it is absurd for men in our present state to teach anything positively about the next world, that there is a heaven or a hell or a last judgement, or that the soul is immortal or that there is a God. It is not that you have not a right to your own opinion, as you have a right to place implicit trust in your own banker or your own physician : but undeniably such persuasions are not knowledge : they are not scientific : they cannot become public property : they are consistent with your allowing your friend to entertain the opposite opinion, and if you are tempted to be violent in the defence of your own view of the case in this matter of religion, then it is well to lay seriously to heart whether sensitiveness on the subject of your banker or your doctor, when he is handled sceptically by another, would not be taken to argue a secret misgiving in your mind about him; in spite of your confident profession, an absence of clear, unruffled certainty in his honesty or his skill. Well, then, if Religion is just one of those subjects about which we can know nothing, what can be so absurd as to spend time on it?

One does not feel disposed to say again anything that Newman has said already—had said, it will be observed, in 1859.

TEMPUS ACTUM[1]

THE more carefully one studies the years between the death of William IV and the accession of Edward VII, the more difficult it becomes to find anything to which the word Victorian can be correctly and exclusively applied. Much to which we commonly give the name, turns out on a closer acquaintance to

1 *As I Remember,* by E. E. Kellett.

be simply nineteenth century, or simply European. 'She had been brought up in one of the most exclusive establishments for young ladies, where three objects are regarded as of the highest importance. First comes French, then the piano, that she may be able to soothe and amuse her husband in his leisure hours; and, lastly, a thorough acquaintance with the principles of household economy, in its highest and most aesthetic sense, including the art of knitting purses.' Now, which is the Victorian element in that passage, the insistence on trivial accomplishments, or the contempt for trivial accomplishments? As a matter of fact, it is not Victorian at all: it is not even English. It is Gogol's account, in *Dead Souls,* of the education of a Russian lady, and I quote it from a Nonconformist periodical of 1868.

Turning over the pages, I come on this. 'If Mr Farrar has been in the habit of meeting such boys as he describes (in *Eric*), we can only say that a most kind and indulgent fate has not permitted us the same advantage. Young gentlemen who do nothing but walk about their school playgrounds with their arms round one another's necks, discussing the various responsibilities of a Christian's duty, deserve to be caged and kept for public exhibition. Boys and girls who are perpetually stopping in the middle of their play to say prayers and sing hymns are simply nauseating. And boys and girls who bristle with texts, quote long passages of Scripture, refreshing themselves at frequent intervals by reference to Dr Watts, are specimens of juvenile humanity whose society would be unbearable.' Again, one asks, which is the Victorian? Farrar and the writers of good books, or their Nonconformist trouncer, who stands by *Tom Brown* and *Alice in Wonderland*?

The truth is that much of what we call Victorianism is a picture at second-hand, a satirical picture drawn by the Victorians themselves. The word does undoubtedly mean something, but what it means has to be built up by going behind the criticism, the invective, and the caricature, and examining the originals. I once heard it suggested that the typical Victorian saying was, 'You must remember he is your uncle', and it certainly brings in one important element: patriarchal order and status in the family group. But I suspect it was heard quite as often in France or

Germany. When Bishop Wilberforce was killed, Mr Gladstone passed some hours in silent depression; then he observed, 'He was a Great Diocesan', and recovered his spirits at once. This impulse to say the right, the improving thing, is more characteristic of the Victorian temper. The gossip columns of the time are full of such pronouncements. Once a servant was sent to meet Sir Bartle Frere at the station. He asked how he was to know him. 'Look for a grey-haired gentleman helping some one.' And, of course, the Proconsul was duly found lifting an old woman's basket out of the carriage. Now there is no harm in saying that, if it is true and you really mean it. The mischief comes of saying it because it is the proper thing to say. And in the Victorian age that mischief was peculiarly rife. Why?

Imagine a large family, and therefore of necessity a well-organized family, framing its life and conversation on Scripture and the traditions of the elders: in most cases a happy family, with minds well occupied and bodies well exercised; conscious of its election, and just a little conscious, perhaps, of its social inferiority to the gentry: it is from such a corner as this that we must learn to think if we are to get the Victorian panorama true. Into such a corner Mr Kellett conducts us. The ordinary educated, evangelical household is in many ways the pivot of Victorian life. Taken as a body, these families determined reputations and decided elections. Their approval gave a composer or a writer rank as a classic. Their abstention from the polls made Disraeli Prime Minister in 1874. Their forgiveness reinstated Gladstone in 1880. They sentenced Parnell and Dilke. 'Whom they would help to a kingdom, these reign, and whom again they would, they displace. Finally, they were greatly exalted.' Over a great part of English society, especially in the ascendant Midlands and North, their way of thinking, acting, and speaking was dominant. They were often surprisingly tolerant; they accepted the infidel Morley and they had a soft place in their hearts for that imp, Lord Randolph. But, on the whole, it was safer to conform and to speak with what, from 1832 to 1885, was the accent of a ruling class, an accent to which Gladstone was born, and which Disraeli never mastered.

'I have seen', Mr Kellett writes, 'no such rapid or complete change as that which took place in the eighties and nineties. It was like one of those catastrophes which the geologist used to postulate in order to explain the alterations in the earth: sudden, immense, and, I think, irrevocable.' He is speaking particularly of the religious outlook of the generation which now took Darwin for granted, and was therefore ready to receive the Higher Criticism. 'What mattered the miracles of Elisha when the point was whether the whole thing was not a huge delusion?' In other ways, too, those decades were a time of catastrophe. The landed interest sank: the lead of the staple industries shortened: the manufacturer made way for the financier: Africa was partitioned: the Liberal Party broke up: the name of Whig was forgotten: the Family was shrinking. In those years of upheaval we can see our present-day mind coming to birth, and of all the elements in the convulsion perhaps the most potent was the transformation of religion from a public and documented system of beliefs, practices and aspirations to a provision for personal needs.

Thus Victorian thought before the catastrophe expresses itself in an idiom which has to be learnt, and Mr Kellett's memories, therefore, apart from the abundant entertainment they incidentally provide, are of real historical value. They take us back into the world of certitude and Special Providences, before the Agora had been deserted for the Waste Land of Specialism. One of his stories I can cap, and one, I think, I can correct. The wife of an Anglican dignitary, invited to open a Wesleyan sale of work, was reduced to painful and unseemly giggles by the initiatory exercise:

O Lord, Thou knowest we are about to have a little bazaar.

And surely the instruction at the head of the Ten Commandments was 'Candidates should attempt the fifth and seventh, and at least three others'. But his central theme is one which can never be emphasized too strongly—the busy, happy, humming vitality at the heart of Victorian life. And, as Mr Kellett is a scholar, the comparison, so unexpected and yet so true, comes naturally to him as he remembers it. In its many-sided curiosity and competence, its self-confidence and alertness, this Late Mid-Victorian culture is Greek. In its blend of intellectual adventure and moral conservatism, it is really Athenian. I doubt if any lines of Tennyson were more often quoted by contemporaries than these:

> Let knowledge grow from more to more,
>   But more of reverence in us dwell;
>   That mind and soul, according well,
> May make one music as before,
> But vaster.

No words could express more perfectly the Victorian ideal of perpetual expansion about a central stability. But would anyone guarantee that they are not a translation from Sophocles?

B. A. KOHNFELDT[1]

*T*HE scale on which the volumes in Messrs Duckworth's biographical series are composed requires us to take them rather as essays, somewhat in the manner practised by the *Quarterly* and *Edinburgh* reviewers a hundred years ago. Judged by this standard, Mr Beeley's brief Life must be pronounced excellent, leaving one only with the regret that he had not a larger space within which to show his gifts. The narrative is compact, and the judgements, on Disraeli and such others as cross the little stage, are framed with good sense and always delivered with good taste.

I was recently talking with an old Gladstonian whose recollections go back to the death of Palmerston and the election of 1868. 'What was it,' I asked him, 'that made your generation so profoundly distrustful of Disraeli?' His answer surprised me somewhat. 'His early Radicalism.' Memories were longer in those days, of course, when the electorate was small, newspapers dear, and tradition was propagated, very largely, by conversation within a closed and responsible circle. The most telling stroke Disraeli himself ever delivered was aimed in 1845 against the Peel of 1828, before an audience to whom Catholic Emancipation and the

1 *Disraeli*, by Harold Beeley.

wrongs of Mr Canning were still living and present recollections. But my friend was right. Disraeli had more to live down than his fantastic attire and his Jewish blood: even in 1868, he was still remembered as the man who had stood in with O'Connell and the Radicals in 1832, who had suddenly discovered the superior advantages of Lord Lyndhurst's patronage in 1835, and who was at least suspected of having purchased those advantages by surrendering his mistress to a man twice his own age. To be diabolically clever, as his books and conversation showed him to be, is not in itself the best passport to political success. To be ridiculous, and to be thought immoral to boot, is weight enough to drown a man. It was simply impossible for Peel to give him office in 1841. What place was there for this belated young Regency rip among those virtuous youths, Canning, Lincoln, Gladstone, Sidney Herbert, who would call themselves, some day, by no other name than Friends of the Late Sir Robert Peel?

'The bitterest and least sincere of Peel's adversaries.' So Morley, speaking in the Peelite tradition, characterized the man who had described Conservative Government as 'an organized hypocrisy'. A generation which has rediscovered that Protection and Free Trade are not principles but expedients, can afford to take the great controversies of the past more coolly. The bitterest?—'It is impossible for me to deny that there is too much ground for the reproaches of those who, having a second time trusted the Right Honourable Baronet, find themselves a second time deluded. I cannot but see that it has been too much his practice, when in opposition, to make use of passions with which he has not the slightest sympathy, and of prejudices which he regards with profound contempt. As soon as he is in favour a change takes place. The instruments which have done his work are flung aside. The ladder by which he has climbed is kicked down. I am forced to say that the Right Honourable Baronet acts thus habitually and on system. The natural consequences follow. All those fiercest spirits whom you hallooed on to harass us, now turn round and begin to worry you. Did you think the day of reckoning would never come?—it has come. There you sit, doing penance for the disingenuousness of years.' Bitterer words have hardly ever been

spoken in the House of Commons. But they are not Disraeli's
words; they are Macaulay's. The topic is the Maynooth Grant,
and not protection at all. But they contain the substance of all that
Disraeli ever said on those famous nights when the House rocked
and Peel sat frozen into helplessness under the icy blast of his
invective. The ladder by which Peel had climbed was the Tory
gentry; the instrument which had done his work was the Landed
Interest; and the passions with which he had no sympathy, the
prejudices which he regarded with such contempt, were the
prejudices and passions of his own party.

Peel fell, and the Gentlemen of England found themselves with
Disraeli on their hands, stabilized somewhat by his quaint and
perfect marriage and his alliance with Lord George Bentinck, but
still neither liked nor trusted. So the years passed; a scramble into
office and out again in 1852, in and out again in 1858 and 1859,
but never into power. 'For twenty-two years', Mr Beeley writes,
'he accepted the position of chief mate, creating by his patience
and loyalty a claim to the captaincy which in the end the Tories
could not decently ignore.' But by then he was sixty-four. Once,
indeed, a great chance seemed to have been put, not into his hands,
it is true, but into Derby's. Suppose Derby had consented to form
a Government in 1855, with Disraeli leading the Commons—
Disraeli, at fifty-one, with the high aspirations of Young England,
a little faded, perhaps, but not yet worn out in the endless criss-
cross of coalitions and Franchise Bills? But in 1855 the country
wanted Palmerston, as definitely as it wanted Pitt in 1756, and
Derby knew it. In 1858 came another chance, and this time it was
Disraeli who threw it away. Mr Beeley has no light to shed on
the most unaccountable error of his career. In its second year the
Derby Administration was attacked on the ground that it had
failed to preserve the peace of Europe. They had, in Lord
Malmesbury's dispatches, a complete answer. The answer was in
print. Disraeli declined to circulate it, and they were out for
another seven years.

When he became Prime Minister in 1868, Disraeli had less than
three years of office behind him, and only six to come. First and
last, Gladstone had over twenty-five. A Lord of the Treasury while

Disraeli was still wavering between Radicals and Tories, love, fashion, and epic poetry, when Gladstone last left office Disraeli was already fading into history. Peace with Honour, Cyprus, the Fleet in Besika Bay, Indian troops at Malta, the Queen an Empress among Emperors; England had rejected his Imperialism and his diplomacy alike. A Socialist came to him in his last days to expound the natural affinity of Socialism and Conservatism. 'You can never do it,' the old man warned him, 'with the Conservative Party. They would thwart you at every turn. They and their women.' But whether it was they, or their women, or Peel, or Derby, he had been thwarted. Compared with the majestic evolution of Mr Gladstone into the world-honoured figure of 1898, Disraeli's career is as strangely fragmentary as it is persistent. He got all that he wanted to get, but he did little that he meant to do. His early writings are rich in political wisdom, and richer perhaps in political suggestion. Read them, and you will soon see why, at political gatherings still, a reference to the greatest leader this great party has ever had is as sure of its round of cheers as a reference to Mr Pitt in the days of Cousin Feenix.

One day last summer, like Matthew Arnold,

> I saw the meeting of two
> Gifted women.

Somehow the conversation got on to the topic: 'Suppose the garden boy came in with the message: "there's one of the Prime Ministers at the gate, but I didn't catch his name, not rightly", which should we wish it to be?' No one wanted Gladstone. The Colonel hoped it would be Pam, having certain views on foreign policy for which he desired a more sympathetic audience than the company provided. If it were Peel, they said, I might have him to myself, and I should like nothing better than an hour alone with Peel. The men were afraid that Canning would talk them down. Johnny, we agreed, would start pouring himself out a cup of tea without noticing that anyone else was there. But the better half were unanimous for Disraeli. 'After all,' said one, 'he is the only man I could ever have married.' 'Do you know,' cooed the other, 'he once kissed me?' For one tense moment we all thought that the scene would close with slapped faces and pulled hair: but someone was inspired to quote:

Esser baciato da cotanto amante[2]

and peace was preserved.

Yes, but consider his time in office, and what he did with it. There are brilliant feats of Parliamentary strategy and tactics; in 1858, when

the whole of the Opposition benches became one great dissolving view of anarchy,

and again over the passage of the Reform Bill of 1867. But at seventy, in power at last, he was losing his political mastery. 'He that runs against time has an antagonist not subject to casualty.' In history, the Parliament of 1874-80 deserves to be known for its legislation as the Useful Parliament. But Cross did the work, and the leadership of the House slipped into the avid but inadequate hands of Northcote, while the old Jew dreamed Imperially and made love to ladies little younger than himself. Below the ashes there was still a fire. Bismarck, who could measure a man, saw that Excellenz B. A. Kohnfeldt, as the street humorists of Berlin called him, meant business, and there was not a tremor in the hand that began the never-finished portrait of Joseph Toplady Falconet.

Rosebery once had the audacity to ask Joseph Toplady what he really thought of Peel. 'He was not,' the old man said severely, 'quite a gentleman. He corresponded with Under-Secretaries direct.' It would be far more interesting to know what he really thought of Disraeli. In the index to Morley's Life, two entries stand in piquant juxtaposition:

Beaconsfield: tribute from Gladstone.
Beaconsfield: deterioration in public life due to.

What searchings of heart that tribute cost, readers of Lord Acton's letters will remember. The other, delivered to a smaller, and perhaps a more submissive, audience, was at least unambiguous:

2 'To be kissed by such a lover.' Dante: *The Inferno*.

'Democracy has not saved us from a distinct decline in the standard of public men. For all this deterioration one man and one man only is responsible—Disraeli. He is the Grand Corruptor.' Ages hence, students of our dead tongue in Lhassa or Melanesia will learn from the *Oxford Dictionary* that his name is associated especially with 'an odious system of bluster and swagger, and might against right'. But if they study the man in his career, they may think that in the essentials of virtue, in sincerity of mind and kindliness of heart, he did not fall conspicuously short, even when measured by the standard of his sainted antagonist; and, if they pursue him to his books, they will find themselves in converse, not perhaps with the most vigorous, and not the most massive, but the most trenchant and sensitive intellect that has ever applied itself to the government of England.

KATHERINE STANLEY AND JOHN RUSSELL[1]

I WAS grateful to the snowstorm of February 28th which gave me an excuse for sitting over the fire and reading *The Amberley Papers* all day. It is not a dipping book, but a complete story, with a beginning, a middle, and an end, which was perhaps less tragic than it seems. The Amberleys had had the best of life: what was to come might not have been so well. He might have come to shrink from her vitality: she might have grown tired of mothering him. But she died at thirty-two of diphtheria caught from one of her children: he followed her soon.

John Russell, Viscount Amberley, born in 1842, inherited many of his father's qualities, without that toughness which kept the old Prime Minister alive to eighty. He had the Russell shyness and courage, and all the Russell aptitude for upsetting coaches, their own or other people's. On his mother's side he was an Eliot, grave, uncompromising Protestants from the Border. But there was, in

1 *The Amberley Papers*, edited by Bertrand and Patricia Russell.

Fanny Lady Russell, much mirth behind the earnestness, and the character which emerges from her letters is that of a far livelier woman than the editors, drawing perhaps on the memories of a grandchild, would lead us to suppose. Her definition of a 'charming evening'—

not a word of gossip: many words on many high matters—

is to be treasured, and if it suggests a somewhat tense intellectual atmosphere, the impression is very happily corrected by the thumb-nail sketches of persons and incidents in other letters. Lecky in love is inimitable; Lecky on his honeymoon must be quoted:

Willy had seen the well-known long and lanky form twisting and turning and forcing its way through the streets of Lausanne some days before and we tracked him out. We were all very much taken with her. He blushes when he calls her Elizabeth: she doesn't blush when she calls him William. He has learned to carry cloaks and shawls for ladies, but has not learned to put them on. He is revising his book on the Irish leaders. She said she didn't approve of his writing so much during a wedding tour, to which he replied, 'I should grow so very tired of doing nothing.'

In Amberley himself this strain seems missing. He was, it is all too plain, a rather dull young man, and I found the tepid amorism of his school and college days very trying. 'Personally insignificant' was the judgement of an American acquaintance, who relates how, Amberley having got out of his depth at an intellectual party, his wife drove over the next day and insisted on having the conversation repeated with herself in charge. But Katherine Stanley, Lady Amberley, is a superbly vigorous and independent creature: a true grand-daughter of the adorable Maria Josepha Holroyd, one of whose letters to Gibbon opens with

Mon âme est sans culottes

and is signed

Citoyen! Ton égale Maria

and who, it seems strange to relate, was still living, as Grandmama Stanley, and as much interested in the world as ever, when Kate's journal opens. 'It is dreadful', the grand-daughter writes, 'not to be willing to die at 91', and she warns her brother not to talk to the old lady about Jowett because it would excite her too much.

But, in and about 1860, Jowett was one of the most exciting men alive, and it was difficult not to talk about him. Kate was not allowed to keep his essays on the Pauline Epistles, but she had made extracts which she circulated among her friends. Her brother Lyulph was at Balliol, quite under the spell; and in so disputatious a family as the Stanleys every heresy was sure of a hearing and a defender.

> The candid incline to surmise of late
> That the Christian faith proves false, I find;
> For our Essays-and-Reviews debate
> Begins to tell on the public mind,
>   And Colenso's words have weight.

The grand assault had opened; the air was as thick with contending banners as the streets of a county town on polling day; and exactly where Jowett, with his little hands on his little knees, stood, or rather sat, in these matters, was one of the questions on which the public mind would have been most glad to have satisfaction.

Indeed, in the early sixties, when John Russell and Kate Stanley were growing up, there was not much beside theology to think or talk about. These were the halcyon years of politics, when a Queen's Speech might contain no promise, or threat, of any legislation whatever, and, simply for want of something to do, the Leader of the Opposition once had to ask for a return on the subject of Noxious Vapours. The educated classes were using their leisure from State affairs to reconsider their attitude to God, Duty, and Immortality. No generation, I suppose, has ever been more thoroughly penetrated with religious ideas, more attentive to religious observances and obligations than that which was young and active from 1830 to 1850, the generation of Mr Gladstone. Ten years later, though the mood or temper was much the same, the traditional beliefs which gave it body were disappearing under the dissolvent action of science. It is one of those epochs when the gap between the generations seems wider than usual. Jowett spoke of Clough's *Dipsychus* as 'a kind of English Faust'. 'But I expect,' he added, 'it is intolerable to anyone over fifty.' One knows so well the sort of book which is intolerable to people over fifty; aggressive, irreverent, hard to make up one's mind about. Shall we try to keep up, like Grandmama Stanley, or shall we drop behind? Shall we mask our fears with a bland superior smile, or frankly take to scolding? We have only to look about us to see how many attitudes are possible when old-established opinions are under fierce revision, and in these papers we may observe their counterparts sixty and seventy years ago.

There are the young people growing slowly, earnestly, and sometimes painfully, out of the convictions into which they had been born or educated. There are the believers in Youth as Such, with Mr Carlyle to tell them that belief in Youth is the greatest mistake of the day. There are those whose charter is Mill on Liberty, those to whom Darwin is a new revelation, and those to whom Comte is the final revelation, as it might be Marx now. Some, particularly the girls, are resolved not to allow themselves to be unsettled; some, particularly the boys, are bent on unsettling everybody. They read heavily, they think hard, they correspond persistently. Victoria Russell is engaged to Mr Villiers. The proposal took place while they were buying a tea-kettle in Soho. He is going to be a curate. Mother is much shocked by Frank Newman's *Phases of Faith*. But she is strongly in favour of the Utilization of Sewage. I want a really good book on Physiology to teach the village girls. From what I took in of Dr Temple's essay on the nature of Christ's mission, it seemed to me to be excessively fantastic. Jowett has heard of monkeys praying every morning with folded hands on the seashore to the rising sun. Would it be possible to omit the reference to the Trinity from the marriage service? Arthur Stanley says no, but he has an explanation which seems to make it all right. It is very bad taste to call us a 'godless couple'.

Let them be shocked and pained if it must be so. We will ask them to confess, if not at once by the force of reason, then later by the force of facts, that the fruits of the Spirit may be granted to those who have flung off the ancient creeds like chaff, and stand upright, pure, and noble, without their aid!

Does this strike anyone as silly or sentimental or superficial prattle? It interests me so much that I don't care if it does. In the correspondence and journals here preserved we catch a large and important section of English society, the enlightened Whig aristocracy, under the guidance of its intellectual advisers, Grotes, Mills, Carlyles, Buckles, Huxleys, Leckys, Morleys, and the rest, in the very act of making up its mind, a process usually as elusive to the observation of those without as the freezing of the sea. And the Whig aristocracy is still the statelier half of the ruling class, its splendour little dimmed, its indifference to the Court, and its dislike of Royal manners, as lofty as ever. When the frozen stream of political energy is released by the death of Palmerston in 1865, its younger, and more adventurous, members naturally go Radical, and Radicals, who like a lord almost as much as Americans do, are very glad to have them. Grote had high views of Amberley's future. But it seems doubtful whether, if he had lived, he could ever have been more than an earnest writer and occasional speaker. For Lady Amberley, at least in Mrs Grote's affectionate fancy, the brilliant destiny seemed to be reserved of being to the new Radical, or perhaps Republican party, what Mrs Grote herself, with immensely fewer advantages, had been to the Philosophic Radicals forty years before; making of Chesham Place a new Holland House for reformers, agnostics, positivists, and trade unionists; and a forum for the issues of the coming time, Women's Suffrage and education, birth control (over which poor Amberley, with true Russell inopportunism, burnt his fingers badly), the organization of labour, and public health. She had all her lines thrown out, and Kate, it is clear, was a strategist of no mean capacity. But I question whether even she could have overcome that dissidence between the social exclusiveness of the Whigs and the intellectual arrogance of the Radicals, the consequences of which are with us to this day.

The bridge-like quality of the sixties, where Mill and Grote, ageing and revered, wait ready to pass on to Morley and Leslie Stephen the torch they had lighted from Bentham and Malthus and another Mill, stands out more forcibly in these pages than in any other record I can recall. I must own that there are rather many of them; Amberley was a long-winded fellow, and some of the details relating to the arrival of the little Russells struck me as being, in our grandmothers' use of the word, unnecessary. Yet I am not sure that this very abundance of trifling intimacies was not required to make the picture complete, giving it a kind of aerial perspective in which the Nottingham election, and the South Devon election, and the Hyde Park riots, and the Fenian descent on Chester, appear as they really did appear to people who were all the time thinking quite as much about their babies, and their nurses, their mothers-in-law, and their gardens, and who took their position at the head of affairs and society for granted. Certainly that Devon election, fought chiefly on an innocent question put by Amberley to the doctors at a private meeting of the Dialectical Society, was a foul business, the chief difference between reformed Plymouth and unreformed Eatanswill being that Eatanswill was, by comparison, decent, and Pott and Slurk, by comparison, fair. But the lovely, suggested background of those closing years of aristocratic rule goes to one's heart—the deep peace of the West, of the woods and meadowlands of Rodborough, which Lord John had bought in 1855 to save himself from despair, in his hour of political extinction, 'when other men would have shot or drowned themselves', and when, as the editors point out, Greville was acidly commenting on his unruffled self-complacency. The long rides of the lovers, too, over the Cotswolds or by the Severn, remind us that the Ruling Class is still the Riding Class. Life goes by at a horse's pace, and the figure of greatest dignity in the whole book, I think, is Lady Strangford's coachman, who was so little acquainted with the East End of the town that he returned from the Mansion House to Regent Street by way of Islington. The most vehement is the little Princess Beatrice, who, asked to choose her birthday present, spoke out bold and plain:

The head of Bismarck on a charger.

But the heroine, no question, is Katherine Stanley.

MAITLAND[1]

$\mathcal{S}$OME years ago it was proposed in Cambridge to issue, with due comment and annotation, Maitland's Collected Papers. 'The Syndics of the University Press did not, however, see their way to a new edition on these lines, and another project was suggested. This was to select certain of the papers likely to be most useful to students in law, history, and politics, to edit them and publish them in one volume. . . The editors venture to think that they (the students to wit) have here all that is of practical use to them; and they have put them upon their inquiry as to where they can find the rest.' In other words, if you want to get marks, you will read Maitland's *Selected Essays*: if you want to waste your time, you will read Maitland.

I cannot think this attitude accords either with the function of an Academic Press, or the respect which a university ought to show to the memory of a master. Granted that some of Maitland's work, now forty years old and more, is 'touched with obsolescence', no passage of time can dull the genius which vibrates in every paragraph he wrote. As Bentley said of Bishop Pearson, 'the very dust of his writings is gold'. But it does not follow that the dust heap is the proper place for them: and such an edition as Professor Hazeltine and his colleagues first proposed would be not only a noble memorial to a scholar of incomparable inspiration, but a history of the progress of the studies in which he was a master. I hope it will still be undertaken. After all, Syndics are not like other publishers. They can always cover their losses by bringing out a Prayer Book in red, white and blue, or a new Bible with camera studies of Behemoth and the Pygarg.

Someone may ask what right I have to speak, and I fully admit that much of Maitland's work is above my head. But it so happens, thanks to a good teacher, that on one subject which he treats of I am not altogether uninformed, and never shall I forget the evening when I took down *Domesday and Beyond*; and read, and read, till the owl in the fir tree began audibly to wonder why the

1 *Selected Essays:* F. W. Maitland.

lamp was still burning; the little breezes that stray down the dene from Wansdyke turned chilly; and the dawn came. I have just opened it again, and if I do not shut it quickly, this paper will not get written today, or tomorrow: no great loss, perhaps, were it not that I have one or two things to say about Maitland which I believe to be worth saying, and, at this particular time, needful to be said. In passing, I invite the Syndics (and Delegates) to look at the last paragraph of that book—and blush, if Delegates (and Syndics) can.

But before I go any farther, I should like to define to myself the character of Maitland's mind: and the first thing that strikes me is its companionable quality. He is never telling you: he is always, most genially and modestly, arguing, never so far ahead that you cannot follow, with a deliberate invitation at every turn to tell him something of your own, and an unforced humour playing over the whole debate. Our intelligent Press periodically sets as a competition: Whom would you most like to take a country walk with? The entrants must be much less modest or self-conscious than I am, because, of their two favourites, I doubt if Dr Johnson would have thought me worth talking to, and I am sure I should cut but a poor figure after ten miles' unmitigated Socrates. I should without hesitation choose Maitland, not so much for anything he might have to say, as to observe his gift of entering into 'the business, projects, and current notions of right and wrong' in other ages; and his power of 'making the thoughts of our forefathers, their common thought of common things, thinkable' once more.

By taking the history of law and institutions for his province, Maitland planted himself in the position where his genius for thinking other men's thoughts could operate with most effect. Law, as he understood it, is fundamentally a system of common thought about common things: the things and the thoughts, the actual doings, for example, of a villein or a trade unionist, and the reflections thereon of Bracton or the judges in the Taff Vale Case, reacting on each other, and modifying each other into a pattern of such shifting intricacy that the most comprehensive vision will not take in the whole pattern, and the keenest eye will misread some of the incidents. They say now that his theory of the defensive origin of the boroughs is 'wrong', or, what is worse, 'imaginative'; and I am reminded of the warning in my school edition of *Julius Caesar*: 'Do not talk about Shakespeare's mistakes: they are probably your own.' But very likely his critics are right. As he says himself, 'the new truth generally turns out to be but a quarter truth, and yet one which must modify the whole tale': and in a world so perplexingly contrived as this is, a frank and joyous acknowledgement of ignorance is the only way of wisdom. 'We must go into the twilight, not haphazard, but of set purpose, and knowing well what we are doing'; and, when all the other classes have been abolished, there will remain the distinction between those who know that all hypotheses, interpretations, creeds, programmes, and what not, are questions, and those who suppose them to be answers.

At no time did this truth need to be more frequently or emphatically restated than today, and I am glad that the Syndics have allowed the editors to print the essay on the Body Politic, written apparently for a dining club, in which Maitland delivered his profession of faith, and his warning against the facile acceptance of systems. So entirely does he seem to belong to our own world, that it is with surprise one remembers that he was born in 1850, and was nine years old when Macaulay died. But he grew up in a time when systems were the mode, when Auguste Comte had turned the history of the world into a commodious suburban residence—theology on the ground floor, metaphysics above, and the clear light of positivism shining in at the top-floor windows: and young Darwinians, going far beyond anything that Darwin would have countenanced, were tracing the development of society with as much assurance as if they had been there all the time: just as, with not less confidence, their grandfathers had propounded the Scheme of Redemption or the Wage Fund Theory, and their grandchildren now propound the materialistic conception of history.

So long as historic systems are in vogue, so long that warning voice will be needed. How plausible they all are, each in its day! How much they explain that was dark before! How easy they

make things! How much trouble they take off our minds! Very
well: then answer this question on any system you like. In the
nineteenth century, the European nations borrowed from us the
criminal jury which they had abandoned, and we had kept. Why
had we kept it? Try it on Positivist or Evolutionary or Materialistic
principles, and see where you get to. Maitland's answer comes
with a flash which makes even his editors blink. 'Tut tut', their
footnote says, 'this is a built-up area, and he went through at
thirty-one.' I do not know whether the answer is right, but I
quote it as the best example in this volume of the soar and swoop
which marks Maitland out as the most inspiring of all historical
companions. He made of history the Gay Science. To account for
a detail of legal history, he lifts to the third century, and watches
the Manichean heresies streaming for a thousand years along the
Mediterranean coasts to Languedoc. But we were an Orthodox
Island. Therefore the Church had no need here to enforce the
inquisitorial process proper for the detection of heresy. Therefore
we kept the jury. And the next moment he is on the ground,
searching the year-books for such grains of truth as that a use in
law is not a *usus* but an *opus,* and that medieval lawyers sometimes liked to show their superior education by spelling it *oeps*.

The swiftness with which Maitland moves over the field, and
the microscopic observation which never seems to weary on the
longest flight, together make him, it seems to me, an almost
faultless example of what Bacon called the *intellectus purus et
aequus,*[2] 'never distracted by study of particulars and never lost in
contemplation of the entirety', the *intellectus simul capax et
penetrans,*[3] over which the idols of the Cave and the Theatre have
no power. This volume has set me reading again his *Canon Law
in the Church of England,* which of all his works I have always
most admired for the logical dexterity with which the argument
is sustained, and most enjoyed for the dainty and respectful malice
with which he plants his barbs in the great Bishop. Here he is
fencing with an equal, exchanging secret professional jokes
between the bouts. In his *Constitutional History* and the chapter

---

2 'Intelligence unadulterated and unbiased'

3 'Intelligence at once comprehensive and penetrating'

on the Elizabethan Settlement of Religion, which some may regard as his masterpiece, he is speaking tutorially. Elsewhere, and for the most part, he is the explorer reporting his travels as he goes. It is unfortunate for his fame—which he would not in the least have minded—and, what is more to be regretted, for his influence, that so much of his work was involved in technical matters. But I doubt if he left a page, I am sure he did not leave an essay, which has not startled some fit reader, not so much by the range or the precision, as the appropriateness of the learning revealed—the right detail coming exactly at the right moment— or made him glow with that sense of confident and delighted energy which only the highest genius can communicate. And they who have received it will impart it as they can.

Goethe (or someone else) said of (Winckelmann, I think, but I see that this quotation is not going to be so impressive as I intended): 'Man lernt nichts, aber man wird etwas.' One learns nothing, but one becomes something. I certainly do not think it any more desirable that we should all become historians than that we should all take courses in dentistry, plumbing, and cookery. But it is, I believe, of some concern to the Commonwealth that we should all brush our teeth, wash with reasonable regularity, and eat well-chosen food well prepared, and in the same sense and degree a right historical attitude seems to me of special consequence in an age when a wrong attitude is being so diligently inculcated for partisan ends. The materialistic conception of history is no more than the sectarian perversion of the great and truly philosophic doctrine—first adumbrated by the French and English historians of the eighteenth century—that all historic forces are interconnected. But historic forces have their seat in human observation, reflection, and purpose: 'in business, projects, and common notions of right and wrong': they act through the minds of men, they reveal themselves in—at the last analysis they are—their 'common thought of common things'. There they must be looked for, and there only will they be found. And of Maitland we can say that, in his chosen field, no man ever searched more diligently, and no man ever saw so much.

TOPSY[1]

*T*HESE two volumes, supplementary to the sixteen issued over twenty years ago, complete the publication of William Morris's writings. Except Ruskin, no writer of the Victorian age has been so loyally served and so carefully laid up for posterity. Whether the time has come for a decisive valuation of his work is, perhaps, to be doubted. More than sixty years ago a sharp-eyed critic, writing of the *Germ* and the earliest pre-Raphaelite poetry, had occasion to speak also of Morris's *Jason*. He quoted the lines:

> Meanwhile, all men spoke hotly of the quest,
> And healths they drank to many an honoured man
> Until the moon sank and the stars waxed wan,
> And from the east faint yellow light outshone,
> O'er the Greek sea, so many years agone:

and added the comment: 'No one can deny the magic. But it will not last. At least, in well-regulated minds it will not.' Possibly I have an ill-regulated mind, but I own that criticism of this kind, which calls up the image of a governess bidding her young charges not to be fanciful, irritates me. I find it simpler, and really more illuminating, to say that *The Earthly Paradise* appeared in four volumes between 1868 and 1870, and that it had been reprinted seven times before I read it, all one July, in an enchantment such as no other book has ever cast on me, except, when I was a child, the *Morte Darthur*, and, later, the *Odyssey*. First of April poetry, if you like, as Bagehot said of Shakespeare's Sonnets. Still, April comes but once a year, and why should we neglect its blessings while they are with us, or despise them when October is drawing near?

> Christ guard the Hollow Land,
> All the sweet spring-tide!

The criticism of poetry is not my trade, but this much, I think, one can say with confidence, that, like Byron, Morris is a poet

[1] *William Morris: Artist, Writer, Socialist*, by May Morris.

who must be taken in bulk or left alone; and that what is admirable and memorable in his work is not the intensity, but the diffusion of his poetic mood. His poetry, and to the verse one must add the prose romances, is a complete world, and, 'taken as a whole', Earle Welby said with much truth in *The Victorian Romantics,* 'it is the sanest and most happily ordered world that any modern English writer has made'. At the centre of this world was a personality by no means simple, but in all its intricacies definite, and in all its activities bounded by that 'wiry outline' which Blake demanded of the draughtsman. It is amusing to compare the demeanour of Ruskin and Morris before a Royal Commission. Ruskin having said his piece, is all at sea; Morris knows what he is about from the first question to the last. In his Introductory Essay, very entertaining and very mischievous, 'On Morris as I knew him', Mr Shaw speaks of the 'extraordinary integrity of his taste.' Welby, quoting

> Many scarlet bricks there were
> In its walls, and old grey stone,
> Over which ripe apples shone
> At the right time of the year,

adds: 'if ever a single word gave us a poet's attitude to the world, the epithet "right" gives us the attitude of Morris'. 'What is irresistible in Morris', a German critic has written, 'is the tangible character of his productions. Here culture takes a visible form and becomes reality; one sound mind working for the comfort of other sound minds.' The same masterful and genial precision appears in the technical papers which his daughter and pupil has reprinted. You may think he is wrong. But there is never any doubt what he is after.

Definiteness implies limitation; and in art, in literature, in public affairs, there was much that Morris could not grasp, and much that he could not see. Neither he nor his master, Ruskin, really apprehended, or even faced, the problem of machinery, though, when it came his way, Ruskin could declaim as magnificently on steam engines as on clouds or waterfalls. Speaking of

Bellamy's *Looking Backward,* Morris warns his readers that every Utopia must be regarded as the expression of the writer's temperament, and very shrewdly he observes, of reformers of another brand, that they aimed at turning the working classes into middle classes. Perhaps he was thinking of Fawcett, who seriously looked forward to a time, not far distant, when they would all be so respectable that we should have to import negroes and Chinese to do the dirty work. But if we said that Morris wanted to turn them all into Old English Yeomen, should we be so far from the mark? In Russian galleries, I am told, pictures are now labelled:

> Taste of the financial *bourgeoisie,*
> Taste of the Imperialist *rentier,*

and so forth; and not so long ago a Russian architect, observing our objection to Ribbon Development, acutely diagnosed it as a symptom of *Bourgeois* Ideology. He was quite right. If we must use ugly, and rather silly, words, our common ideology is *bourgeois.*

But one of the most serviceable clues to the tangled pattern of Victorian history is the steady resistance of the country-minded *bourgeoisie,* commonly called gentry, and entrenched in the Universities and the Church, to the encroachments of the town-minded *bourgeoisie.* Wisely, Miss Morris places in the forefront of her introduction a chapter on country life. Morris belonged by birth to the rural stock, the stock of Kingsley and Hughes. He was educated nominally at Marlborough, and really in Savernake and on the Marlborough Downs. He went up to Oxford when Oxford and the English country scene were at the peak of their pride and beauty. He might very well have become a parson, a fighting, reforming, cricket-playing parson of the type of Sydney Godolphin Osborne. He chose to be a designer. But he must have an abbey to design in. He built himself one country house among the Kentish orchards. He took another in the heart of that lovely and still lonely land where the spire of Lechlade looks up to the tower of Highworth; of the ridge under Faringdon he writes: 'the hills are low but well designed', a proper compliment from one artist to another. Mr Shaw tells us that no Fabian ever bothered about *News from Nowhere*. Indeed, it has little connexion with any topic that is ever likely to figure on the agenda of the L.C.C., and it bears, all too plainly for utilitarian approval, the rubric:

Taste of the Squire.

Of the world of Morris one can say, as the man from the Lincolnshire wolds said of wooded Nottinghamshire: 'a very good country for gentlemen', and the prospect, one fears, of having to catch its own dinner and eating it in tapestried chambers by candle-light, drinking claret, and listening to poetry, would almost certainly give the proletariat what the proletariat would call the Ump. But Morris was an inventor, a creative craftsman, of astonishing vigour and fertility, rejoicing in the work of his hands, and, by a natural and generous illusion, he believed that if others could be brought to rejoice also, their work would be as good as his. 'There is a tendency deeply implanted in our best impulses, by which men are moved to make others partners of whatever good they themselves possess, to abnegate all superiority and disclose the very secret spring of it.' I do not think Morris would have rejected this as a statement of his own philosophy of life and society, though it did appear in that Tory organ the *Quarterly Review,* and the writer was Regius Professor of Divinity in the *bourgeois* University of Oxford.

It is to be borne in mind, too, that Morris was not only an extremely capable man; like Owen and Ruskin before him, he was, in his vocation, a highly successful one. Owen in our day would have commanded any salary he liked to name as managing director of a combine. Ruskin, having given away one fortune, made another by a raid on the book market of the kind which is called unscrupulous by those who have not thought of it first. Morris was barely thirty when he was commissioned to decorate St James's Palace, and on Tennyson's death he was sounded for the Laureateship, having in the interim been up for fighting the police. He descended into the arena from an assured and lofty place in both literature and art. A descent it was. Torn from his moorings in the great political storm of 1878, the harbour in which he found refuge was not the true Tiber:

longa procul longis via dividit invia terris.[2]

With the gift of prophecy denied to contemporaries, the historian can now see that the way led through Westminster and not through Trafalgar Square: not through revolution but through the orderly development of the legislation of the seventies. But it was not the way for a positive, combative man, whose imagination, for all his positiveness, was filled with the vision of guilds and common halls, and white villages by unpolluted streams.

Morris in his day was a great power in the world of art and poetry. Now that his day has passed into history, how are we to think of him? A great man, doubtless, and as he is drawn for us in these volumes, less by design than by instinctive sympathy and skill, by incident and comment and reminiscence, a man of uncommon breadth and stature: deep-hearted, laborious, fiery. History needed such a man to close the long succession of those who fought, all through the years of industrialism triumphant, to keep some place for art and beauty in a world grown blear and grey. Before he was born the battle was set between the disciples of Coleridge and the disciples of Bentham. When he was a school-boy Chartist halls were singing Massey's 'Hymn to Labour', with its refrain:

Come, let us worship Beauty.

Young England and the Christian Socialists added their voices to the chorus, and it was from a famous chapter of *The Stones of Venice* that Morris drew his first inspiration. We may be sorry— it is impossible not to be sorry—that he did not remain above and aloof from party strife, content to be the poet and prophet of English Socialism, without involving himself in the Athanasian complexities of its fissiparous federations. But he could no more have taken up the mantle of Ruskin than he could have followed Millais or Leighton down the primrose path to a baronetcy or the House of Lords. His Socialism was the final synthesis of all his

---

[2] 'Far, through far lands, and a long untraced track between.'

Virgil: *Aeneid* iii

purposes: and without it his character would have been unfinished, his life incomplete.

THOMAS HARDY[1]

I

THE movement of English poetry in the century which followed the appearance of *Lyrical Ballads* may be considered as a succession of three phases, each imparting something of its own character to the next. The poets of the mid-century, Tennyson, Browning, and Arnold, were not less affected by the first Romantic group than, in their turn, Rossetti, Swinburne, and Morris were affected by their own immediate predecessors. But, as the century approached its end, the springs of poetry began to sink. A frailer and more deliberate art prevailed.

The poetry of the Nineties has a colour and a personality as unmistakable as the sonnet sequences of the last Elizabethan decade. Like them, it was much influenced by foreign examples: it aimed less at originality than accomplishment: and, like them, it could be very tedious. The accomplishment is undeniable. Almost at random—but the quality of this verse is so uniform that it is not easy to go wrong—I take some lines of John Davidson's:

> As I came up from Dymchurch Wall,
> I saw above the Downs' low crest
> The crimson brands of sunset fall,
> Flicker and fade from out the west.
>
> Night sank: like flakes of silver fire
> The stars in one great shower came down;
> Shrill blew the wind; and shrill the wire
> Rang out from Hythe to Romney town.
>
> The darkly shining salt sea drops
> Streamed as the waves clashed on the shore;
> The beach, with all its organ stops
> Pealing again, prolonged the roar.

[1] First published as an introduction to *Selected Poems of Thomas Hardy* (Macmillan, 1940).

That is the authentic singing voice of the Nineties. But what is this?

> Passing heaths, and the House of Long Sieging,
>   I neared the thin steeple
> That tops the fair fane of Poore's olden
>   Episcopal see;
>
> And still sadly onward I followed
>   That Highway the Icen,
> Which trails its pale riband down Wessex
>   By lynchet and lea.
>
> Along through the Stour-bordered Forum,
>   Where Legions had wayfared,
> And where the slow river-face glasses
>   Its green canopy.

This ancient music? This gnarled and wintry phrasing?

II

Poetry, let us never forget, is not an affair of the great names only, of the one or two immortal lights. They are only those who have done well what scores of others were doing somehow.

> And one a foreground black with stones and slags,
>   Beyond, a line of heights, and higher
> All barr'd with long white cloud the scornful crags,
>   And highest, snow and fire.

Who, we may ask, but Tennyson could have written so in the Thirties? Well, when the spirit was upon her, Felicia Hemans could:

> And then a glorious mountain-chain uprose,
>   Height above spiry height!
> A soaring solitude of woods and snows,
>   All steep'd in golden light!

And is this not Shelley?

> She kept her own immortal form,
> And I came as the breezes soft and warm
> Of which she breathed. I was a sigh
> Within her heart, alternately
> Coming and going.

No; it is John Banim.

In judging the poets, it is well, therefore, now and then, to take a view of the levels from which they rose, even though the exploration may lead us into those barren places of uninspired cravings and unaccomplished labours which memory rejects and history disdains to record. Never, I suppose, was there such an abundance of versifying as in Victorian England: and when we have turned over a hundred volumes bearing names which prolong a vicarious existence in the handbooks, there remains, untold, forgotten, the vast bulk of occasional verse, fugitive verse: anecdotal, descriptive, reflective, hortatory, hymnodic; never collected, never reprinted; magazine poetry, good enough to serve its weekly or monthly turn, and then fade briskly into oblivion: a casual exercise, an agreeable accomplishment, a serious relaxation. Much of Hardy's verse rises no higher.

> The smile on your mouth was the deadest thing
> Alive enough to have strength to die;
> And a grin of bitterness swept thereby
> Like an ominous bird a-wing. . .
>
> Since then, keen lessons that love deceives,
> And wrings with wrong, have shaped to me
> Your face, and the God-curst sun, and a tree,
> And a pond edged with grayish leaves.

So Hardy wrote in 1867. So any young man who had read Browning and Swinburne might have written. It is a copy of verses, nothing more. His work was in the other harmony of prose.

III

Yet to this task, or relaxation, of verse, he brought one gift of rare and curious power. He was steeped in the ancient music of rural England, of song and dance, of psalm and hymn; of village choir and of harvest-home: and the example of William Barnes was there to show him what could be made of it. The musical inspiration, for example, of the verses quoted above is manifest.

When sycamore leaves wer a-spreadèn
          Green-ruddy in hedges,
Bezide the red dowst o' the ridges,
          A-dried at Woak Hill;

I pack'd up my traps, all a-sheenèn
          Wi' long years o' handlèn,
On dowsty red wheels ov a waggon,
          To ride at Woak Hill.

Barnes, as Hardy said, was a spontaneous singer, but a deliberate
artist, 'warbling his woodnotes with a watchful eye on the
predetermined score', a scholar in many tongues. Hardy's cast of
mind was different: his natural powers greater. But without the
practice of Barnes before him, it may be doubted whether he
would ever have achieved that singular purity of rhythm, that
mingling of simplicity and subtlety, which, audible even in his
earliest verses, grew with the years, and with increasing mastery
of the instrument, into the lyrical triumps of *The Dynasts,* where
every measure, from the most trivial to the most august, is
handled with equal aptness and assurance, while again and again
the ear can catch, as so often in our native song, echoes of a still
older music, borne on the hymns and carols of the Middle Ages,
from Provence and far beyond.

We come; and learn as Time's disordered—deaf sands run
That Castlereagh's diplomacy has—wiled, waxed, won.

Companho, non posc mudar qu'eu—nom esfrei
De nouvellas qu'ai auzidas—e que vei.[2]

In the wild October night-time, when the wind raved round the land,
And the Back-sea met the Front-sea, and our doors were blocked with
  sand.

Γλαῦχ᾽, ὅρα, βαθὺς γὰρ ἤδη κύμασιν ταράσσεται
πόντος, ἀμφὶ δ᾽ ἄκρα Γυρέων ὀρθὸν ἵσταται νέφος.[3]

---

[2] 'My friend, I cannot help feeling apprehensive at the news I have heard and seen.'

[3] 'Look Glaucus, already the deep sea heaves with billows, and the dark cloud stands up round the peaks of Gyrae.'   Archilochus

IV

But in the other matter of diction as opposed to music, we may lament that Hardy found no such exemplar. It is doing his fame no service to deny that, of all our writers, he can be, at times, the flattest and the most ungainly. And then, perhaps, we think of Egdon and the Vale of the Great Dairies, and remember, what so many have felt, that craving for Hardy which comes over the exile. The secret, what makes him, some may think, our greatest master in the old pastoral tradition, is the loving precision, the almost professional exactitude with which he specifies those sights —and still more those sounds—of the English landscape, of which we are most conscious when they are not there to be heard or seen. I use the word with intent: because never for long, in reading Hardy, can we escape the accent of a young architect drawing up a specification, and sometimes all the Muses hold their ears in pain. Here he succeeded to no tradition: he was imperfectly educated, cramped by a book-language which he could not shake himself free of, and writing it with a stilted and self-conscious clumsiness. Much of his dialogue is composed in this strained falsetto: much of his narrative savours of the local reporter bent on doing justice to his theme. His errors are not those of an untrained taste, feeling towards a style which will not come. They are errors of practice in following unfortunate models —prose translations of the classics, for example—without perceiving their imperfection. And what is true of his style may be repeated of his craftsmanship more generally: he never overcame his youthful addiction to melodrama: he never mastered the difference between strength and violence. Without the accompanying music of the pastoral theme, would *Tess* be tolerable?

V

With the publication of *Jude the Obscure* in 1895 Hardy, except for the slight fancy of *The Well-Beloved,* closed his career as a writer of prose fiction. His first volume of poems—many of them written at earlier dates—appeared three years later, when he was a man of fifty-eight. For the rest of his life, he wrote verse abundantly: the collected edition of his poems contains nearly a thousand pieces.

Hardy is as much a poet of place as Wordsworth or Cowper: but more than either of them he is a poet of local incident: of anecdote, tragic, humorous, or cynical: of such drama as an earlier age might have cast into a ballad, or his own time into a novelette. But he is a poet of reflection also, of reflection on memory: and, taken together, his verses are, to a greater degree than is perhaps common with poets, a commentary, an old man's commentary on a life that had not been happy, nor, till its later years, much honoured with discipleship or public renown. Here he turns inward: and there is trouble in his eyes.

As a young man, bred on the border-line between rustic commerce and rustic gentility, he had been socially sensitive: susceptible to the charm of grace and breeding, and a little vexed with himself, perhaps, that he was so. He wished to raise himself: he thought of taking Orders, and the Rev. Thomas Hardy exchanging pulpits with the Rev. Leslie Stephen is one of the more piquant might-have-beens of history. Mill and Huxley barred the way: he abode by his profession of architect, and discharged his ambitions in a boyish work, *The Poor Man and the Lady,* reminiscent, it would seem, at once of *Alton Locke* and *Maud.* His profession took him to Saint Juliot. And what happened there was what has happened and will happen from one generation to another. He fell in love with a girl with whom he was not intellectually in key. There was no open catastrophe: only the fire sank rapidly into vacancy and chill. But by some mysterious power Hardy was able to preserve, encysted as it were, this early passion in all its primal intensity; and so it came about that some of the most poignant love-poems in our language were written by an old man out of his memories of forty years before.

VI

A common accident befalling an uncommon man will work out its consequences in uncommon ways. And that Hardy was a man of endowments bestowed on few, *The Dynasts* exists to prove. Not long ago, I had occasion to read it aloud all through, and at the end I thought how far back must one go to find its match in power and beauty? I paused for a while on *The Ring and the Book*: rather longer on *Don Juan,* and came to rest on the Third and Fourth Cantos of *Childe Harold*. Then other peaks showed through the mist: *Hyperion* and *Prometheus*; the closing chorus of *Hellas*; *Manfred* and *Cain*. It is from these heights, among the Titans who walk

> With Death and Morning on the silver horns,

that this poet, I thought, must be viewed and judged.

Titanism, or the spirit of revolt against an order felt to be unjust, first appears, I suppose, in English literature with Milton's Satan. Its strong resurgence in the early years of the last century is in large measure a political phenomenon, because an order which meant Sidmouth and Eldon at home, and the Holy Alliance abroad, was made to be revolted from. With the new Liberalism setting in victoriously after 1830, there was less call for an attitude which always edges perilously towards a mixture of self-pity and swelled head. But towards the middle of the century we see the spirit re-emerging quietly, gravely, ironically: defying nobody, denouncing nothing, simply disapproving.

> We, in some unknown Power's employ,
> Move on a rigorous line;
> Can neither, when we will, enjoy,
> Nor, when we will, resign.

Both in thought and manner that is not very far removed from Hardy, though it was written when he was a child of nine. And this of the same year is nearer still:

> Eat, drink and play, and think that this is bliss:
> There is no heaven but this;
>   There is no hell,
> Save earth, which serves the purpose doubly well,
>   Seeing it visits still
> With equallest apportionment of ill
> Both good and bad alike, and brings to one same dust
>   The unjust and the just.

That is how young men—Arnold's pupils—were thinking in 1849, ten years before the great storm broke.

If I were asked what the total effect of Darwin, Mill, Huxley, and Herbert Spencer upon their age had been, I should answer somehow thus. They made it difficult, almost to impossibility, for their younger contemporaries to retain the notion of a transcendent, governing Providence. They forced the imagination of their time into a monistic habit of thought, of which *The Dynasts* is the great, and solitary, artistic record. To those who pass that way, the various devices with which believers of another sort reconcile Providence with Evil, or with Pain, will almost necessarily seem servile or sophistical. For them, there is nothing to reconcile: because to them, inherent in It, in the essence and operation of It, abides

> the intolerable antilogy
> Of making figments feel.

The injustice of uncompensated pain, the darkening of our hours of happiness by the thought that they, too, are passing towards Nothing, round these two themes Pessimism revolves in a closed circle. Men of an abundant, active temperament will not often think of them: men absorbed in some intellectual pursuit have little time to think of them. But for the meditative man there is no escape, and no consolation, except perhaps in constraining his temper to such an indifference as the ancient philosophies, Stoic and Epicurean, inculcated. And who can be sure that this equanimity will be proof against all shocks, from without, or from within? Against pain, frustration, disappointment, wrong?

VII

Hardy's pessimism is primarily that of the disappointed man, who cannot find the serenity which naturally attends on satisfaction and achievement, and feels himself ill-adjusted to an ill-adjusted world. It is the vast projection of an inner discord, untuning the music of the spheres. And as we follow his work forward from his early pastoral time we become aware that his growing preoccupation with one mode of this ill-adjustment, the disharmony of the Human Pair, is an artistic danger: that if he cannot keep it at the tragic height of *The Return,* it will slide into propaganda.

> The gods approve
> The depth and not the tumult of the soul:

and, as we go on, this tumult seems to be growing louder; there is a shrillness in the voice that pronounces doom, a helpless magnification of the personal discord: and we may feel that unless the Titan returns to his native peak, he will merit the graceless jibe about the Village Atheist brooding over the Village Idiot.

To his native peak? Rather to his native vale.

'The choice', he wrote of *The Dynasts,* 'of such a subject was mainly due to three accidents of locality. It chanced that the writer was familiar with a part of England that lay within hail of the watering-place in which King George the Third had his favourite residence during the war with the first Napoleon, and where he was visited by ministers and others who bore the weight of English affairs on their more or less competent shoulders at that stressful time. Secondly, this district being also near the coast which had echoed with rumours of invasion in their intensest form while the descent threatened, was formerly animated by memories and traditions of the desperate military preparations for that contingency. Thirdly, the same countryside happened to be the birthplace of Nelson's flag captain at Trafalgar.'

Thus it was from incidents of place that he conceived the inspiration of his drama. In place, and music, was his strength. As in Attic tragedy, however far the tale may range, still it is fixed to a few familiar points: here at Colonus the blind and exiled king found rest: here on the Areopagus the ways of God to man were justified: and the war-worn seamen in the camp at Troy think of Sunium, as, by the side of his dying Commander, the Flag Captain thinks

Thoughts all confused, my lord:—their needs on deck,
Your own sad state, and your unrivalled past;
Mixed up with flashes of old things afar—
Old childish things at home, down Wessex way,
In the snug village under Blackdon Hill
Where I was born. The tumbling stream, the garden,
The placid look of the grey dial there,
Marking unconsciously this bloody hour,
And the red apples on my father's trees,
Just now full ripe.

VIII

But the theme, whatever its starting point, gave him something which his own unaided imagination could not provide. What Wordsworth said of Goethe's poetry is true of Hardy's tragedy: it is not inevitable enough. It is not in the nature of things that Tess and Jude should come to their disastrous ends. They are led there by a series of prepared accidents for which their creator cannot convince us that the Immanent Will, and not Thomas Hardy, is responsible. If he is to persuade us that things happen so, he must, like the Greek tragedians, take a story where they did happen so, a real story, such as the Woe of Thebes and the Curse of Atreus were to those who saw them enacted on the stage.

The task, in fact, which Hardy set himself was to create a form in which the busy variety of Shakespearean History should harmonize with the austere and epic progress of an Aeschylean trilogy—its two or three actors, its well-spaced incidents, its long deliverances, its choric comment. 'Readers will readily discern,' he said himself, 'that *The Dynasts* is intended simply for mental performance and not for the stage,' and certainly he has left nothing undone to assist the reader's imagination, to keep it always at the right distance from the scene, and the scene always in focus. Here the professional exactitude of which I have spoken comes to his aid.

From high aloft, in the same July weather, and facing east, the vision swoops over the ocean and its coast-lines, from Cork Harbour on the extreme left, to Mondego Bay, Portugal, on the extreme right. Land's

End and the Scilly Isles, Ushant and Cape Finisterre, are projecting features along the middle distance of the picture, and the English Channel recedes endwise as a tapering avenue near the centre.

DUMB SHOW

Four groups of moth-like transport ships are discovered silently skimming this wide liquid plain. The first group, to the right, is just vanishing behind Cape Mondego to enter Mondego Bay; the second, in the midst, has come out from Plymouth Sound, and is preparing to stand down Channel; the third is clearing St Helen's point for the same course; and the fourth, much farther up Channel, is obviously to follow on considerably in the rear of the two preceding. A south-east wind is blowing strong, and, according to the part of their course reached, they either sail direct with the wind on their larboard quarter, or labour forward by tacking in zigzags.

And he employs the same precision to bring forth 'the unapparent', to penetrate through the 'insistent substance', the atomies by which the drama must be enacted, to 'the thing signified', the immeasurable, impersonal Thing which sustains it.

SPIRIT OF THE PITIES

It is a moment when the steadiest pulse
Thuds pit-a-pat. The crisis shapes and nears
For Wellington as for his counter-chief.

SPIRIT OF THE PITIES

The hour is shaking him, unshakeable
As he may seem!

SPIRIT OF THE YEARS

Knows't not at this stale time
That shaken and unshaken are alike
But demonstrations from the Back of Things?
Must I again reveal It as It hauls
The halyards of the world?

A transparency as in earlier scenes again pervades the spectacle, and the ubiquitous urging of the Immanent Will become visualized. The web connecting all the apparently separate shapes includes WELLINGTON in its tissue with the rest, and shows him, like them, as acting while discovering his intention to act. By the lurid light the faces of every row, square, group, and column of men, French and English, wear the expression of people in a dream.

SPIRIT OF THE PITIES (*tremulously*)

Yea, sire; I see.
Disquiet me, pray, no more!

The strange light passes, and the embattled hosts on the field seem to move independently as usual.

The result is that nowhere are we conscious of any unreality, or any hollow place. The whole piece, apparent and unapparent, is compact, coherent, and convincing. Given the initial surrender of the imagination which every work of art requires, this, we feel, in the world here displayed, is how things must happen.

IX

And what is this world? It is the same as that of the Tramp Woman, and the ill-motherings of Pydel Vale—perhaps Hardy's most tragic ballad—and a hundred personal pieces. It is a world of almost unimaginable contrasts, not reducible, yet, to any satisfying synthesis: and of these the greatest, the most insistent, the most oppressive, is the disproportion between the effort of the individual, his aspirations and intentions, his capacity for good or evil, joy or pain, and the silent impersonality of that Universe out of which he is mysteriously projected into a short consciousness, by which for a brief while he is sustained, and into which he is again and for ever absorbed. But Hardy has in many places expressly disclaimed both the pretentions of a philosopher and the name of pessimist. 'My alleged pessimism', he wrote in the preface to *Late Lyrics and Earlier,* 'is in truth only "questionings" in the exploration of reality, and is the first step towards the soul's betterment, and the body's also.' Not indeed that even from this betterment much is to be hoped: only 'that pain to all upon the earth, tongued or dumb, shall be kept down to a minimum by loving-kindness, operating through scientific knowledge, and actuated by the modicum of free-will conjecturally possessed by organic life when the mighty necessitating forces—unconscious or other—that have "the balancing of the clouds" happen to be in equilibrium, which may or may not be often'. His pessimism, in other words, is not to be read as despair, but as a resigned waiting on events which he will never see, and which very likely will never come to pass: especially on one event, transcending and transforming all the others, which he contemplates with wistful speculation: on the emergence of consciousness, or loving-kind-ness—a favourite word—in the necessitating forces themselves.

X

I have spoken of Hardy's lyrics as a commentary on his own life, a commentary redeemed from egoism by its obvious and intense sincerity, and rarely, if ever, sounding that note of self-pity which is so persistent in much Victorian poetry. But among them there is a group, *In Tenebris,* written about 1895, which seems to me to be an interpretation of the commentary, and to place Hardy, more exactly than anything else he has left, in relation to his contemporaries, and to the movement of poetic thought in his time.

It opens with a slow movement in a minor key.

'Percussus sum sicut foenum, et aruit cor meum.'[4] Ps. ci.

> Wintertime nighs;
> But my bereavement-pain
> It cannot bring again:
> Twice no one dies.

> Flower-petals flee;
> But, since it once hath been,
> No more that severing scene
> Can harrow me.

> Birds faint in dread:
> I shall not lose old strength
> In the lone frost's black length:
> Strength long since fled!

---

[4] 'I am cut down like the grass, and my heart is dried up.'

> Leaves freeze to dun;
> But friends can not turn cold
> This season as of old
>   For him with none.
>
> Tempests may scath;
> But love can not make smart
> Again this year his heart
>   Who no heart hath.
>
> Black is night's cope;
> But death will not appal
> One who, past doubtings all,
>   Waits in unhope.

Note here the simplicity of the metrical structure, the perfect carrying-through of the stated theme; contrasted with this, the awkwardness in places of the diction, the obstinate choice—as it seems, for careless it is not—of the lifeless word

> No more that severing scene
> Can *harrow* me:

and the quality of the vision disclosed in the line

> In the lone frost's *black* length.

With the gift, so widely diffused in the Victorian age, the power of bringing word and image together in one movement of the mind, Hardy was not abundantly endowed. Now and then his observation flowers into a sudden and exquisite perception as in the magnificent epithet

> O the opal and the sapphire of that *wandering* western sea.

But for the most part his landscape is thought out, and must be thought again by the reader before the reader sees it, as he does not need to think when Tennyson, for example, takes up the poetic brush. 'The lone frost's black length' is not a direct picture: it is, for all its brevity, a composition, and will hardly, perhaps, convey its full meaning till it has recalled the vivid blackness of hedge and covert seen against the snow.

In the second movement Hardy shifts, with a satirical intent which the metre at once discloses, to the high-spirited recitation-couplets of popular poetry.

'Considerabam ad dexteram, et videbam; et non erat qui cognosceret me . . . Non est qui requirat animam meam.'[5]   Ps. cxli.

When the clouds' swoln bosoms echo back the shouts of the many and
    strong
That things are all as they best may be, save a few to be right ere long,
And my eyes have not the vision in them to discern what to these is
    so clear,
The blot seems straightway in me alone; one better he were not here.

The stout upstanders say, All's well with us: ruers have nought to rue!
And what the potent say so oft, can it fail to be somewhat true?
Breezily go they, breezily come; their dust smokes around their career,
Till I think I am one born out of due time, who has no calling here.

Their dawns bring lusty joys, it seems; their eves exultance sweet;
Our times are blessed times, they cry: Life shapes it as is most meet,
And nothing is much the matter; there are many smiles to a tear;
Then what is the matter is I, I say. Why should such an one be
    here? . . .

Let him to whose ears the low-voiced Best seems stilled by the clash of
    the First,
Who holds that if way to the Better there be, it exacts a full look at
    the Worst,
Who feels that delight is a delicate growth cramped by crookedness,
    custom, and fear,
Get him up and be gone as one shaped awry; he disturbs the order here.

So much for Robert Browning, and Rabbi Ben Ezra, and all who never doubt that clouds will break!

Near the end of his life he chose that line,

Who holds that if way to the Better there be, it exacts a full look at
    the Worst,

as the watchword of his 'questionings': and perhaps the line before it hints at the secret of his private trouble. It does not matter: a child's sorrow over a dead bird can be as keen as a man's over a

---

[5] 'I looked on my right hand and saw; and there was none to recognize me. . . There is none to care for my life.'

broken life, and remembered as long. The trouble was there, and it was not to be put by. Like his age, Hardy was growing tired: tired of compromise and conventions: of customs and conformities: but only in passive revolt. Still, now and then a note sounds, surely recalling an older voice, and the rebel of an earlier age. For three hundred years, as I have said elsewhere, what may be called our poetic attitude to the world was in the main Spenserian, and to Spenser, Donne, in his intellectualism and his rejection of the romantic lure, is the obvious antithesis. But not more obvious than Hardy. How Hardy might have written had he been born an Elizabethan, it is amusing to conjecture, if impossible to say. But how Donne might have written if he had been a younger contemporary of Meredith it is easier at least to guess.

> Yes; we'll wed, my little fay,
> And you shall write you mine,
> And in a villa chastely gray
> We'll house, and sleep, and dine.
> But those night-screened, divine,
> Stolen trysts of heretofore,
> We of choice ecstasies and fine
> Shall know no more.

> The formal faced cohue
> Will then no more upbraid
> With smiting smiles and whisperings two
> Who have thrown less loves in shade.
> We shall no more evade
> The searching light of the sun,
> Our game of passion will be played,
> Our dreaming done.

But what to an Elizabethan could only be a turbulence of the spirit, to be atoned for at the right time by a passionate repentance, was to a Victorian, to a man living under the new cosmogony disclosed by science, no turbulence but a profound questioning and one that went down to the very roots of life, the springs of destiny. It is always the same contrast, but this time in its most intimate, haunting form: the vast power of Nature to create, and the impoverished, strained, conventional material which our

social discipline has made for Nature to work on. It was the riddle
of his day: not to be solved, only to be felt: only to be endured:
in rare bright hours perhaps to be forgotten, and to be remembered
the more keenly for that brief oblivion.

'Heu mihi, quia incolatus meus prolongatus est! Habitavi cum
habitantibus Cedar; multum incola fuit anima mea.'[6]   Ps. cxix.

There have been times when I well might have passed and the ending
    have come—
Points in my path when the dark might have stolen on me, artless,
    unrueing—
Ere I had learnt that the world was a welter of futile doing:
Such had been times when I well might have passed, and the ending
    have come!

Say, on the noon when the half-sunny hours told that April was nigh,
And I upgathered and cast forth the snow from the crocus-border,
Fashioned and furbished the soil into a summer-seeming order,
Glowing in gladsome faith that I quickened the year thereby.

Or on that loneliest of eves when afar and benighted we stood,
She who upheld me and I, in the midmost of Egdon together,
Confident I in her watching and ward through the blackening heather,
Deeming her matchless in might and with measureless scope endued.

Or on that winter-wild night when, reclined by the chimney-nook
    quoin,
Slowly a drowse overgat me, the smallest and feeblest of folk there,
Weak from my baptism of pain; when at times and anon I awoke
    there—
Heard of a world wheeling on, with no listing or longing to join.

Even then! while unweeting that vision could vex or that knowledge
    could numb,
That sweets to the mouth in the belly are bitter, and tart, and
    untoward,
Then, on some dim-coloured scene should my briefly raised curtain
    have lowered,

6 'Alas that my stay is prolonged! I have lived with them that live in Cedar;
my soul has been long away from home.'

Then might the Voice that is law have said 'Cease!' and the ending
have come.

But it does not come.

XI

Hardy was of no school and he created none. From the great
procession of nineteenth-century poetry he stands aloof, a lonely
figure, always observant, not ready of speech; rooted in his native
soil, and responsive to every passing warmth, or bitterness, in the
air; shrinking and stubborn, compassionate and austere. Here we
shall not find the romantic gusto of Meredith or Browning, or the
classic graces of Arnold and Tennyson; or the joyous energy with
which William Morris created his happily ordered world. Often
in reading Hardy, especially in reading the muted blank verse of
The Dynasts, I have recalled the words in which he describes the
Christmas mummers of his childhood, and 'the curiously hypno-
tizing impressiveness of their automatic style, that of persons who
spoke by no will of their own'. At the end, it is to the simplicity,
the unpretentious integrity, of Hardy's verse that those who have
once caught the note find themselves returning. His poetry is all
of a piece, the utterance, often harsh, often casual, of a mind that
knows itself, that is content with no derived philosophy, seeing
things as it must see them and speaking about them as it must
speak. His style has not the natural grandeur of Wordsworth, to
name the poet with whom his meditative habit of mind most
closely associates him. Rather, its characterizing note is a certain
impersonal dignity, such as we may still often find, in company
with a surface clumsiness of manner and a tongue-tied difficulty
of speech, in men of Hardy's country and Hardy's stock.

The wind bloweth where it listeth, and the spirit of the age may
choose to speak, now in the accent of a rebel prince, as it did
when Byron filled Europe with his voice, and now in the tone of
an ageing man watching the fire die down, and thinking of old
tunes, old memories: moments remembered at railway stations
and lodging-houses; sunsets at the end of London streets, water
coming over the weir, the rain on the downs. But what we hear is

the voice of an age, of a generation carried beyond sight of its old landmarks, and gazing doubtfully down an illimitable vista, of cosmic changes endlessly proceeding, and ephemeral suffering endlessly to be renewed. Twilight was coming on: an evening chill was in the air.

Of that chill, that twilight, and all its memories of noontide gone, Hardy is the poet. But more is needed of a poet than that he should say acceptably what his own generation is most ready to hear, though that, doubtless, is needed too, if his voice is to be heard; and among the accomplished versifiers of his later time Hardy was listened to with respect rather than acclaim, and with little of such regard as incites to imitation. Nor is it enough that a poet should record for future ages the life and landscape of his day, as Shakespeare has preserved the shearing feasts of Cotswold, or Mistral the Provençal scene, unless like them he has the art to make the record a thing of poetic price itself. Besides this, what the world asks of its poets and what it remembers them by, is a certain mastery, as we may say, of the meaning of their time, and a certain power to bring this meaning—thought, and feeling about thought, and reflection upon feeling—home to other ages.

The volcanic inroads made by science and invention upon the ancient fields of life and belief in Europe were, with us, for a long time masked, and partly concealed, by the tenacity with which we clung to our traditional institutions, the vigour with which we defended them from imminent, inevitable change; the attachment they inspired. We misread the Victorian age if we do not apprehend how deep, how intimate, and how sincere were the feelings that gathered round, and sustained, its customary life, its religion, and its domestic order. But a time will always come when custom, no longer needed as a defence against precipitate innovation, becomes a burden and an impediment. The adjustment is no longer instinctive but deliberate, and, being deliberate, brings with it a sense of uneasiness, of weariness, of resentment. And of all this Hardy is the poet too. This is what the Late Victorian age meant, this is what it stands for in the history of the English mind. Here we see with what presuppositions men of a good intelligence thought, what themes engaged their minds and

stirred their sympathies, by what canons they judged of things:
the pressure of custom, the breaking up of custom, the anxious
view into a world where custom had dissolved: the craving, no
longer for certitude of mind—that dream has gone—but for
serenity of soul, not sovereign over circumstance, but at least in
harmony with itself. And there we may leave the poet, as the
darkness gathers about him and his world, wistfully speculating
on an alliance, by means of 'the interfusing effect of poetry',
between 'religion, which must be retained unless the world is to
perish', and 'complete rationality', without which the world will
also perish, and, for the last time, circling home to the place
from which he had come, to the prayers, the music, and the very
stones of the village church.

THE NEW CORTEGIANO

I RECENTLY picked up a tale in one of our more trivial
magazines. There was nothing in the story: a benighted
motorist receiving hospitality from an old gentleman in a decayed
house. But my eye was caught by one sentence. The host said:

'I wish the place was in better trim';

and the narrator comments:

In better trim! Who but he could have said it?

Well, I might have said it myself. I had never realized before
what picturesque old johnnies those of us who have passed the
years of discretion must seem to those who have not yet reached
them, or how much innocent pleasure we can give by saying our
pieces right.

While I was indulging, not without complacency, the mood
thus indicated, the library sent me Mr Compton Mackenzie's
Literature in My Time. I read it with great and increasing interest
as I found that, starting from different points and pursuing
different paths, we had arrived at the same end. Mr Mackenzie
and I are of an age: he is more concerned with the proceedings of
literature, I am interested in the movement of thought which they

disclose. But we are both in the throes of the same nightmare. The culture which the nineteenth century received and we supposed it would transmit is over and done with. We are left carrying the baby, and the baby is dead.

'Montaigne is the first French writer whom a gentleman would be ashamed not to have read.' That sentence of Hallam's has always seemed to me to place our nineteenth-century culture with perfect aptness. It was still the culture of the Renaissance. We had added, for historic reasons, certain moral and political requirements of our own. But in all essentials, Hallam's gentleman, like Macaulay's naval officer, 'a man versed in the theory and practice of his calling, and steeled against all the dangers of battle and tempest, yet of cultivated mind and polished manners' was still the Cortegiano. And the Cortegiano is no longer required.

I approach the question from another side and I try to call up the picture of Bagehot and George Grote as Tired Business Men. Some years ago an international memorandum on Tariffs, of English authorship, was sent about the Continent for signature. It covered much the same ground as the Merchants' Petition of 1820, and while I deplored, I could not help sharing, the amused contempt with which foreign business men regarded it. I have always thought that one of the most remarkable achievements of our early nineteenth-century thought was the assimilation of the new science of economics into the general body of culture, as a topic within the common framework of reference. The Petition of 1820 was a theorem in economic philosophy. The Memorandum of 1924 was just the talk of bread-winners in the 9.15. To Grote or Bagehot it would have seemed incredible that such flimsy, uninformed, ill-reasoned stuff should ever be put forward as the considered view of the commercial community of England. I do not suppose the average business man of 1820 was really more familiar with Adam Smith than the average squire with Montaigne. But if they were not in the stream, they were on the bank, they knew the stream was there. That stream seems to have plunged into a gulf.

It may reappear, as ancient culture re-emerged at the Renaissance, or the Middle Ages in the eighteenth century, and,

inasmuch as modern life moves in quicker tempo, the world may
not have so long to wait. The recapture of medieval feeling by
the Romantics was like the reopening of a channel long dammed
by a convulsion of the past. In the mid-nineteenth century, the
educated man had a clear run back to his own origins, to Homer
and the Parthenon along one line, to Rome or Palestine along
another, by way of Kemble to his Germanic cradle, by way of
Max Müller to those misty heights inhabited by the virtuous
Aryans, who seemed to bear so signal a resemblance to Rugby
boys preparing for New Zealand. His education, his religion, the
sight of his fields if he was a countryman, of his streets if he was a
townsman, all impressed upon his mind the antiquity and
continuity of his civilization, while the social order at home, the
balance of land and industry, the counterchange of urban and
rural ideas, preserved and emphasized its unity. I was thinking,
while I read Mr Mackenzie's book, how a writer, as competent
and serious, would have treated Literature in My Time in 1884.
Half the book at least would have been concerned with history,
theology, economics, public affairs: we should read of the sensation provoked by *Vestiges of Creation,* of the impact of Mansell
on an angry world and of John Mill's response. To Mr Mackenzie
literature means novels, poetry, and Mr Santayana. Whatever
hopes we may nurse of the continuity of our culture into the
future, its unity is shattered.

Whether that continuity is really ended, whether 'Plato, and
Dante, and Shakespeare' are, as Mr James Stephens thinks, really
finished, whether it is not that we are too nervous to face them,
or whether after all we are not simply passing through one of
those recurrent phases of spring-cleaning when the second-rate,
the less important, the rubbish are sorted out for the back passage,
the spare room and the bonfire—ἄδηλον παντὶ πλὴν ἤ τῷ θεῷ.[1] But
that unity of culture is socially desirable, that it is of the very
greatest importance that there should be a common framework
of reference by which men of all avocations can make their ideas
known to each other, will not, I imagine, be denied by anyone.
And to judge by certain symptoms that occasionally come to one's

---

[1] 'unclear to all except to God'

notice, I am afraid we must go down very deep to build it up again. Macaulay was much incensed to find that a young peer of intellectual tastes had never read *Don Sebastian*: he put it down to Puseyism, whereas, really, it was a case of spring-cleaning. What would Macaulay have said if he had known that some day in his own University, 'serious and professed students of English literature' would never have heard of the Flood, would not recognize a sonnet when they saw one, would not know what *encroachment* meant till they had looked it up in the dictionary and would then complain of it as a 'hard word'? Yet, from Mr I. A. Richards's *Practical Criticism* it would appear that so it is. I once saw a little Yorkshireman emerging, flushed and resentful, from a Committee where he had been badgered, and muttering as he went 'Beasts at Ephesus, beasts at Ephesus'. I thought it was a *trait de mœurs* worth relating at a dinner-party. But it fell very flat. What beasts? Why Ephesus?

A common vocabulary is not so difficult to create. Broadcasting and crosswords coming together have already greatly enlarged our *copia verborum*. In the last few years I have noticed that villagers now use without self-consciousness many words which twenty years ago, if they had known them in print, they would never have uttered. They may still get them wrong: an old railway porter the other day reminded me that in the eye of the law the Bank of England was a Private Interview. But that will soon be mended, and I can foresee, though I cannot quite define, the consequences that must follow when we have learnt, like the Latins, all of us to speak with the whole of our language, and to speak it without shyness or resentment. In a scuffle over tickets in a Milan tram I discovered the Italian for 'Now then, none of that'. 'Basta, basta', it ran, 'no fatte quì delle polemmiche'. Broadcasting, too, might restore our sensitiveness to speech-rhythms and so make good, in part at least, the harm we have sustained by the decline in church-going. The Church of England service is a great literary function, and it would be difficult to assess the atmospheric effect on our culture of such diction and such cadences reiterated to audiences, necessarily, if unconsciously, in a mood of special receptiveness, from one generation to another.

This increased command of language seems to me, in making up the account, to be the most positive advantage with which we have to reckon. Against it, I set the failure of the common stock of reference and allusion. In *Fiction and the Reading Public,* Mrs Leavis insists, with justice, on the strongly literary character of the self-made culture of the Victorian working classes. The earnest young workman—Cooper in real life, Alton Locke in fiction—really gave himself a classical education not different in essence from the curriculum of Oxford and Cambridge. He read the great books—Milton, Locke, Adam Smith, Gibbon—and as they were written in an unfamiliar idiom he read them attentively, sentence by sentence, with dictionary and notebook, as his more fortunate contemporaries, if of like inclinations, might have read Thucydides and Tacitus. The writings and addresses of that famous and, to my taste, very disagreeable, rhetorician, W. J. Fox, are the result and the proof. They assume that 'Plato, and Dante, and Shakespeare', or at least the range of ideas which those names stand for, really mattered to the lower middle classes or the respectable working man. And the audience thought so, or pretended they thought so, too.

Was it pretence? Did Northcliffe, Pearson, and Newnes only call a bluff which had really ceased to take anybody in?; not altogether. My belief, from what I have read and what I remember, is that there was, in the mid-nineteenth century, certainly to the eighties and even into the nineties, a far more widely diffused interest in the culture-bearers and their doings than we have known before or since. I cannot find it in the eighteenth century: Johnson was something of a national figure, 'Oddity, they call him', but no one else. From the fifties onward, I can trace a growing pride—such as I imagine an Athenian must have felt in the possession of Sophocles—in having such men among us. And this pride, or interest, went a long way down in society. I was standing on a railway platform one day in the summer of 1896 when a man, certainly not of the aesthetic class (I guessed him to be a Gravesend pilot), opened his paper and exclaimed to a friend, 'Millais is dead.'

There was about the mid-Victorian culture, in the after-glow of which Mr Mackenzie and I grew up, a certain unitary quality, of doing, thinking and appreciating, which will be found, I believe, to be the note of all great and characteristic cultures. One can, of course, see the dangers ahead of a universal competence and a universal connoisseurship. The Victorian culture escaped them, but at a cost which we are still paying. It did not run down into a universal amateurishness. But it was doubly fractured: vertically, into professionalism, laterally, along its weakest stratum into—let us adopt the later word and call it high-brow and low-brow. The warning note was struck by the P.R.B. The artists of the forties, Landseer, Mulready, the cartoonists of the Houses of Parliament, meant to make, and were accepted as making, a universal appeal. When the dust of the fifties has settled down, we find the artists out for different game. Whether the pictures on Mr Millbank's walls were better or worse than those which a generation later his successors were meekly ordering from Rossetti and Burne-Jones is not now the question. But there is no doubt that even to see a Burne-Jones requires some special training, while everyone, from that standing authority on art, Henry Marquess of Lansdowne, to the Academy porter, could get the point of Mulready's 'Wedding Gown'.

But art, as a certain exhibition has so ignominiously demonstrated, is not our business in the world. *Excudent ali!*[2] The break-up of the mid-Victorian reading and writing unity was a far more serious matter. A certain failure of absorptive capacity is perceptible in the sixties: in a private library formed about that time, for example, one is fairly certain to find Grote and Milman, and quite certain not to find Gardiner. The sphere of interest is contracting: it had room for the new biology—Darwin and Huxley naturally struck home on a nation still preoccupied about its religion and always fond of natural history. But the new physics made little appeal; Faraday, who died in 1867, had long been an object of popular regard; Hallam's gentleman would have been ashamed not to know, in general terms, what he, or Lyell, had done and what they stood for. Clerk Maxwell was beyond the scope of the gentleman's ideas.

2 'Others may mould [the bronze].'   Virgil, Aeneid VI

One example, because it lies in the way of my own studies, has always struck me forcibly. Our national habits, the excellence of our communications and the small area within which we have to live, early combined to create a type of literature which still has a very great diffusion, the literature of the road. One of the rules of composition is that it should contain a modicum of instruction in antiquities, architecture, local history and so forth. I have constantly observed that the information thus agreeably imparted represents the state of knowledge in about 1850. I can trace Kemble and Wright everywhere—usually in fragments of long-exploded theories. Isaac Taylor and, within a narrowing circle, Seebohm were still capable of being absorbed; Maitland and Haverfield were not; and it would be safe to guess that Taylor had more purchasers in one county than the Place Name Society has subscribers in all England.

It is not, or not altogether, I think, that Liberal Curiosity is extinct, that Hallam's gentleman has failed out of the land. The interest, for example, in anything which Sir James Jeans or Sir Arthur Eddington writes is rather like the old excitement over Huxley. But curiosity has undoubtedly turned away from what was, from what always had been, its most obvious food, the art, the literature, the memorials of the past. Looking back, I think it did not so much turn of its own accord, as it was frightened off. Mr Mackenzie speaks of 'making things difficult for machine man' as an ideal which we should all pursue. I most heartily agree. Only, if he is scared away, he will not know whether you are being difficult or not. If, as the newest culture tells us in verse of strange construction, 'the pianola replaces Sappho's barbitos', surely the right thing is to see that machine man gets good tunes on the pianola, not to take the barbitos and beat the poor fellow about the head with it, as the late Victorians of all degrees were only too prompt to do.

This vertical comminution of a universal culture into separate provinces, each of which is nobody else's business, was no doubt assisted by the development of modern studies at the newer public schools, and the gradual conversion of the Universities— through the development of competitive examination for the

Indian and Home Civil Services—from *studia generalia* into professional training courses. They resisted stubbornly, and by their resistance did protract the survival of the unitary culture. One of the characters in *Sinister Street* speaks of 'the spirit, filtered down through modern conditions, from Elizabethan England. Take a man connected with the legislative class, give him at least enough taste not to be ashamed of poetry, and enough energy not to be ashamed of football, and there you are.' To poetry add history, theology, scholarship and the like, and you have, I think, the corresponding man of the fifties. And when we go back to that mid-Victorian time we find, I think, that the culture thus defined was not only less constricted in quality but more widely diffused. Brassey, the contractor, was, in his way, a man of that type: so was Armstrong the engineer: so pre-eminently was Bagehot the country banker. Indeed, anyone can verify the facts for himself by taking down a volume of the *Athenaeum* at random, for any year between 1850 and 1880, observing the range of interests it serves, and then reflecting that the *Athenaeum* yielded its fortunate proprietor an income of over £7,000 a year. For the general movement of English thought in the mid-Victorian period, and somewhat later, it is the prime and indispensable document and I sometimes wonder whether hereafter the *Listener* will not serve the same purpose, whether a unitary middle-brow culture is not coming into existence again, to gather up once more the specialisms into which Victorian culture split.

But when I try to forecast the content and animating drive of the next culture, I am at a stand. At times I feel that our troubles are only the rush and fret of a stream at a stickle and that there may be clear deep ranges close ahead: the golden freshness of the fifties was won by the grimness and lucidity, the set teeth and open eyes with which the early Victorians fought down their own fears. At other times, I feel that precedents are useless, that the moral continuity of Western history has been broken at last. Society in the mid-nineteenth century was still primitive Indo-Germanic society with some slight speeding up of cart-wheels and looms, and it thought of itself, for the most part, less as a departure than as a consummation. The fundamental conceptions of the West—

Lords and Commons, Patriarch and Family, Farmer and Craftsman, Combat and Chastity—still persisted. What is becoming of
them, I do not know. What will come out of them in the next
age, I cannot guess. But, to follow one line of reflection only, I
doubt very much whether there can be any continuity between a
civilization based on automatic child-bearing and a civilization
based on regulated child-bearing. The detachment of sex from its
primeval framework of social union and domestic authority, has
in my own time produced consequences so observable that I can
set no end to the consequences it may still produce. Among them,
perhaps, is the solution of the problem over which Mr Mackenzie
and I are distressing ourselves.

This is going rather deep. More immediately, I seem to be aware
of a shortening of the span of attention, an increased susceptibility
to distraction, which as it proceeds must tend to make all responses
shallower and less memorable. Miss Sitwell has somewhere
compared the old rhythm of life to the clop-clop of a horse's hoofs;
of the new, to the *brrr* of motor traffic. I am clear at least that,
like books, events had a much longer life even forty years ago
than they have now: they sank in, they were absorbed into
tradition, whereas now they seem to bound off into oblivion like
pebbles thrown on to a frozen stream. One could still see tradition
being made in the ancient way, by the recital and collation of
precedents, the loss of the *Victoria,* for instance, bringing up the
loss of the *Captain* and the *Birkenhead,* just as culture was made
by the acceptance and inculcation of the standard books, pictures,
music, and even journeys.

One cannot hold the newspapers to blame because they could
hardly have helped themselves. It is no doubt unfortunate that
capital should be committed to the enterprise of keeping the
public mind in the easily fluttered, easily satisfied state of
barbarism or childhood. But when once a race has lost the conception of Liberal Curiosity it is lost to civilization, and whether it
succumbs to the boosters of the press or the terrorists of the higher
culture makes no matter. Of the two, the terrorists seem to me to
be the worse enemies of civilization. A true, a sound, a social
culture must be middle-brow, the high-brow elements serving as

exploratory antennae, to discover and capture new ideas for the middle-brow mass to assimilate. The better it is fed, the freer, and more various its diet, the less likely it is to get poisoned or lose strength. The mid-Victorian culture was essentially middle-brow: in judgement it was not selective, in creation it was not masterly. But it did lay hold: it furnished a very large class—broadly, the ten-pound householders and their leaders—with a common stock of philosophy and a medium of inter-communication, and as it had little or no use for books which only 'trained critics' could get through, so it was under no necessity of soothing the alarms of the little clerk by addressing him as a Tired Business Man.

Of one of his more disagreeable characters, that is to say, of one of his characters, Mr Aldous Huxley makes an acquaintance remark, 'She had excellent table manners. People of that class always have.' There are people who cannot afford to eat cheese with their knives or touch pie-crust with their fingers. And just as those who are habitually well fed at home are most readily content with cold boiled beef abroad, so, one has noticed, people who are really grounded in the tradition—Saintsbury was a fine example—can take their ease with *The Green Hat* or *The Bridge of San Luis Rey* without the uneasy feeling which afflicts the others that they ought to be construing their next ten pages of *Ulysses*. They are in no danger from the terrorists, whose standard-bearer in this age seems to be Mrs Leavis. They do not go into precipitate mourning every time the really final decease of Scott or Byron is announced. They do not quail when they hear that Jane Austen (unlike Aphra Behn) could not write, though they may blench a little when they find that Mrs Leavis (unlike Jane Austen) can write *religio-ethical*. 'Obsequies ain't used in England no more, now—it's gone out. We say orgies now, in England. It's a word that's made up out'n the Greek *orgo*, outside, and the Hebrew *jeesum*, to cover up.'

An attentive, discriminating and judical attitude to literature is what we all desire to see as widely diffused as possible. I own that the popularity of *If Winter Comes* made me miserable, and what the Christ Child was doing in its blurbs I have never yet been able to make out. Perhaps that phenomenon will some day be taken to mark the nadir of our age in sense and taste. But the mischief of the sniff-brow pose, even when it does not frighten the young out of the honest, immature enjoyment which is the lure of attention and the foundation of judgement, is that it makes criticism the clap-trap of a coterie and scholarship contemptible. 'It is difficult to account for the acrimony of a scholiast', though Disraeli offered an explanation which modern psychology would perhaps confirm. For Mr Richards's own work I have a great regard. But when I compare the lucubrations with which certain of his pupils are beginning to favour us, and, for example, a piece of criticism, so perceptive, so truthful and so old-fashioned as Mr Sitwell's *Dickens,* I foresee for Mr Richards the fate which has already overtaken Strachey, and which of old befell the sage *quem discipuli trucidaverunt stylis suis.*[3]

The statisticians tell us that certain phenomena, weather for instance, move in cycles of different periods, and that when the crests or troughs of two or three cycles chance to coincide, the result is a climatic Age of Gold, or Mud. We are, I suggest, just now in such a trough, the coincident point of two calamities which are working themselves out. One of course was the stoppage of education in the war. I am not speaking only of the schools and Universities, but far more of that intangible instruction which forty imparts to twenty-five, twenty-five to twenty-four and so on down the line. For some years the natural processes of youthful education, the discoveries, the enthusiasms, the repulsions, the eternal dialectic of assertion and denial, were suspended in the interests of the quick decision, and of all the consequences the one that is most abundantly clear to me and my contemporaries is that though we were probably quite as foolish as Mr Richards's pupils we were incomparably better informed. We had heard of the Flood. Though 'no ornithologists', we did not query Miss Rossetti's statement that a robin sings in the holly-bush. We were not 'serious and professed students' of anything very much, but we did not move in a great fog of ignorance, fitfully illuminated

---

[3] 'Whom his disciples murdered with their pens.'

with flashes of a feigned, and unconvincing, contempt for everything we happened not to know.

The other cycle is of longer period. We are, *in hoc interim seculo*,[4] footing the bill for the great Victorian omission. It is curious to observe in history how inexplicably things go wrong: there was for example nothing in Roman history, law, or temper, to suggest that the Romans would muddle their Christian problem. I suppose an under-secretary was down with influenza, the clerk looked out the wrong precedent, and the machine once started could not be stopped. If one could take a stand in 1837, look round and ask: 'They have reformed Parliament, the Municipalities and the Poor Law: Free Trade is only a matter of time: I hear they are drafting a County Councils Bill. What will they do next?' I do not think the imaginary observer could hesitate to answer: 'Look at Brougham and his Institutes: look at Grote and his London University: they will reform the Grammar Schools. They will probably create a Board of Intermediate Education and I should not wonder if they brought Arnold from Rugby and put him in charge.' It was so obviously the next thing to be done, and no one thought of doing it.

This was the line of weakness along which Victorian culture was fractured. The Middle Classes, 'the wealth and intelligence of the nation, the pride and glory of the British name', were stratified along the seam where the public schools met the grammar schools. With the social and political consequences I am not concerned. For our culture it was a major disaster. A culture is an area of inter-communication, living and alert in all directions at once, and in the late Victorian age the educated classes, already splitting into specialized interests, were dragging behind them a growing mass with no interests at all. It had thrown up the sponge, and was becoming to all intents and purposes a proletariat, and it was Northcliffe, I think, who first apprehended its existence and diagnosed its quality.

My impression is that in the decade before the war it was recovering its tone, was seeking as it were reunion with its better half. I have read somewhere that an instructive series issued

4 'In this age of transition.'

about 1900 by Dent—attractive little books written by excellent hands—was a complete failure. Ten or twelve years later, a similar series but of larger range was selling like hot cakes. The peak of Meredith's influence falls about the same time and Meredith could be cited as the symbol of continuity recovered, because he was bred of the ferment of the fifties—*Richard Feverel* appeared with *The Origin of Species: Modern Love* is the counterpart of *Ecce Homo*—and he seemed to us in those days to have already some of the timeless quality of the immortals. I was never quite captured. But I certainly felt that, flashing through the murk, a clear note above the affectation, was the same kind of genius that one looked for and recognized in the greatest, old or new. 'No! Vernon, oh! not in this house!' is the way the women of Euripides speak, and to my ear still, 'Kill Claudio', and 'Sirius, papa', come with the same unexpected inevitable propriety of the classics.

With Meredith at the top of popular recognition, Hardy still living, a prodigious absorption of the classics and the instruction provided by publishers who still professed the old faith—the faith of Knight and Macmillan—in good books, the first decade of this century was a kind of mirage of Victorian culture, a false sun that refused to set and was swallowed up in the cloud of war. I was never able to see anything profoundly original in the satire of Mr Shaw: it always seemed to me to be the old Victorian tricks played on the old Victorian characters: most of the ideas came from the Philosophic Radicals or Ruskin and most of the jokes from Oxford or *Punch*. Mr Wells was different. I shared Mr Mackenzie's experience of hearing him spotted by a Wise Youth of seventeen, on the strength of *When The Sleeper Wakes,* as the great man of the coming age, and after forty years I must agree with Mr Mackenzie that the wise youth was right. When foreigners have recited to me their Triad, Shaw, Wells, and Galsvozzy, I have often replied, 'Never mind Shaw and Galsworthy: but read *Kipps*.' Foreigners do not wish to understand us: they only want to gratify the feeling, to which Shaw and Galsworthy minister so comfortably, that they are not after all quite so much our inferiors as in their hearts they know themselves to be. And only an Englishman can apprehend the power, the depth and penetration of Mr Wells's social diagnostic.

Nothing, I know, is more exasperating than to be told that 'it is all in the *Theaetetus*'. No doubt it is—all except the application. It would not be very difficult to argue that Mr Wells is all in the Utilitarians or all in the Christian Socialists. But the clue I find in his work, what has always interested me profoundly, and what explains, I believe, his power over the last generation, is his quest for the Cortegiano of a world which is no longer indefinite in space and contracted in time, but unimaginably extensive in time and insignificant in space. How suggestive it is that his first books should have been *The Wheels of Chance* and *The Time Machine*! Mr Wells, it seems to me, has done more than any man to adjust the modern imagination to the materiality of its framework. No doubt it was 'all in' George Stephenson when he made the Rocket run, and 'all in' Boucher de Perthes when he indentified the flint implements of the Somme. But it was not articulated, and therefore not apprehended. In his efforts to adumbrate the new Cortegiano, Mr Wells seems at times to have in mind something like an Assistant Poor Law Commissioner of the eighteen-thirties, at times something like a muscular Christian of the eighteen-fifties. But with his diagnosis, as a moralist and philosopher, of what needs to be done, my own diagnosis of what went wrong, exactly coincides.

When the New Cortegiano comes will he find culture on the earth? Will he be 'ashamed not to have read Montaigne'? But for one thing, I should mournfully answer no, and that one thing is, that the Cortegiano may come first. In the days of the Interesting Deathbed it was customary to inquire of the Departing 'Are your feet on the Rock?' I have an impression of increasing strength and comfort, that the women have their feet on the rock from which the men are being swept away. Women, they say, are more conservative, more realistic, more dutiful than men; very likely. Certainly the combination is no bad equipment for the work of continuing, enlarging, consolidating a culture. Men, I feel, will be less and less disposed to take that interest in the subject-matter of tradition, which gives the inducement to observe it further, whether as a work of art, an historic process, or an operation of the human intelligence. Women—but there, in another minute I shall be pointing out that woman is not undeveloped man but diverse. I will therefore say no more than this. For some time past it has seemed to me that the old-fashioned quality of distinction is fading out from the writing of men and becoming more noticeable in the writing of women. I feel it in books, for example, of such different weight and quality as Miss Sharp's *Fanfare for Tin Trumpets* and Miss Wilson's *Sidney*, in Miss Waddell's *Abelard* and Miss Ramsay's *Peel*, and the only stylist of our day whom the reader instinctively matches with the great artists of the past is a woman. Culture is surely not extinct in the age of *The Common Reader*. Could its future be in safer hands than those which shaped the prose of *The Years*?

PRINTED BY
HEADLEY BROTHERS LTD
THE INVICTA PRESS ASHFORD KENT
AND 109 KINGSWAY
LONDON WC2